The Reading Figure in Irish Art in the Long Nineteenth Century

The Reading Figure in Irish Art in the Long Nineteenth Century

Tricia Cusack

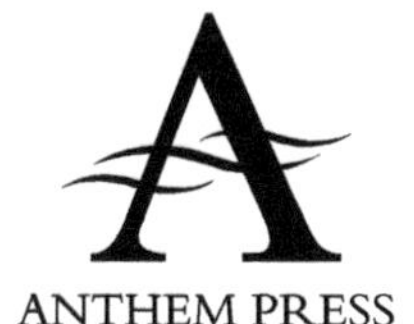

Anthem Press
An imprint of Wimbledon Publishing Company
www.anthempress.com

This edition first published in UK and USA 2023
by ANTHEM PRESS
75–76 Blackfriars Road, London SE1 8HA, UK
or PO Box 9779, London SW19 7ZG, UK
and
244 Madison Ave #116, New York, NY 10016, USA

First published in the UK and USA by Anthem Press in 2022

British Library Cataloguing-in-Publication Data
A catalogue record for this book is available from the British Library.

Library of Congress Control Number: 2023932273

ISBN-13: 978-1-83998-870-7 (Pbk)
ISBN-10: 1-83998-870-3 (Pbk)

Cover credit: Sarah Purser, Miss Jane Barlow, D.Litt. (1894).
Collection & image © Hugh Lane Gallery (Reg. No. 232)

This title is also available as an e-book.

CONTENTS

FIGURES

ACKNOWLEDGEMENTS

Many individuals and organisations have assisted in the course of this project, with critical comments, support and encouragement, answering diverse questions or helping to source images. My warm thanks especially to Michael Purser, Sarah Purser's nephew; John O'Grady, Sarah Purser's biographer; Yvonne Scott, Fellow Emerita, Trinity College Dublin; Julie Anne Stevens, School of English, Dublin City University; Adam Pearson, Adam's Fine Art Auctioneers, Dublin; Amy Boylan, Marsh's Library, Dublin; Logan Sisley, acting head of collections, and Philip Roe, registrar, Hugh Lane (Dublin City) Gallery; Louise Morgan and Brendan Maher, Publications & Images, National Gallery of Ireland; Emer McGarry, director, and Daniel McDonald, curatorial assistant, The Model, Sligo; Alan Hobart, Pyms Gallery, London; Hilary O'Kelly, Faculty of Visual Culture, National College of Art and Design, Dublin; Angela Griffith, director, Trinity College Irish Art Research Centre; David Britton, former director, Adam's Fine Art Auctioneers, Dublin; Arabella Bishop, head of Sotheby's Ireland, Dublin; Adelle Hughes, head of art, Whyte's Fine Art Auctioneers, Dublin; Ellen O'Flaherty, Manuscripts and Archives Research Library, Trinity College Dublin. I would like to thank the anonymous reviewers of an initial proposal for their helpful comments. I am enormously grateful to the anonymous reviewers of the full draft of the book for their detailed, constructive and perceptive critiques. Thanks to Megan Greiving, acquisitions editor, Anthem Press, for her support, care and advice. My husband, Igor, and our son, Rhodri, have provided constant encouragement and thoughtful critical comments.

Finally, I am extremely grateful to Christopher Catling, director, and the trustees of the Marc Fitch Fund for their generous award of a grant towards publication costs for the illustrations. Sadly it has not been possible to illustrate every picture discussed. However, I have included repositories where known or noted a website containing the image.

INTRODUCTION

My own early enthusiasm for reading began properly through a serendipitous encounter with George Eliot's (or Mary Ann Evans's) novel, *Silas Marner* (1861), picked from the shelf of my school library in Taupo, New Zealand. At the first page, I was enthralled by the language, so complex, yet so clear and its vivid evocation of a strange race of peripatetic weavers that lived on the fringes of a suspicious village community. Such writing not only engaged the reader but also demanded full concentration. Art has its own modes of engaging an audience. It is effective in making abstract ideas concrete, for example, the notions of concentration or studiousness, as we shall see later when examining images of readers. Not being explicated, art invites interpretation. I am intrigued by how art, like literature, not only forms part of culture but helps to constitute it in different historical contexts. An image of a reading figure does not merely show a figure that reads but is a concatenation of signs incorporating a host of historical and cultural references. Often unrecognised, art transmits ideologies.

Continuing a long fascination with literature and art of the late nineteenth and early twentieth centuries, I decided to examine visual representations of readers during that period. My focus on Ireland in this context is for several reasons. Until relatively recently, Ireland was better known for its production of literature than for its art.[1] Yet Ireland, particularly Dublin, had a lively art scene prior to independence and the onset of the Catholic state. The Municipal Gallery of Modern Art, established in Dublin in 1908, constituted 'the first real attempt at a representative collection of Modern Art to be found in the British Isles'.[2] In particular, contemporary Irish art included some distinctive and intriguing representations of readers. This art and period are the focus of the present volume. I use the shorthand chronology of the 'long nineteenth century' in preference to a less flexible delineation relying on the end of one century or the start of another one, with which historical events may not neatly concur. The long nineteenth century commonly refers to the period from the French Revolution of 1789 to the start of the First World War in 1914. In an Irish setting, I apply it to the period from approximately 1801, marking the Union of Ireland with Britain, to the watershed of the Irish Rising of 1916.

The reading figure has been a recurrent theme in Western art, especially from the nineteenth century. Yet despite being the subjects of countless public portraits, men are rarely depicted reading at this time. Women readers are a constant theme in European art but with a predominant emphasis on their bodily appearance. In Ireland, especially, a number of images mainly by women artists depict women absorbed in a book, oblivious to any imagined spectator. These distinctions invited explanation and were a starting point for the current volume and its argument that in a patriarchal society those images of serious women readers helped to constitute the idea of the New Woman in Ireland.

This volume examines Irish portraits during the long nineteenth century in which people are shown reading or holding a book. It explores the different assumptions and values that were ascribed to reading and contemporary constructions of the reader. Portraits had often contained accessories that were deemed appropriate for the subject, such as a fan or flowers for women, or for male figures a range of objects from a quill to a gun, and this practice continued into the nineteenth and early twentieth centuries. However, in Ireland and elsewhere, a book was an increasingly common accompaniment, especially in portraits of women.

Over this period, depictions of male subjects with a book usually follow the tradition in male portraits of accessories functioning as professional or status symbols. In Ireland, both imperial and nationalist ideologues fostered dominant notions of manliness that depended on the construction of an aggressive masculine nature checked only by self-management and without call for gentle occupations or contemplation. Reading for pleasure, especially fiction, was not valued as a manly pursuit. Nonetheless, some men are depicted absorbed in reading and failing to embody a manly attitude. Complementing such notions of manliness, a patriarchal ideology that was prevalent across Europe framed women as inferior to men in both physical and intellectual power.

However, in Dublin in the long nineteenth century, there existed a space for women, at least among those from the privileged classes, to be productive and creative. The new prevalence of 'silent reading', alongside the spread of the novel, allowed women of the middle and upper classes to engage privately with a new range of imaginative and intellectual reading materials, while silent reading also offered seclusion from patriarchal surveillance. Visual images of women as serious readers contradicted common constructions of women as consumers of lightweight romances. Images of female subjects absorbed in reading could also serve as a trope for an independent woman with private thoughts. Such images drew on and contributed to the emergence of the 'New Woman' in Ireland.

In a study of women readers in Britain between 1837 and 1914, although without reference to Ireland, Kate Flint found that the 'woman reader' was a topic in many different contexts.[3] Yet there are few studies of the woman reader as represented in art. Writing about depictions of women readers in American visual arts, Linda Docherty observed that such images remained 'a largely untapped source of information'.[4] Images of readers in Irish visual arts have been even less studied. Tina O'Toole's *The Irish New Woman* (2013) discusses history, politics and literature in relation to the 'New Woman' in Ireland, but her book is not concerned with visual art.[5] *Literacy, Language and Reading in Nineteenth-Century Ireland* (2019), a collection of essays on reading, writing and literacy in nineteenth-century Ireland, edited by Rebecca Anne Barr, Sarah-Anne Buckley and Muireann O'Cinneide, is relevant to the theme of readers but again is not about visual art.[6] Maria Luddy's useful *Women in Ireland, 1800–1918: A Documentary History* (1995) covers aspects of Irish political and social history in relation to women, but her collection omits any reference to contemporary women artists.[7]

Catherine J. Golden's *Images of the Woman Reader in Victorian British and American Fiction* (2003) discusses book illustration in relation to representations of women readers but without Irish examples. Kathryn Brown's *Women Readers in French Painting 1870–1890: A Space for the Imagination* (2016), which explores images of *liseuses* (readers) during the first two decades of the French Third Republic, has some parallel themes to the present volume. Brown is concerned with how pictorial innovations were applied to the theme of reading in relation to female literacy, and she notes that her period of focus provides 'a transition to the fragile autonomy of the New Woman, and the social impact of French educational reform'.[8]

Some publications offer visual images of reading figures from diverse periods and countries but without reference to Ireland, for example, *Reading Women* (2006) by Stefan Bollmann which includes images of women reading across a wide chronological and geographical span. *Books Do Furnish a Painting* (2018) by Jamie Camplin and Maria Ranauro has copious European examples of men, women and children reading over the past five hundred years, but none from Ireland.

Fintan Cullen's comprehensive study, *The Irish Face: Redefining the Irish Portrait* (2004), does focus on Ireland, with an examination of portraits from the seventeenth to the twentieth centuries in relation to Irish history and national identity. Cullen explains that 'the key focus is on the examination of Irish subject matter in portraiture rather than in arguing for an Irish "look", a Celtic physiognomy or [...] an identifiable Irish school of portraiture'.[9] His study concerns the public portrait, resulting in most of the images being of men.[10] As in Cullen's study, there is no attempt in the present volume to seek an essential 'Irishness' in artists or sitters, nor to identify an 'Irish School' of portraiture. However, there is no particular focus on public portraits nor on 'history painting', allowing domestic portraits of women, as well as informal portraits of male figures, to be included. Moreover, the term 'portrait' is not necessarily used to imply a recognisable individual. Identification might be precluded, for example, by the angle of vision, such as a back view, or by a modernist blurring of facial features. Cullen suggests that the interconnectedness of Ireland and Britain, given their shared colonial history, meant that any discussion of the Irish face involved an English aspect.[11] The present study argues that this interconnectedness was particularly true of Anglo-Irish artists, who had close links not only with England but also with the European continent.

The long nineteenth century was a period of large political, social and cultural shifts for Ireland. The Union with Britain in 1801 was an attempt to tighten British control following the unsuccessful Irish rebellion of 1798. Although Ireland's status then oscillated between that of a province and a colony, it remained effectively a colonial adjunct of Britain.[12] The period up to the Easter Rising of 1916 saw the Great Famine and its aftermath, the growth of Irish nationalism, the slow erosion of Anglo-Irish landlord power and moves towards Home Rule. It was a time of expanding mass literacy and also a period when 'English-reading Ireland was part of an England-centred literary system'.[13]

The cultural historian Stuart Hall observed that representational practices 'always implicate the positions from which we speak or write – the positions of *enunciation*'.[14] Most of the artists and their sitters discussed in this volume were Anglo-Irish Protestants, that is, members of the still powerful ruling classes, although a number of them had Irish nationalist sympathies. The following sections of this introduction explore three themes that for those unfamiliar with Irish history and culture at this time provide some contextualisation for the chapters and arguments that follow. The first, 'The Anglo–Irish Hegemony', considers what being Anglo-Irish meant at this time and indicates how the foreign travels of Anglo-Irish women activists and artists facilitated exchanges of ideas about women's rights and the New Woman. The second theme, 'Cultural Nationalism and Reading', explores the contentious contemporary issue of cultural nationalism, which incorporated both those hostile to the Anglo-Irish as well as to the notion of women's independence, and those among the Anglo-Irish who supported the goal of Irish independence and celebrated Ireland's history and culture. Lastly, 'The Objectives of Literacy' offers a brief overview of the expansion of literacy in Ireland in this period and the persistent inferior educational status of girls and women.

The Anglo-Irish hegemony

According to Ina Ferris, the term 'Anglo-Irish' came into use only in the early nineteenth century following the Union with Britain.[15] It was then used pejoratively to distinguish the 'English-Irish' Protestant 'settlers', many of whom had lived in Ireland for generations, from the 'Irish-Irish' Catholic dwellers. Northern Protestants were often Presbyterians or Methodists from Scotland, although many landed families in Ulster had converted to the established church.[16] Anglo-Irish identity was imbricated in the exercise of power as a ruling elite (the Ascendancy), but it was also the product of a long and close association with Ireland.

The Anglo-Irish considered themselves Irish, but many adopted a unionist and imperialist stance, and their Big House estates, spreading across to the west, constituted a power base for British control of Ireland. The dominant, patriarchal Ascendancy culture was based around the Union and the empire, together with its military exploits. Following a tour of Ireland in May 1856 with his Irish common-law wife Mary Burns, a fervent Irish nationalist, the German intellectual and revolutionary socialist Friedrich Engels wrote to his associate Karl Marx about the parlous state of 'England's first colony', mocking the Anglo-Irish landowners:

> These fellows are droll enough to make your sides burst with laughing. Of mixed blood, mostly tall, strong, handsome chaps, they all wear enormous moustaches under colossal Roman noses, give themselves the false military airs of retired colonels [and] travel around the country after all sorts of pleasures.[17]

However, the Anglo-Irish did not comprise a homogeneous community. The landed class itself was a mixed socio-economic group, their domains ranging in size from 500 acres to over 100,000 acres, and a few of the large landlords were Catholic.[18]

Over the course of the nineteenth century, the Protestant Ascendancy lost ground, literally and figuratively. In the 1870s, however, fewer than a thousand landlords still owned half of Ireland.[19] The Church of Ireland, although disestablished in 1869, continued to be a wealthy institution, uniting many Anglo-Irish adherents.[20] Prestigious institutions such as the Royal Hibernian Academy (RHA), founded in 1823, remained part of the Anglo-Irish, as well as masculine hierarchy. The National Education system, developed from 1831, continued to be an agent of cultural imperialism, overlooking Ireland to focus on Britain's colonies.[21] Anglo-Irish and Protestant interests were well provided for by Irish newspapers and magazines. The *Irish Times*, founded in 1859 by

Lawrence Edward Knox, from a well-connected Anglo-Irish family, retained Anglo-Irish editorship throughout the long nineteenth century. The paper's politics were Protestant nationalist until a change of ownership after Knox's death in 1873, when it became unionist, and later independent.[22] Various Protestant magazines were launched, such as the *Irish Evangelist*, a Methodist journal established in 1859, the year of the Ulster Christian Revival which generated huge meetings and conversions.[23]

Contemporary imperial and religious/racial ideologies sharpened divisions between Protestants and Catholics. Protestants, whether Anglo-Irish, English or Scottish, regularly represented Irish Catholics as less civilised than themselves.[24] For example, Protestants claimed for themselves such virtues as rationality, enlightenment and orderliness, in opposition to the irrationality, ignorance and disorderliness attributed to Catholics. These ideologies were promulgated and reinforced through visual art and fiction. For instance, the English magazine *Punch* regularly portrayed Irish men as brutal and mindless. In *The Real Charlotte* (1894), a satirical novel by the Anglo-Irish authors Edith Somerville and 'Martin Ross', her second cousin Violet Martin, the narrator sets a scene of washerwomen with 'a slatternly woman or two […] pounding the wet linen on a rock with a flat wooden weapon, according to the immemorial custom of their savage class', while the novel's social-climbing protagonist, Charlotte Mullen, has 'a detestation of Roman Catholics'.[25] The English in turn were liable to regard even the Protestant Anglo-Irish as less civilised than themselves. Among the many exchanges between Ireland and England, teams from Alexandra College Dublin and Newnham College, Cambridge, played hockey matches. On one occasion, 'A Lady' writing in the *Irish Times* observed that 'the Newnham team evidently came over here prepared to verify their previous conceptions of the "wild" Irish […] I overheard an English girl saying, with a charming air of condescension, "You played so *nicely*, not at all *roughly*, you know!" '[26]

Not all Anglo-Irish were part of, or supported, Ascendancy culture or politics, or were hostile to Catholics. Many Anglo-Irish artists and writers mixed with a variety of artists, intellectuals and political activists, including Catholics and others, and also supported the notion of Home Rule for Ireland. The artist and nationalist Cesca Chenevix Trench, from an affluent Anglo-Irish family, wrote disparagingly about it to her sister Margot, 'the cousins make such idiotic jokes and talk about such idiotic things and look at life in such an idiotic way, with their dogs and their horses and their swans and their crops and the weather and their neighbours, it's too awful'.[27] William Orpen's large commissioned work *The Vere Foster Family* (oil on canvas, 1907, Figure 1) presents a slightly ridiculous image of the dominating Anglo-Irish aristocratic figure of Sir Augustus Vere Foster of Glyde Court, Louth, cradling a double-barrelled gun and accompanied by his wife, Lady Charlotte, who appears to

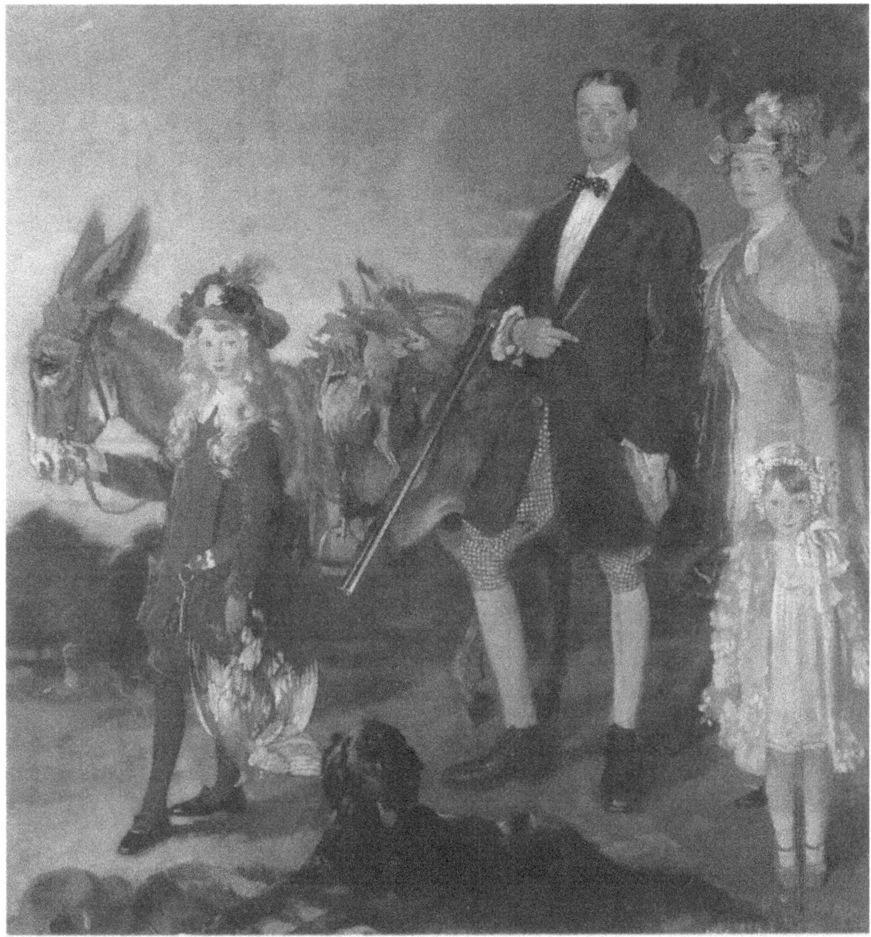

Figure 1 William Orpen, *The Vere Foster Family*, oil on canvas, 198 × 198 cm, 1907. NGI.1199. Photo © National Gallery of Ireland.

be somewhat overdressed, and her little girl Dorothy, whose sister Philippa carries a dead bird while leading a donkey laden with further game.[28] Orpen, himself from an affluent professional Protestant family, stayed with the family at Glyde Court for the portrait and 'as it rained a lot […] the family's favourite donkey was often entertained in the drawing room for a sitting'.[29] The family was not happy with this painting and Sir Vere Foster commented that 'the donkey and all of us seem to share the same expression'.[30]

'Anglo-Irish' was therefore a complex term. It signified the ruling class exercising colonial authority, as well as a broader, distinctively Irish segment of the population. It encompassed those who tended to fall outside of Ascendancy culture and politics, including a number of artists discussed in this volume. Those Anglo-Irish artists, however, remained part of a privileged and well-connected sector of Irish society. Their international associations, especially with England but also with the Continent, were important for the mutual sharing of ideas, including the nascent notion of the New Woman.

Cultural nationalism and reading

The cultural nationalism of what became known as Irish-Ireland was generally opposed to the international cross-currents that helped produce campaigns for women's suffrage and access to higher education and the associated idea of the New Woman. Some Irish nationalists in this period focused on a collective identity that excluded the Anglo-Irish. In addition, some strands of Irish Catholic nationalism placed restrictions on women's role in society. Proponents of Irish-Ireland such as David Patrick (D.P.) Moran explicitly opposed votes for women. The nationalist paper *The Freeman's Journal* emphasised that the point of further education for women was to enhance their mothering skills: 'While acknowledging the fascination of the "fair sex" it was diplomatically suggested that she whose mind is refined with the spirit of learning was fairer still and in a position to transmit knowledge to the next generation.'[31]

It was evident to Irish nationalists that English educational publications were designed to shape British imperial subjects. Moran claimed it was not English rule but the predominance of English culture that was most problematic.[32] Cultural nationalism flourished alongside political nationalism. Gerry Smyth defines cultural nationalism as a theory that 'there is a natural link between culture and nation – that is, that the kinds of artefacts and narratives produced by individuals and communities are related to the peculiar national system of social organisation, political order and historical identity from which they have emerged'.[33] Such a conception assumes a homogeneous national cultural identity, as well as a neat congruity between political and social organisation and culture.

Efforts were made to bring an autonomous national culture into being. There was a growing interest in specifically representing Irish localities, for instance, in book illustrations which from the early 1800s showed Irish topographic views and portrayals of Irish life.[34] In journalism, alongside the stream of English publications, and Methodist and other Protestant magazines, a nationalist press was nurtured. *The Freeman's Journal* founded in 1763 changed its politics several times and in the nineteenth century was a nationalist paper supporting the Irish Parliamentary or Home Rule Party. New nationalist newspapers like *The Nation* were launched. Henry McManus's *Reading 'The*

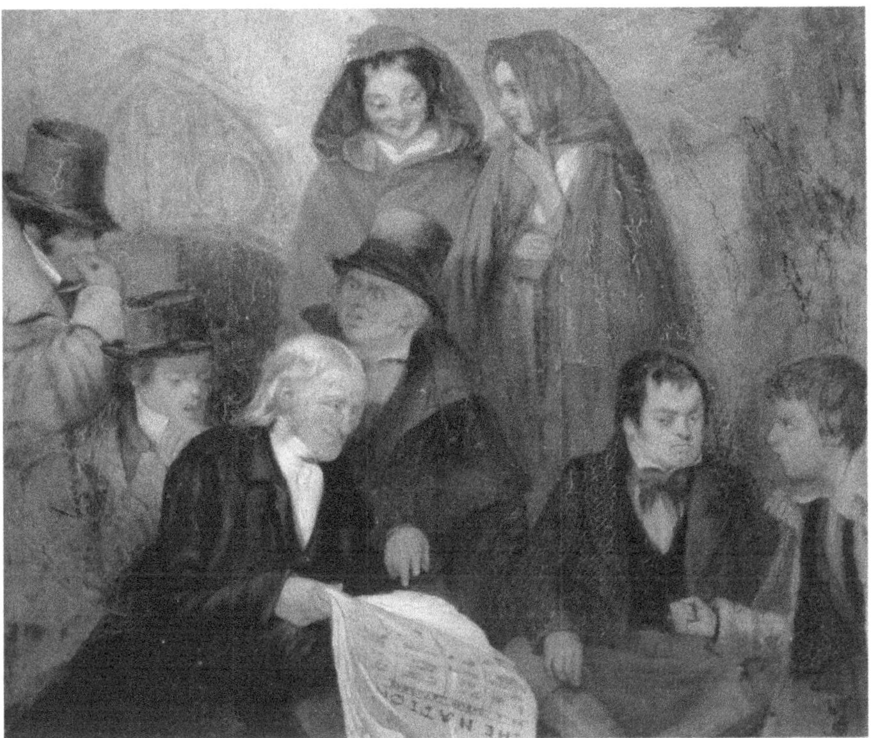

Figure 2 Henry McManus, *Reading 'The Nation'*, oil on canvas, 30.5 × 35.5 cm, 1850s. NGI.1917. Photo © National Gallery of Ireland.

Nation' (oil on canvas, 1850s, Figure 2) suggests that its contents were a popular topic of debate among men, while the two women in the picture are shown content but distracted, or not being addressed. A Dublin newspaper, *The Irish People*, was founded in 1863 by James Stephens and edited by John O'Leary as a mouthpiece of the Irish Republican Brotherhood or Irish Fenians, and therefore more militant than the *Nation*. The first issue observed of the Irish establishment: 'Its existence is an injury and an insult to the majority of the people of Ireland. But [...] it can not be abolished, as long as British connexion lasts; for it is a necessary part of the Imperial system.'[35] The paper was suppressed two years later.

Moran founded and edited *The Leader* from 1900, espousing a Catholic and Gaelic nationalism. In the first decade of the twentieth century, newsagents in Dublin were warned not to sell English newspapers, and clergymen were active in this campaign. The Catholic Truth Society of Ireland, established in 1899, aimed to combat the spread of English popular literature. The

Archbishop of Dublin in 1908 chastised 'vendors of immoral and irreligious books, newspapers, and other publications', and in 1911 the Irish Vigilance Committee reinforced this message with personal visits to newsagents.[36] A. M. and T. D. Sullivan produced an edited collection in 1913 titled *Irish Readings*, asserting that the earlier development of a national literature had been stymied by 'the subjection of this country by a foreign people [which] crushed out the old laws, literature, and language [...] The National Literature of the Irish People is of recent growth. It is fresh, and bright, and vigorous [...] [it] is now essentially patriotic'.[37]

As Irish political and cultural nationalism developed, so too did the discourse concerning the 'Irishness' of Protestants in Ireland. There were various efforts to unite Catholics and Protestants under the rubric of a collective, authentic Irishness. For instance, George Petrie, an Anglo-Irish artist and antiquarian, sought to establish an early shared Christian history for Ireland.[38] The *Dublin Penny Journal*, produced from 1832 to 1836, was largely shaped by Petrie. It was aimed at a national Irish readership and had a reported weekly circulation of 30,000.[39] By 1863 a rare copy of the *Dublin Penny Journal* was advertised perhaps surprisingly in the militant *Irish People*, its woodcuts of old castles and Round Towers incorporated into the newspaper under the rubric 'To the Lovers of Nationality'.[40] The *Dublin University Magazine: A Literary and Political Journal*, founded by graduates of the Protestant university, Trinity College Dublin, staked a claim to Ireland's past history, and published illustrations of prominent cultural and political figures, such as the Irish writer Anna Maria Hall. Hall is depicted in an image of 1840 engraved by John Kirkwood after Henry McManus; fashionably dressed and coiffed, 'her hand rests on a book of Irish subject matter'.[41] A couple of columns in *The United Irishman: A National Weekly Review* in 1903 signed by 'An Irish Protestant' found it necessary to argue that 'The Protestant Irishman is as much an Irishman as the Catholic Irishman', while also seeking a voice for Protestants.[42] Stephen J. Brown S. J., a Jesuit priest, teacher and writer born in Co. Down, in 1912 analysed the contentious issue of Irish nationality, which he saw as common to all those living in Ireland, whether Catholic, Gaelic or Anglo-Irish: all had a right to be called Irish, including 'that large body of the population which, though at present politically hostile to the majority, has, nevertheless, a right to call itself Irish [...] the Irish people of today is, *in nationality*, not Gaelic, nor Anglo-Irish, but simply Irish'.[43]

Irish nationalism itself had many strands, some of which accommodated or were produced by the Anglo-Irish. For example, members of the Anglo-Irish 'artistic classes' became part of 'that largely Protestant and to some degree fashionable Irish nationalism of the pre-Great War period'.[44] Michael Purser describes 'Celtic mist and twilight all over Dublin [...] One Stokes relative even dressed in an emerald green gown, with golden interlaced appliqué, to play the harp every St Patrick's morn, on top of the Hill of Tara'.[45] The Gaelic League, founded in 1893 to promote the Irish language as part of a cultural nationalism, was open to women members, unlike most contemporary political and other societies.[46] It was supported by Anglo-Irish artists and publishers such as Lolly and Lily Yeats who made Irish cultural history a focus at both Dun Emer, their craft cooperative, and the Cuala Press.[47] Mary Cottenham Yeats (Cottie) produced female saints for Catholic sodality banners, and illustrations for the nationalist magazine *The Irish Homestead*.[48] Cesca Trench, a Protestant nationalist, 'read voraciously' about Irish history.[49] Typically, Trench attended school in Switzerland, boarding school in England and trained in the Paris ateliers.[50] She produced a poster for the Gaelic League in 1913, juxtaposing a proud spear-bearing female Eire with a mendicant West Britain. Maud Gonne, from an Anglo-Irish family, founded *Inghinidhe na hÉireann* (Daughters of Erin), intended 'to combat in every way English influence'.[51]

The Anglo-Irish hegemony was therefore increasingly challenged by Irish nationalists in both political and cultural terms. A number of nationalist activists were Anglo-Irish, and many of the Anglo-Irish artists discussed in this volume sympathised with the broad aims of Irish political and even cultural nationalism. At the same time, they often participated in a community of artistic and intellectual interest that made a space for members with varying beliefs. Their art training commonly included study in London, Paris or Amsterdam as well as in Dublin. By the latter nineteenth century these international connections, including an acquaintance with European literature, facilitated exchanges of ideas about women's role in society and the 'New Woman', as well as about art and modernism, far from the ideals of Gaelic nationalists.

The objectives of literacy

In late eighteenth- and early nineteenth-century Ireland, an informal literary culture existed among well-off Anglo-Irish families, based on manuscripts written and circulated privately.[52] Eighteenth-century Ireland also had a lively publishing industry and profitably reprinted English books. However, after 1801 the Union with Britain brought British copyright laws, and the Irish printing trade together with book publishing collapsed, after which most of Ireland's reading materials, whether popular novels, newspapers or magazines, came from England.[53] This included novels by Irish writers and, as pictures in novels became popular, books illustrated by Irish artists.[54]

National literacy was a shared goal of the British government and of Irish nationalists, with divergent ideological objects. The National Education system developed from 1831 constituted

> a classic example of 'cultural imperialism', directed towards the moral and intellectual advancement of a hitherto backward people [...] the Irish reading books paid little attention to Irish geography or history, instead giving detailed information on Britain's overseas colonies and their picturesque peoples.[55]

Against this, a policy of 'Irish-Ireland' was proclaimed by Irish nationalists, looking instead to the Irish language, the Catholic faith and to reading that enshrined a singular, uncontaminated Irish culture that reified an Irish past of heroic folk tales.

Gender divisions in education that privileged boys operated at all levels of Irish society. In Anglo-Irish families, boys were formally educated at school, often in England and then university. Meanwhile, their sisters were tutored at home with a view to marriage.[56] These discriminatory practices were to lead to campaigns for women's access to higher education and the concomitant formation of the New Woman. Mass literacy grew slowly from the mid-nineteenth century and boys were treated more favourably than girls in school. Boys spent longer there, and as reading was taught before writing, fewer females learned to both read and write.[57] Literacy rates also differed according to religion, particularly among girls and women, the advantage being with Protestants. The 1861 census showed that Protestant women, including members of the Church of Ireland and Presbyterians, were more likely than Catholic women to be able to both read and write.[58] In 1871, 60 per cent of Irish Catholics could read compared to 90 per cent of Irish Presbyterians.[59] Insofar as the Catholic Church discouraged Bible study without priestly mediation, this discouraged reading. The established Church of Ireland and especially dissenting Protestant religionists, by contrast, promoted personal Bible study. 'Improving' fiction, such as William Carleton's *Father Butler*, as well as visual portrayals of religious readers dramatised this distinction.[60]

Various facilities enabled reading for men and gradually also women on a voluntary basis. Marsh's Library Dublin, founded and financed as a public library in 1707 by Archbishop Narcissus Marsh, by mid-century had acquired collections that covered theology, chemistry, medicine, mathematics and astronomy and a large collection accessioned in 1745 added poetry and plays.[61] Marsh's Library permitted women readers from the mid-nineteenth century. The first recorded woman visitor was Miss L. Crampton on 26 March

1850, probably accompanied by two men named Crampton whose entries are next to hers in the Visitor Book.[62] Between 1850 and 1911, there were over a hundred women visitors.[63] In 1863, a Mrs Glancy visited the library after hours with two children to look at several items including Faulkner and Clarendon.[64] Later that year, Mrs Pakenham and three other ladies viewed these.[65] Faulkner referred to an eighteenth-century newspaper, *The Dublin Journal, being the freshest advices, foreign and domestick* (Dublin: G. Faulkner, 1720–75). Edward Hyde Clarendon's *The History of the Rebellion and Civil Wars in England, begun in the Year 1641,* was first published in 1707 and annotated by Jonathan Swift.[66] An entry in the Visitor's Book for 1877 includes a number of named Reverend gentlemen and their friends, 'Two Catholic Clergymen' and two anonymous 'Lady' visitors.[67] The Visitor's Book in 1877 also recorded, 'A Lady to make references to Lodge's Peerage, 4 vols.'[68] This would be John Lodge's *The Peerage of Ireland: Or a Genealogical History of the Present Nobility of That Kingdom with Engravings of Their Paternal Coats of Arms,* updated in 1789 (Dublin: James Moore), the reference suggesting that the reader was an interested member of the Anglo-Irish Ascendancy.

The Public Libraries (Ireland) Act in 1855 encouraged, although it did not mandate, local authorities to establish libraries, and the first local authority public library was established in 1858 in Dundalk, Co. Louth.[69] The National Library of Ireland was established in 1877 and women were likely to have been admitted from that year.[70] Photographs of the National Library Reading Room between 1880 and 1895 show women reading alongside men. A sketch by the Dublin artist Sarah Purser of about 1891–92 depicts an older woman in coat and pince-nez reading at a table by lamplight, likely to be located in a library.[71] Educative reading was also encouraged by bodies such as the Mechanics' Institutes. The Dublin Mechanics' Institute, founded in 1824, aimed to promote scientific education for artisans, and from 1839, women were allowed to attend lectures.

Literacy was widespread towards the end of the nineteenth century. Judge Richard Paul Carton in the 1870s noticed a large increase in novel reading,

> the gaudy boards of cheap editions are familiar to our eyes, and find ready purchasers on every railway bookstall [...] [regarding] the number of novels which were read within a circuit of twenty miles round Dublin, during the past summer months [...] the figures would be rather alarming.[72]

The protagonist of Somerville and Ross's novel *The Real Charlotte*, Charlotte Mullen, has bought a 'railway novel' on a journey from Dublin.[73] By 1871, 33 per cent of those over 5 years old remained illiterate, but by the turn of the century there was near universal literacy and reading spread, especially of popular publications.[74]

Literacy and reading therefore expanded across the population in Ireland over the long nineteenth century, although educational opportunities were restricted for girls and women compared to boys and men. Public libraries were beginning to allow women access for informal reference and reading. The increase in literacy brought a concomitant expansion in the production of novels, which was important in extending the choice of reading matter. This also brought a high visibility to the prevalence and use of novels, accompanied by criticisms of novel reading, directed especially at women readers (see Chapter 2).

Whether part of a cultural nationalist recuperation of Irish-Ireland, or of a transnational culture bearing on women's role in art and society, reading constituted a cultural and political statement: 'To read in Ireland, to read while being Irish, was to […] take part in constructing national identity after the Act of Union – but a national identity whose boundaries, inclusions, and significance were up for perpetual debate and re-definition.'[75] Despite the increase in general literacy, portraits of readers however remained limited to mainly Anglo-Irish middle-class artists and sitters, a number of whom were women. Nonetheless, those portraits further extended the social and cultural implications of reading and of art in contemporary Ireland and produced a new kind of representation of women readers.

This volume examines portraits of both women and men readers executed in Ireland or by Irish artists during the long nineteenth century. It suggests that contemporary constructions of manliness at this time discouraged reading for pleasure among men, who are seldom depicted reading. The book focuses on a distinctive array of portraits of women readers, mostly by women artists, and their relevance to the developing concept of the New Woman. It also considers how some of these artists and their sitters might themselves be seen to embody aspects of the New Woman. Ireland at this time was a patriarchal society constrained by powerful gender ideologies of femininity and masculinity. Some contemporary Irish writing introduced female characters who radically transgressed gender and sexual norms.[76] The Irish portraits of women subvert dominant gender ideology in a less overt but equally consequential way. Through the visual depiction of subjects absorbed in reading, rather than conforming to conventional feminine modes of self-presentation, the portraits present an iconography of the New Woman as an independent thinker.

The following chapters are arranged thematically, each engaging different questions arising from a study of the portraits, their artists and sitters, and the emergence of the New Woman as a cultural and social phenomenon in contemporary Ireland.

Chapter 1, 'Imperial Man, Manly Nationalism and the Unmanly Reader', questions why so few among many Irish portraits of men depict them reading. It argues that reading, especially of fiction, was incompatible with contemporary notions of dominant masculinity in Ireland, whether imperial or nationalist. Imperial and nationalist ideologues argued for a kind of tempered aggressivity and the value of decisive action and military preparedness over sedentary or contemplative occupations. This was reinforced by the Protestant ethos of 'Muscular Christianity' or by 'Muscular Catholicism' which made team games carriers of manly strengths. The chapter concludes that when men are portrayed with books, these generally function as markers of their status or profession. This chapter is concerned with the dominant ideologies of masculinity and how they impinged on imaginative reading. There were also committed male readers who enjoyed fiction. Some of these are depicted in recumbent poses, unready for action, reinforcing the idea that reading for pleasure was not a manly habit.

Chapter 2, ' "Creatures of a Different Breed": Women Readers and Patriarchal Discourse', outlines the patriarchal ideology consistent with dominant masculinities that was prevalent in Ireland and elsewhere in Europe and which situated women as inferior to men not only in physical strength but also in intellectual ability. It shows how many European portrayals of women readers, mostly by male artists, incorporate such ideology by focusing on a feminine body displayed for a male gaze, or on elaborate sartorial arrangements, rather than on the intellectual and imaginative act of reading. Some Parisian artists, such as Berthe Morisot, did represent women, often family members, primarily as readers. This chapter suggests that in Ireland at this time portraits of women readers that emphasise the figure's body are unusual, although women's dress is sometimes a preoccupation.

Chapter 3, 'The Shaping of the New Woman in Ireland', explores the idea and embodiment of the New Woman, setting the scene for a detailed examination of the reading figure in Irish art in Chapter 4, and a study of four New Women in Dublin in Chapter 5. Chapter 3 suggests that for women in the more privileged, typically Anglo-Irish, classes Dublin in the long nineteenth century was a creative space. Anglo-Irish artists had close connections both to England and Europe, and the concept of the New Woman emerged in the context of campaigns for women's suffrage and access to higher education in Dublin and London. The New Woman was constituted in relation to a reading habit and New Women emerged as protagonists in European and Irish fiction. The New Woman was increasingly represented in visual art, and in various guises from English cartoons to the Irish portraits.

Chapter 4, 'The Silent Reader and the Fictive Viewer', explores the concept of silent reading and the private relation of reader to text, with its implications especially for women readers and for the constitution of the New Woman. This chapter shows that many Irish portraits of the woman reader depict her as solitarily engaged in reading, without acknowledgement of a viewer. It considers how such images convey a notion of the 'absorbed reader' and construct an illusion of the 'absent viewer', in fact drawing the viewer in to focus on the reader and her absorbing activity. Alternatively, a visual trope of the 'interrupted reader' is introduced that both acknowledges a viewer, and suggests the temporariness of disturbance and so the urgency of the reading postponed. The significance of windows and curtains as part of the private setting of depicted readers is also examined.

Chapter 5, 'A Room of Her Own: Four New Women in Dublin', focuses on two Dublin artists, Sarah Purser and Estella Solomons, and the subjects of two of their portrayals of readers, Jane Barlow and Alice Milligan. It shows how all four were key figures among the successful women artists and writers of this period, and how in their creative work, cultural leadership and political engagement, each embodied the idea of an independent and active New Woman.

Chapter 1

IMPERIAL MAN, MANLY NATIONALISM AND THE UNMANLY READER

Most Irish portraits of this period found in art galleries, other institutions such as the Royal Irish Academy (RIA) or Irish country houses are of men. Many displayed the achievements, status or wealth of the Anglo-Irish. It is noticeable that relatively few among them represent men reading, or even holding a book. This chapter asks why so few men were shown with books and, when they were, what those books might signify. It argues that reading, especially fiction such as novels for pleasure, was incompatible with dominant notions of masculinity, whether imperial or nationalist. Portraits that do show men with books often follow an earlier use of accessories to indicate rank or profession, and reading matter tends to be explicit and instrumental, such as a Bible. Although some nationalists advocated the reading of old Gaelic tales, this was often to serve a practical purpose offering exemplars of masculine valour, rather than to provide an intellectual or imaginative experience. Homeric epics played a similar role in preparing privileged British and Anglo-Irish pupils and students for imperial service. Not all men subscribed to the dominant ideas of masculinity and some were committed readers who enjoyed fiction. The chapter concludes by considering some visual examples of unmanly engagement in reading for pleasure.

Imperial man and manliness

In *Manliness and Culture*, a booklet in its third edition by 1877, John Brookes enumerates exemplary manly qualities such as decisiveness, heroism and a rejection of domesticity, justified by an appeal to religion. Thus he proposes a Christian conception of manliness that entails '*openness* to God's Light and Love [and] cheerful *decisiveness* […] It is unmanly to be doubtful, timorous, uncertain'.[1] Brookes further notes, 'There can be no manliness […] without heroism' and that 'A brave man has contempt for […] cushions, and easy-chairs'.[2] Brookes assumes that cushions and easy chairs are available, suggesting he is not addressing the poor or working-class man. Robert Baden-Powell, a

British army officer, in 1908 reiterates the undesirable 'softening' effect of domesticity on boys in his manual for boy scouts.[3] As an aggressive imperialist, 'when Baden-Powell organized his Scout movement he did so with one primary motive – to prepare the next generation of British soldiers for war and the defence of the Empire'.[4] In Ireland, scouting was quickly introduced, the first event pursued in 1908 by the Dublin City Boy Scouts in Phoenix Park.

In his study *Masculinities and Culture* (2002), the cultural theorist John Beynon distinguishes a hegemonic embodiment of masculinity that he dubs 'imperial man', current in Britain from the second half of the nineteenth century until the start of the First World War.[5] This ideal was characterised by 'action, authority, the celebration of the will and [...] British racial superiority'.[6] According to Beynon, a corollary of the attributes of manliness again was an avoidance of domesticity, and a devaluing of the quieter traits associated with femininity: 'Masculinity is associated with mobility, toughness and adventurousness, femininity with immobility and the softness of faraway home.'[7] David Jackson's comments on a later fictional derivative of 'rugged masculinity', the British working-class comic book hero Alf Tupper, raise another correlate of tough, action-based masculinity: 'He didn't seem to have an inner world. His whole focus was on public actions in the public domain.'[8]

Irish and Victorian masculinities in this period overlapped, especially for the Anglo-Irish. In *The Myth of Manliness in Irish National Culture, 1880–1922* (2011), Joseph Valente further analyses the notion of manliness in Victorian culture which, like Beynon, he perceives as a tool of masculine hegemony.[9] Valente proposes that 'manliness' was built on an idea of masculinity that characterised it as inherently bestial. 'Manliness' consisted not only in possessing animal qualities of passion and aggressiveness but also in exercising the ability to control or sublimate such passions to moral and Christian ends.[10] He argues that manliness required a balance between animal passions and their sublimation, in order not to be too aggressive, nor too feminised.[11] As these qualities of manliness were only inherent in the masculine gender, women could not attain them. Furthermore, Victorian manliness was conflated with Protestant Englishness and with the metropolitan gentleman. Manliness was a quality or state that while in theory was attainable through effort, in effect was restricted not only to the Protestant English but to the metropolitan gentleman, who alone could achieve the requisite balance between animal spirits and appropriate restraint and sublimation of those spirits.[12]

Imperial masculinity in this period therefore has been variously, but not very differently characterised as decisive and action-based, characterised by a natural aggression controlled for Christian (Protestant) ends and naturally a property of the privileged classes. It was uniformly understood to be alien to domesticity and/or femininity, and to eschew the stillness and contemplation that might characterise the committed reader, instead favouring vigorous physical activity. It also had overtones of racial superiority.

In a study of British travel writing in the Victorian period, Marjorie Morgan found that Protestantism connoted 'rational inquiry, enlightenment and open-mindedness', while '[Protestant] depictions of Catholics include such words as "dark" [...] "ignorant" and "strange"'.[13] L. Perry Curtis Jr. and others have documented the increasingly savage denigration of Catholic Irish men in this period who were represented in the English press, for example, in *Punch*, as simian, irrational and inarticulate.[14] However, as Roy Foster pointed out, *Punch* had a somewhat ambivalent attitude to the Irish and depicted all 'class enemies' as brutish.[15] Meanwhile, contemporary characterisations of 'Celts' claimed that they were 'feminised'. Ernest Renan in 1854 wrote that 'la race celtique [...] est une race essentiellement feminine'.[16] (The Celtic race [...] is an essentially feminine race.) Matthew Arnold in 1867, like Renan taking the normative Celt to be male, followed Renan's thought when he wrote that 'the sensibility of the Celtic nature, its nervous exaltation, have something feminine in them, and the Celt is thus peculiarly disposed to feel the spell of the feminine idiosyncrasy; he has an affinity to it'.[17] In Valente's terms, the Catholic Irish were regarded as other to Protestant Englishness and as such were represented as possessing the wrong balance for the expression of manliness, either too bestial or too feminised.[18]

Irish Protestant landlords tended to share the ideology of imperial man. They had close social, cultural and political connections with England, and commonly maintained loyalist credentials. For example, the Brabazons, earls of Meath, who had been awarded lands by King Henry VIII in the sixteenth century, welcomed members of the royal family to their home, Kilruddery Co. Wicklow, including King George IV in 1821, and the Prince and Princess of Wales in 1868. Reginald Brabazon recalled that in 1896, 'the germ of the future Empire Day Movement took up its residence in my brain'.[19]

Anglo-Irish boys attended British public schools and often British universities where they imbibed doctrines of manliness that were transplanted to Ireland to be nurtured among the Anglo-Irish elite. Well-placed Catholic families also sent their children to school in England, or their boys attended private schools in Ireland that emulated the British ones, especially in an obsession with manliness.[20] Greek and Latin classics, a core element of the curriculum in English public schools and universities, provided students with ancient epics as models for imperial endeavour. For instance, it was said that during the Indian Uprising, 'examples from [...] the *Iliad* provided reassurance regarding British martial spirit'.[21]

Sport was a key element of public school and university life, and team games of rugby and cricket were held to improve physical strength and moral character, a manly condition from the 1850s dubbed 'Muscular Christianity'.[22] One of its proponents, Charles Kingsley, observed that 'in the playing field boys acquire virtues which no books can give them' and he saw manliness as an 'antidote to the poison of effeminacy [...] which was sapping the vitality of the Anglican Church'.[23] Muscular Christianity was regarded as a preparation for imperial service.[24]

Men of the landed classes in Ireland regarded leisure and sports, which they associated with the Ancient Greeks, as integral to their social position.[25] Hunting, a manly pursuit among the Ancient Greeks, was popular. Domestic hunts were joined by Ascendancy women, such as the artist Edith Somerville. Although her drawings made fun of traditional Anglo-Irish pursuits, Somerville belonged to and conformed to the culture of the Anglo-Irish Ascendancy in many ways, participating in 'sporting tournaments and riding to hounds'.[26] However, Big Game hunting was a masculine sport. The masculinity of the Irish Protestant Ascendancy was displayed in their country house interiors, ornamented with imperial trophies such as tiger skins and elephant tusks.[27]

For the Anglo-Irish Ascendancy, aggressive manliness was bolstered by strong imperial military traditions so that 'military commissions provided employment for members of most families of Irish gentry, the pool of officers remaining virtually closed to the middle classes and to Catholics until the First World War'.[28] Anglo-Irish interest in the empire and its military exploits was provided for by empire news in both national and local Irish papers, which were addressed principally to men.[29] The *Irish Times* in the 1870s reported regularly on the wars in South Africa, in which members of the Ascendancy fought and died. In May 1877, the paper reported, 'The announcement that the Transvaal has been annexed to the British Empire has taken the public – if not, indeed, foreign nationalities – by surprise, and excited a good deal of comment.'[30] In February 1879, the paper's heading 'The Zulu War' was followed by sub-headings announcing '500 men and 30 officers killed' and 'Five thousand Zulus killed'.[31] In the summer season of 1879, a local paper such as the *Kilrush Herald*, from July renamed the *Kilrush Herald and Kilkee Gazette*, was primarily concerned with daily reports from the 'Imperial Parliament' (the House of Commons and the House of Lords) and continuing items of international imperial concern such as 'The Zulu War'.[32] Participation in and widespread newspaper headlining of the war fitted the bellicose manliness that characterised the image of Ascendancy menfolk, as well as reinforcing the imperial ties of the Anglo-Irish. A corollary of imperial manliness was a devaluing of gentle and non-instrumental imaginative pursuits like reading, especially novels. The libraries of Anglo-Irish 'Big Houses' were furnished with books on hunting expeditions, travel, military campaigns and other imperial writings.[33]

Manly reading

Various publications offered men guidance on what to read or to avoid, and it
is evident that many of these endeavoured to cultivate a manliness that would
avoid any charge of effeminacy, while reinforcing the attribution to women
of a low level of intellect. Some of these were aspirational texts for men who
wished to acquire the habits of the superior classes. *Advice to Young Men on Their
Duties and Conduct in Life* was first published in Boston in 1848 and in London in
1855 by T. S. [Timothy Shay] Arthur, a prolific American writer, moralist and
temperance campaigner. Arthur's book is aimed particularly at young men
who had not benefitted from 'high advantages' and needed to educate themselves through study.[34] It accords particular value to informational texts and
recommends that young men study science and moral philosophy.[35] Arthur
attached little or no value to fiction, which he regarded as lacking intellectual
substance:

> Reading is resorted to by very many as a means of making an idle hour
> pass more pleasantly; others have a natural desire to obtain information
> on a variety of subjects, and read [...] history, biography, travels, and
> the current publications on all the various subjects that generally interest
> readers of taste and intelligence. The first class are mainly novel-readers.
> These, if they do not actually stand still, make but little advance in intel-
> lectual improvement.[36]

According to Arthur, men who read novels spent the remainder of their
leisure time attending the theatre and visiting, and, in an aside that indicates
his low opinion of women's intellect, he notes of novel-reading men that 'such
persons generally make agreeable companions in mixed companies, where
conversation is light and rambling'.[37] Arthur also recommended 'every young
man to read carefully one or more books on etiquette and good-breeding, and
thereby acquaint himself with the laws that are observed in polite society'.[38]
The aspiration to pragmatic manliness is associated with one for gentility.

The English writer William Rathbone Greg, like Arthur, regarded reading
novels as an occupation that failed to engage men's brains. Greg suggested
that men among the idle rich, as well as businessmen released from work,
turned to novel reading. '[Novels] are the reading of most men in their idler
and more impressionable hours, when the fatigued mind requires rest and recreation; when the brain, therefore, is comparatively passive.'[39]

In *Manliness and Culture*, Brookes comments directly on the value of books
for the cultivation of manliness, concluding that 'it is a folly to overburden the
mind with books [...] Experience gained from actual life is more important

than mere *book-learning*.[40] On what men should read, Brookes again emphasises useful, not imaginative reading, although poetry is allowed some value, urging, 'how much better to read History, Travels, Biography, Poetry, than a lot of *senseless* novels! [...] Novels are not the bread and meat of our mental life, they are only the dessert thereof'.[41] Novels are regarded as a subsidiary and not necessarily healthy indulgence that may follow factual reading.

Some commentators held more ambivalent and even favourable views on novel reading, such as Judge Richard Carton. Carton, born in Rathgar, Dublin, was educated in a Jesuit school and, although he took up law as a profession, remained an active member of the charitable Catholic St Vincent de Paul Society. In the 1870s, he offered his views to 'a society of young men who had been trained by the Brothers of the Christian Schools' whom, he observed, had not had the benefit of a university education. Carton advocated novel reading as a diversion from 'real life', and regarded it as a useful alternative to undesirable entertainments among men: 'A taste for novels will keep many a young man away from the billiard-table, the singing saloon, and the pit of the theatre, and preserve him unscathed amidst the temptations [...] of cities.'[42] However, Carton admitted,

> I have been, and am still, an inveterate reader of novels [...] Even as a means of amusement, if they were nothing more, novels cannot be too highly valued. They take men out of themselves. They lift them for a time, at least, above the [...] hard realities of daily life. They fill up odd gaps of time with bright and pleasant imaginings.[43]

Judge Carton himself was, as he suggests, a bookish man, and he also advised his audience, 'There is more to be got out of novels than mere amusement. They may in many ways be made a means of intellectual cultivation and of educational advancement.'[44] Such advocates of men's reading were unusual. The incompatibility of imaginative reading with ideas of manliness was reinforced by the popular guides that disparaged men who read novels. It is unsurprising then that men are not commonly portrayed with books, rarely with novels and hardly ever actually reading.

Irish nationalism as a man's project

Irish nationalism took many shapes over the long nineteenth century. Much of the growing nationalist project was directed by, and aimed at, men, apart from the role allocated to women of nurturing nationalist sons. Ireland was symbolised as a woman, to be defended by its menfolk, so that 'women [...]

are not merely transformed into symbols of the nation, they become the territory over which power is exercised'.[45]

The group that became known as the Young Irelanders aspired to create a nationalist consciousness celebratory of Ireland's historical struggles, with an educated populace capable of independent government, and they regarded public literacy as essential to their project.[46] To further this aim, 'a small group of intellectuals', Thomas Davis, Charles Gavan Duffy and John Blake Dillon, founded *The Nation* newspaper in 1842.[47] Davis and Dillon were graduates of Trinity College Dublin and had each been president of Trinity's Historical Society. Addressing the Historical Society, Davis called the nation's history 'the birth-right of her sons'.[48] Davis would be addressing an all-male audience but all the same, the national citizen is here unequivocally male. Duffy saw the goal of Young Ireland as the conversion of the Protestant middle classes to the cause of repealing the Act of Union, reconciling Catholics and 'ordinary' Protestants, while condemning acts of the Ascendancy landlords.[49] This approach therefore wished to persuade the Anglo-Irish that they had a role in an independent Ireland.

Advertisements in *The Nation* were aimed at a readership 'solidly middle class and prosperous'.[50] In Henry McManus's oil painting *Reading 'The Nation'* of the 1850s (Figure 2), the named newspaper functions as an advertisement for itself and by extension the nationalist cause.[51] The picture depicts an elderly, bespectacled man holding up the newspaper among five serious animated men, while two women standing behind them and excluded from the group smile together about a different matter. The figures appear well-fed and well-dressed, one of the men wearing a kind of cravat. The painting suggests that Irish nationalism as promulgated through the *Nation* is a popular topic of debate, particularly among middle-class men.

James Quinn, writing in 2019, argues that 'Young Ireland was crucial in helping to establish print culture as an integral part of nationalist movements'.[52] In 1845, the group produced a series of publications in history, poetry and fiction intended to form a new national literature for a 'Library of Ireland'.[53] Although publications for the 'Library of Ireland' focused on past deeds, they were supposed to be emulated in the present. Gerry Smyth in *The Novel and the Nation* (1997) suggests that in Ireland over the nineteenth century, the discourse of a '*past*-oriented culture *of* the nation' was subsumed by that of a '*future*-oriented culture *for* the nation'.[54] The 'Library' promoted a putative masculine heroism and fighting spirit. For instance, in his biography of a medieval chief, the author Thomas D'Arcy McGee hoped for a contemporary revival of 'manhood […] chivalry, the love of native land'.[55] Again, the manly ideal is a bellicose one.

The Irish Republican Brotherhood (IRB), counterpart to the Fenian Brotherhood in America and established as a secret body by former Young Irelanders, was set up explicitly to cultivate a militaristic manhood in readiness for an uprising. The IRB was an entirely male organisation and supported by a new newspaper, the *Irish People*, which in 1863 claimed that 'every Irishman, worthy of the name, believes once more that he has a soldier's heart and arm'. A war of independence with 'sacrifices and heroic deaths' was wished for and regarded as 'ennobling'.[56] Unlike the *Nation*, the *Irish People* reified manliness by eschewing any female input.[57]

Valente argues that Irish nationalists, such as advocates for Young Ireland or the IRB, who aspired to manliness found themselves in a double bind of engaging in violent or militaristic actions when they were seen as uncontrolled and brutish, or exercising manly restraint, behaviour interpreted as feminised.[58] The IRB adapted a cult of manhood popular in Britain and Europe that included 'qualities of physical courage, chivalric ideals, virtuous fortitude [...] military and patriotic virtue'.[59] This combination of militaristic ideology with aspirations to valour and chivalry does not sound so far removed from the manly aspirations of Valente's gentleman. The IRB attracted the middle and especially the lower middle classes in thousands, and by the mid-1860s it had over 50,000 adherents.[60]

The Gaelic Athletic Association (GAA), founded in 1884 by Michael Cusack, a teacher, sportsman and native Irish speaker from Co. Clare, had IRB links although the extent of Cusack's own involvement with the IRB is debated. John O'Leary, former literary editor of the *Irish People* and nominal head of the IRB, was a GAA patron.[61] The GAA stood for a putative retrieval of the Irish games of hurling and Gaelic football and set out to substitute them for the English games of football and cricket.[62] The GAA also had ties to Roman Catholicism and its first patron was Thomas William Croke, Catholic Archbishop of Cashel, Ireland.[63] The close connection between the team sports and Protestant masculinity of 'Muscular Christianity' is mirrored in the term 'Muscular Catholicism' to refer to a new Catholic masculinity.[64] Patrick McDevitt suggests that a new notion of manhood was created that instead of being based on Protestant elitism drew on a Catholic communalism.[65]

The GAA promoted the ideal of an aggressive yet tempered Irish manliness. The earlier violence of the Irish games, especially hurling, was controlled through standardisation, just as the English games had recently been codified. The Irish games were to be violent within limits, thus making them suitable for manly men, who would be tough yet civilised, countering both the brutality and the effeminacy placed upon them by a colonising people, as well as building an athletic body against the image of the body weakened by Famine.[66] 'Founding members and patrons of the GAA favored a masculinized figure – the Gaelic body – performing on a sentimental pitch, the Gaelic field.'[67] This new Irish manhood was set not only against the English and the Anglo-Irish but also against Irish women, while independent women such as those who fox hunted were deemed irredeemable and incapable of motherhood.[68]

As part of the efforts to recover a putative Irish historical culture, further recreational activities such as dancing were co-opted for the nationalist cause. For example, a popular guide to Irish dancing written by a prominent member of the Gaelic League, John Sheehan, and published in 1902, addressing male dance partners, advised, 'Don't hug your partner round the waist English fashion […] be careful to avoid any straining after "deportment" […] be natural, unaffected, easy – be Irish.'[69]

A women's nationalist organisation *Inghinidhe na hÉireann* (Daughters of Erin) led by Maud Gonne was established in 1900 with the aim of complete independence for Ireland, combatting English influence and teaching Irish language and culture to the young.[70] In 1908 it produced the first women's paper in Ireland, *Bean na hÉireann* (Woman of Ireland).[71] However, the nationalist cause remained generally dominated by the men's organisations and publications, although its history has also elided women retrospectively.[72]

Sinn Féin (We Ourselves), as founded by Arthur Griffith in 1905, was a 'broadly based, non-extreme organisation' committed to a policy of economic nationalism such as the use of boycotts.[73] Unusually, women were elected to its executive in 1907. However, advice proffered to universities the following year is for men: 'If the new Universities are to be a benefit to Ireland, the demand of Sinn Féin that they shall teach young Irishmen to regard commerce and industry as the main pursuits of Irishmen must be honoured.'[74] In this modern nationalist version of Irish manliness, the ideal occupation is as a businessman.

The Irish Literary Renaissance that grew out of the preoccupation with Ireland's Gaelic heritage and flourished from the later nineteenth century had many strands. Revivalists included Anglo-Irish authors and poets such as W. B. Yeats, John Millington Synge and Lady Augusta Gregory. Introducing his first volume of Irish folk tales in 1888, W. B. Yeats described them as 'full of simplicity and musical occurrences'.[75] By contrast, *In the Celtic Past* (1904) by Anna MacManus presents violent stories of warrior battles.[76] Despite its female contributors, the Literary Renaissance constituted 'essentially a male narrative'.[77] However, again there has been a retrospective elision of women's considerable creative output at this time (see Chapter 5).

The brothers A. M. and T. D. Sullivan, who edited the *Nation* for many years, continued on the earlier path of Young Ireland and in 1913 edited *Irish Readings*, a miscellany of history, poetry, fiction, essays, lectures and speeches based on the premise that 'our national literature is now essentially patriotic', and intended to be brought into 'the homes and hearts of all our countrymen' to inspire 'the mechanic, and the peasant, and the schoolboy'.[78] Clearly boys and men are the intended audience for such cultural inspiration. *Irish Readings* is threaded through with stories of Ireland's heroic past bids for freedom. For example, John O'Donnell's poem, *On the Rampart: Limerick*, has the constant refrain:

> Where Freedom's seed was sown in blood
> To blossom into ashes[79]

As in the *Nation*, the Anglo-Irish have a role. It is notable that in *Irish Readings* an Anglo-Irish Protestant revolutionary like Theobald Wolfe Tone is regarded as exemplifying 'how thoroughly fused into the Irish race are the descendants of many who came over to our shores in hostile guise'.[80]

Irish nationalism therefore encompassed a range of views and proponents, but it remained predominantly a men's project. Some versions of nationalism accommodated the Anglo-Irish while others were militantly hostile towards them. Catholic and Gaelic nationalism, like imperial masculinity, tended to value physical and practical activities over imaginative and intellectual work. While literacy was regarded as necessary for an independent populace, reading was valued particularly for its inculcation of a valorous manliness.

Portraits of reading men

Across different professions, the normative national historical figure in Ireland was male, and art galleries are full of manly actors.[81] The National Gallery of Ireland, founded in 1864, assembled portraits of national figures that were collected and viewed as history paintings and represented men who had been active in national and military events. When the Municipal Gallery of Modern Art in Dublin was launched in 1908, its founder, Hugh Lane, unusually envisioned it as displaying the portraits of modern Irish figures, both men and women.[82] However, eventually, the Hugh Lane collection was typical of many galleries in that 'the visual record of the political elite is overwhelmingly male'.[83] Only a small minority of those portraits depict the subject reading or with a book. This section examines some of those which do, and suggests that the books featured tend to be functional and symbolic of the subject's social status.

The politician and the cleric

A curious early example in this period is Maria Spilsbury's *Portrait of Henry Grattan MP, in a Library* (oil on canvas, c. 1817, Figure 3). Spilsbury was born in London in 1776 but moved to Ireland with her husband, John Taylor, in

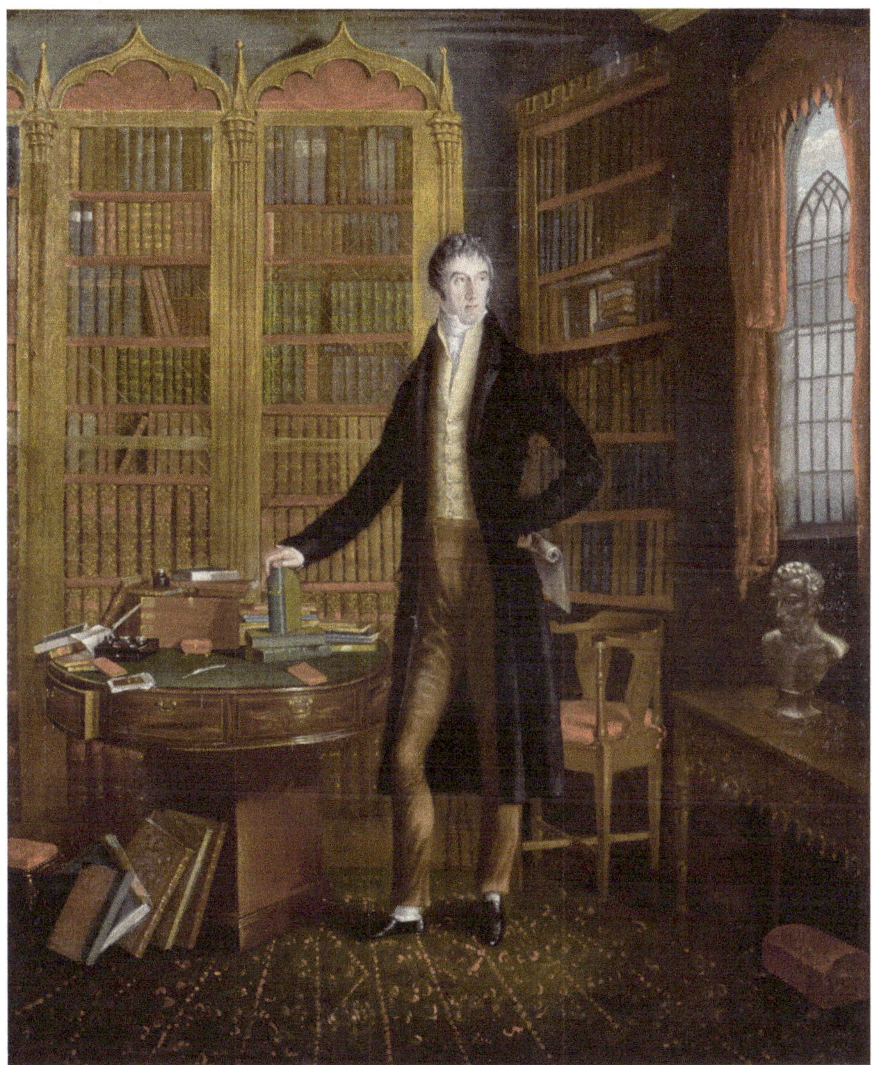

Figure 3 Maria Spilsbury, *Portrait of Henry Grattan MP, in a Library*, oil on canvas, 96.5 × 79.5 cm, c. 1817. Courtesy of Sotheby's.

1813–14, where she lived until her death in 1820. Spilsbury's work as an artist in Ireland was greatly helped by her family's connections with the Protestant elite there, especially through the Tighe family. Spilsbury's father had taught drawing to the daughters of Sarah Tighe, an Evangelical Methodist with landed estates in Ireland.[84] Spilsbury's subject, the politician Henry Grattan, was born in Dublin and was baptised in the Church of St John the Evangelist.

He was a member of the Anglo-Irish Protestant landlord class and a habitué of Daly's, an exclusive gentleman's club in Dublin patronised by members of the Irish Parliament. Grattan supported Catholic Emancipation and campaigned for greater freedom for the Irish Parliament, although he later became an MP in the British House of Commons, where he continued to speak on the 'Catholic question'. He believed it would benefit the Protestant Ascendancy to grant rights to Irish Catholics, arguing that 'the progressive adoption of the Roman Catholics does not surrender, but ascertains the Protestant Ascendancy'.[85]

Spilsbury's portrait depicts Grattan standing by a table in a library, or his study, his right hand supporting a history of Ireland on end, and which at the same time symbolically supports him. Grattan had studied classical literature and oratory at Trinity College Dublin and was known for his oratorical skill:

> His eloquence was of a very high order [...] In the constant stream of a diction replete with epigram [...] was poured forth the closest reasoning, the most luminous statement, the most persuasive display of all the motives that could influence, and of all the details that could enlighten his audience.[86]

He is an embodiment of imperial man, characterised by decisive action, whose oration is designed to influence and direct others. Grattan's pose is suitably histrionic, with one arm outstretched to place his hand on the book, the other arm on his hip, his fingers holding a scroll, one leg stepped forward, the other straight, mirroring the asymmetry of his upper body. This is a curious portrait which shows Grattan as exaggeratedly tall and thin, conveying a sense of authority but also of asceticism. His thin tallness is echoed in the towering bookcases topped by Gothic arches and finials, and full of weighty tomes, and a Gothic-leaning window. Grattan is placed at the commanding centre of the space with a physical link to the book-learning it represents. The room itself seems heavy with learning and history, while the window offers perhaps an aspirational glimpse of blue sky and cumulus. John Henry Foley's later bronze statue of Grattan facing Trinity College on College Green, erected in 1876, retains a histrionic element as the figure steps forward, one arm raised. Placed on a tall limestone pedestal, the statue was formerly at the centre of four gas lamp standards, reinforcing its importance as a public monument.

Alongside political portraits, there is a tradition of portraits of Irish male clerics and these may have books as the sign of their profession and implied learnedness. Martin Archer Shee's formal portrait of Walter Blake Kirwan

(c. 1800–1803) shows him accompanied by books, scrolls and quill. Spilsbury's portrait *The Revd. B.W. Mathias, AM, Chaplain of Bethesda and of the Lock Penitentiary, Dublin* (mezzotint, engraved by Charles Turner, 1821, Figure 4) is a persuasive example of the reader as evangelical proselytiser. Spilsbury's and her husband's move to Ireland may have been motivated by a wish to join a pan-evangelical movement that had spread in Ireland following the Union with Britain.[87] Spilsbury was admitted to the Moravian Church in London to which her father, Jonathan Spilsbury, belonged, which encouraged engaging in evangelism.[88] The Moravian Church had established bases in Ireland in the mid-eighteenth century.[89] It valued visual art and portraits of Church leaders were seen to embody exemplars of the faith and of missionary work.[90]

Charlotte Yeldham has pointed out the significant religious content of Spilsbury's art.[91] Spilsbury's earlier work often depicted women and children reading the Bible outside humble English cottages. For example, in *The Bible Reading in the Cottage Garden* (oil on canvas, c. 1808, Private Collection), a young woman and two children are the attentive audience for an older woman reading aloud.[92] Spilsbury's frequent inclusion of books and female readers, with children listening attentively or reading themselves, gives women a family role that extends beyond cooking and cleaning to educating themselves and their offspring. However, in such pictures the woman's role is as mother, nurturer and moral guide, and reading materials are dominated by the Bible.

Spilsbury executed portraits of Anglican clerics sympathetic to Evangelicalism, as well as Calvinism. She painted her friend Reverend Thomas Kelly, a Calvinist, his fingers keeping a place in his Bible. In one portrait, he sits half-turned from his desk in his study (*Reverend Thomas Kelly*, oil on canvas, c. 1815, Private Collection) and in another, he is again shown in his study and keeping his page (oil on canvas, n.d., Private Collection).[93] There was a connection between Kelly and the Tighe family, as he had married Sarah Tighe's daughter, Elizabeth. Reverend B. W. Mathias was curate to Mr Tighe, and an Anglican preacher, again with Calvinist leanings, whose work widely promoted evangelical thinking in the Anglican Church.

Like many subjects of portraits of readers, particularly women, Mathias was a committed reader, growing up from a well-behaved and bookish child into a polite and studious graduate of Trinity College Dublin,

> the young Benjamin [...] manifested great love for reading, even when a mere child [...] [and] he used when very young to lay out every sixpence he could command in buying books, and when he had collected a few, fixed some shelves in his trunk, which he turned on the end to form a book-case, and over these he used to bend, looking at them with as much delight as ever miser gazed on his gold.[94]

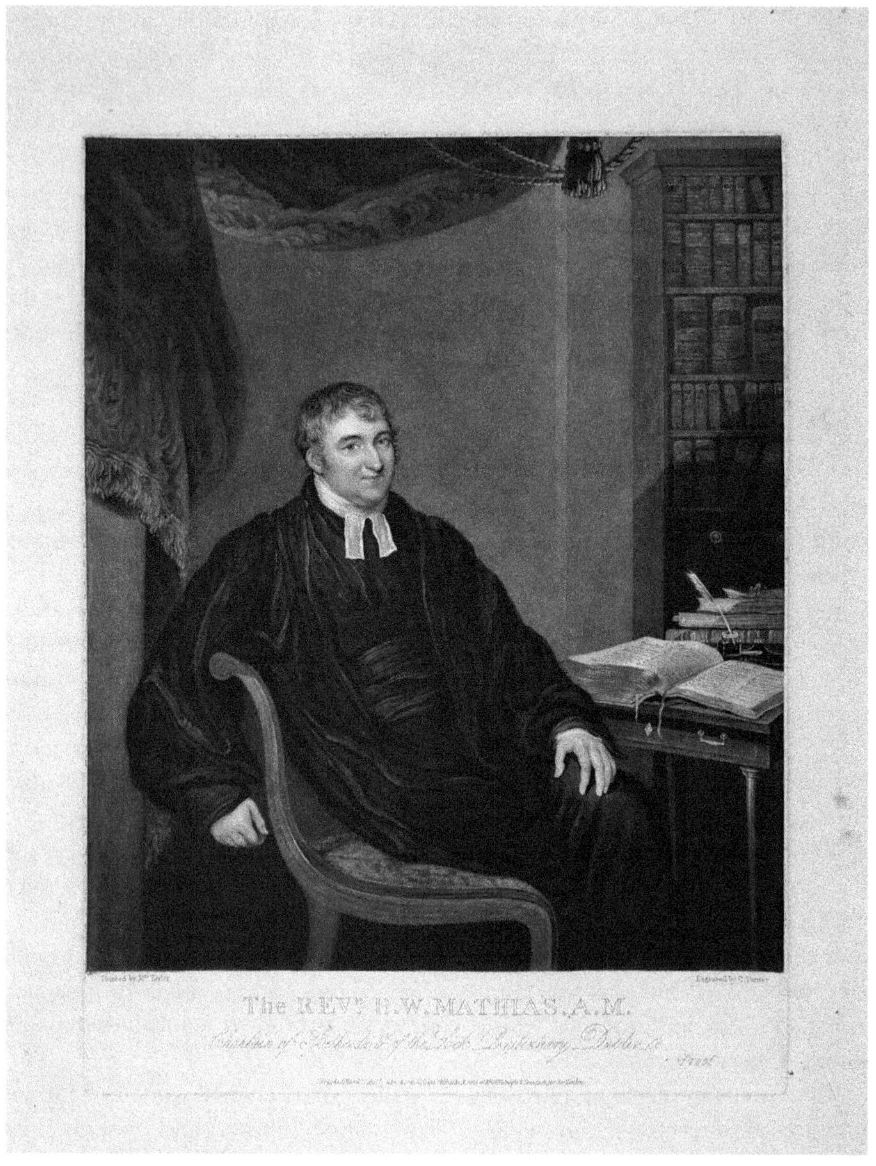

Figure 4 Maria Spilsbury, *The Revd. B. W. Mathias, AM, Chaplain of Bethesda and of the Lock Penitentiary, Dublin*, mezzotint, engraved by Charles Turner, 35.3 × 20.5 cm, 1821. © The Trustees of the British Museum.

Mathias practised for 30 years as chaplain of Bethesda Chapel, Granby Row, Dublin, known as 'the only evangelical Anglican place of worship in Dublin', and his work has been claimed to be 'the most important single factor in the spread of evangelical principles throughout the Established Church'.[95] Mathias has been described as a 'moderate Calvinist' adhering to the idea of universal salvation, not predestination for the select, and he believed that the best life was one lived with meekness.[96]

Spilsbury's images might be seen to embody aspects of evangelical thinking. In her portrait of the Reverend Mathias, the sitter is turned temporarily from the act of reading a large Bible. The Bible is especially significant in evangelical doctrine, which emphasises the personal relation between penitent and God. The Moravian Church held that the Bible should be read directly by people and it produced the earliest Bible in the vernacular.[97] The cleric's attitude is informal. The temporariness of the pose is emphasised by the relaxed yet slightly awkward hang of his right arm over the back of the chair as if to anchor him in position. A heavy curtain and the shadow to the right indicate that the window and light source are behind the figure, while light falls on the Bible, and also on Reverend Mathias's face, collar and hands. The open Bible references the Gospel according to St John. Behind the Bible stand an ink well and quill and further books, making a bookish working desk. According to Moravian belief, a 'cheerful or serene facial expression indicated a state of grace'.[98] Mathias wears an amicable facial expression, encouraging the viewer to share his activity as he gazes at the viewer with quiet optimism. The weighty dimensions of the Bible, which may have been for ease of reading or for effect, gives it additional prominence. The Bible is emphasised by the light that falls on it, which also illuminates Mathias's face as he looks out at the viewer. Like Spilsbury's other pictures of religious men, this depicts a professional man momentarily suspending his dutiful work, not someone engaged in the reading for pleasure.

Evangelical doctrine may have encouraged less emphasis on the presentation of ecclesiastical hierarchy than might generally be the case in portraits of Anglican or Catholic clergy. However, despite the informal pose, and benevolent expression, the sitter represents a figure of authority. He is dressed in his official garb. His full desk and the bookcase packed with heavy tomes confer scholarly status. The Bible signifies his profession, as with the accessory objects in earlier painting traditions. If Evangelism/Calvinism had an ascetic image, his portly well-fed figure does not embody it.

Many nineteenth- and early twentieth-century portraits of women were designed for the male gaze. In Spilsbury's portraits of ecclesiastical figures, as in her portrait of Henry Grattan, there is an unusual reversal of the traditional arrangement of male artist and female sitter. If Grattan looked histrionically off to one side, ignoring the gaze of the artist/viewer, in the case of the portrait of Mathias, the female artist gazes at a male sitter who looks back at her and the viewer. Yet although Spilsbury might control aspects of how Mathias appears, her subject's equable gaze conveys a quiet patriarchal authority. The sitter engages with the viewer, who consequently takes the part of the person diverting the preacher from his study and the witness to his spiritual efforts. In both the portrait of Grattan and that of Mathias, the accoutrements surrounding the men, especially the books, contribute to defining their professional status.

In a later example of the use of a book to signal a professional religious identity, Patrick Tuohy's *Priest by Stained Glass Window* (oil on canvas, c. 1915, Figure 5) depicts a Catholic priest in three-quarters view, one hand on his hip, the other holding a missal, symbol of his faith and profession. Tuohy himself had a Catholic education. However, the model here was not a priest but Tuohy's friend, Dominick Bowe, a sculptor.[99] Behind the priest's head and shoulders is a stained glass window, functioning as a sort of elliptical halo, drawing attention to his 'natural' habitat of a church and to his special professional status. The figure looks directly, even challengingly, at the viewer, although the import of his interrogative gaze remains obscure.

Signalling scholarship

A bronze statue of the eighteenth-century Irish novelist and playwright Oliver Goldsmith shows him standing with an open book in one hand. The statue is unusual in its inclusion of a book and the figure's active engaged stance as he looks down at it. The figure was sculpted in 1864 by John Henry Foley and erected in 1866, mounted on a granite plinth on the lawn near the main entrance to Trinity College Dublin. The statue's location aligns the figure and book with academia, while the height and solidity of the plinth, which requires the viewer to gaze upwards at it, contribute to ensuring that the work represents an impressive public commemoration of a famous alumnus.

Sarah Purser's portrait of John Kells Ingram (oil on canvas, 1897, Figure 6) again uses a book to signal intellectual status. This painting also represents a public celebration of its subject, although viewing is mainly confined to members of the RIA, where it hangs. Ingram was an internationally recognised scholar at Trinity College Dublin, with publications on subjects ranging from mathematics to Shakespearean criticism. He was president of the RIA from 1892 to 1896. Purser's portrait, commissioned for the RIA and completed in early 1897, presents Ingram as a scholar in academic dress, looking up from an open book. It is designed to be a public portrait of a prominent academic

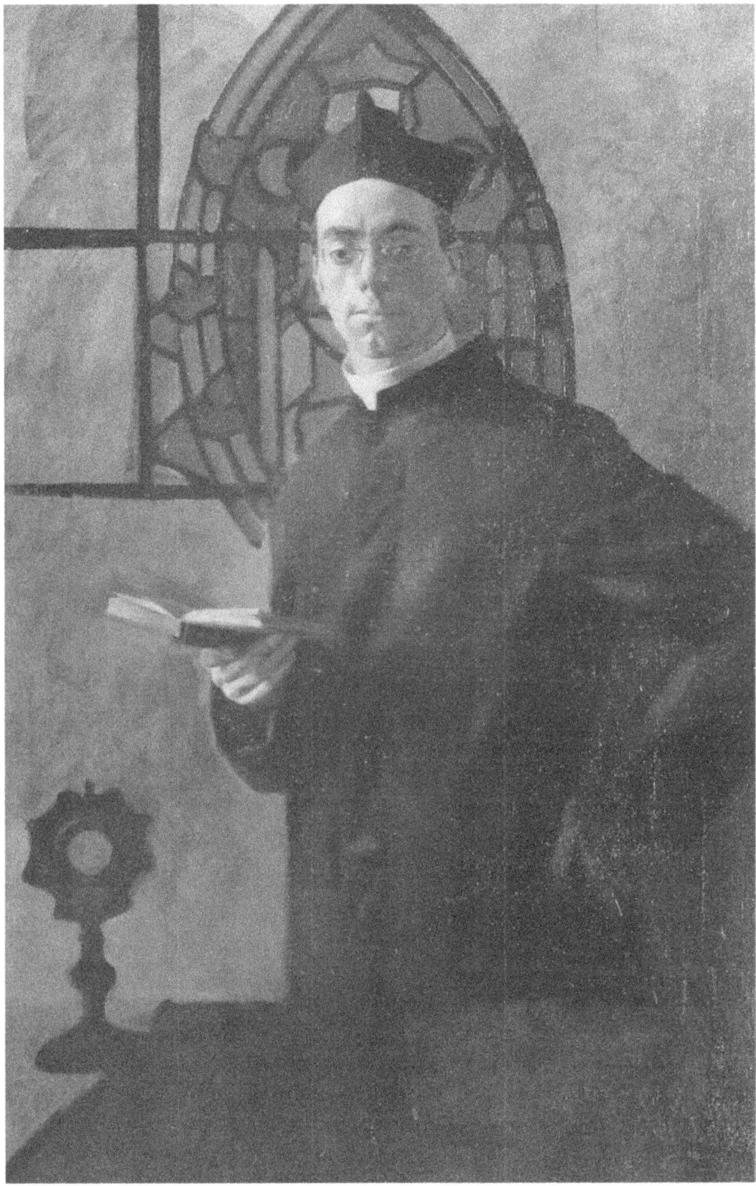

Figure 5 Patrick Tuohy, *Priest by Stained Glass Window*, oil on canvas, 122 × 76 cm, c. 1915, Private Collection.

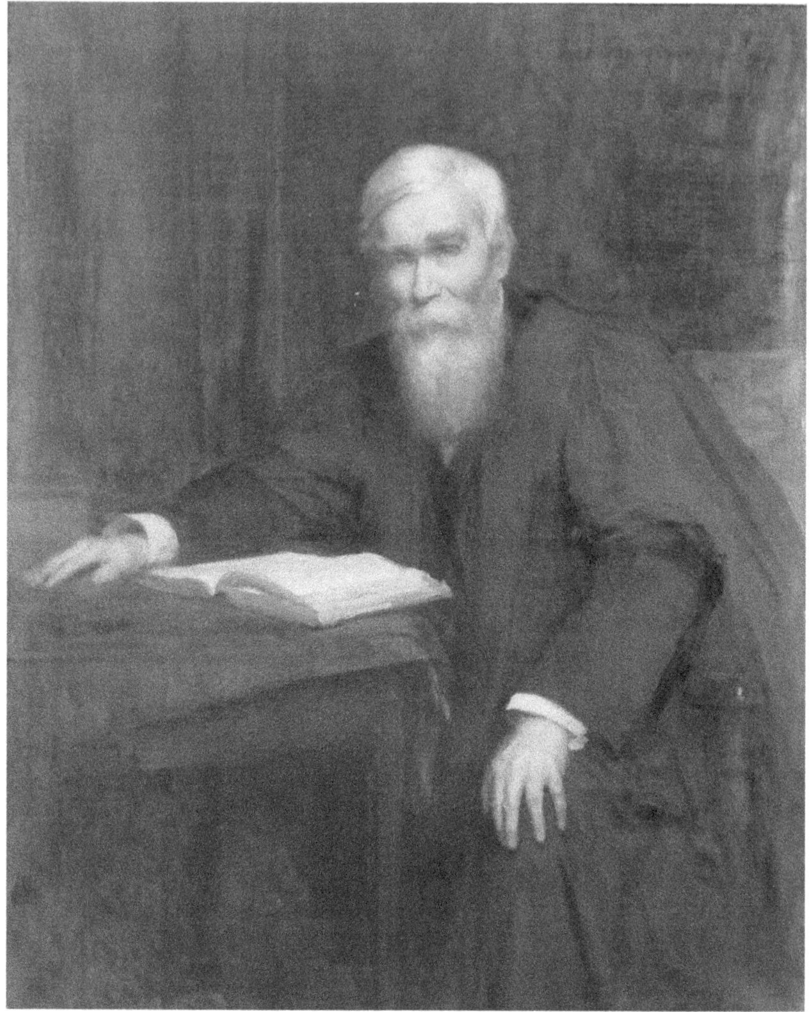

Figure 6 Sarah Purser, *John Kells Ingram*, oil on canvas, 125.5 × 100 cm, c. 1897. By permission of the Royal Irish Academy © RIA. Courtesy of Michael Purser.

figure in one of Dublin's most prestigious Anglo-Irish institutions, the book symbolising his scholarly status.[100]

However, Ingram became especially well-known in Ireland as a result of a patriotic poem about the 1798 rebellion that he had penned in one night in 1843, *The Memory of the Dead*, which was published in the next edition of the *Nation*.[101] In the context of contemporary notions of manliness, Ingram's poem has a heroic patriotic refrain which with slight variations ends each of his six verses:

> And we will pray that from their clay
>
> Full many a race may start
>
> Of true men, like you, men,
>
> To act as brave a part.[102]

However, Ingram stated in 1900 that he had little sympathy for rebellion then in completely different circumstances.[103] His liberal views included advocacy for women's admission to college.[104]

The Exile from Erin

Jack B. Yeats's oil painting, *The Exile from Erin* (c. 1913, Figure 7), depicts a male figure reading a newspaper in an office.[105] Yeats's politics were republican, and this painting might be regarded as a nationalist text contributing to the complex nationalist formation of contemporary Ireland. Yeats was brought up in Sligo and he celebrated the men of the West in his art, for example, in *The Man from Aranmore* (black chalk and watercolour on board, 1905, National Gallery of Ireland) which represents a proud island man.[106] Yeats had lived and worked in London and Devon but looked to Ireland as his home and by 1913 he had returned to settle in Ireland permanently with his wife Cottie. *The Exile from Erin* could draw on his experiences of attachment to Ireland, especially the West, and of working abroad. It was painted for inclusion in George A. Birmingham's book *Irishmen All*, published in 1913. George A. Birmingham was the pseudonym for Rev. James Owen Hannay, a Church of Ireland minister, Gaelic League activist, and prolific novelist and playwright. *Irishmen All* takes a mildly satirical view of 12 Irish types, each type accompanied by an illustration from Yeats's paintings. However, Yeats based his 12 paintings on just the chapter headings for Hannay's book, and there was no communication between illustrator and author, who did not see each other's work until completion.[107]

Hannay satirically compares Ireland to a picture full of dots that shape themselves into a beautiful view only from afar: 'London is the nearest place from which a person of normal vision can see Kathaleen ní Houlahan [*sic*] […] the inhabitants of places like Athlone and Mullingar only see Irishmen, not Ireland.'[108] Hannay's characterisation of the 'Exile from Erin' is not a flattering one. Noting that 'the exiles from Erin whose whole lives are spent in London are far the most patriotic Irishmen there are', Hannay portrays such

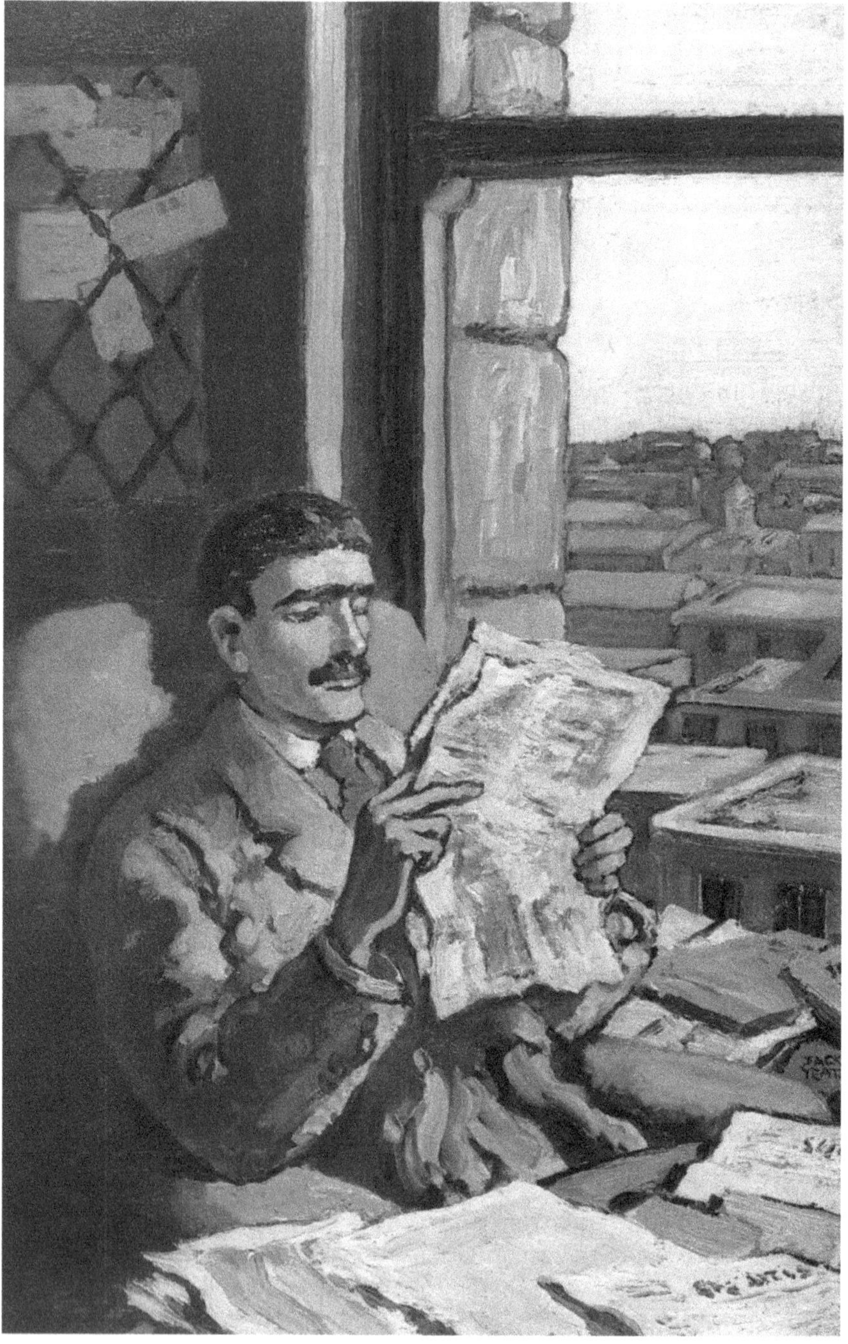

Figure 7 Jack B. Yeats, *The Exile from Erin*, c. 1913, Private collection. © Estate of Jack B. Yeats, DACS London/IVARO Dublin, 2020. Image courtesy of Pyms Gallery, London.

patriots as overly serious and slightly ridiculous in their cultivation of things Irish.[109] Hilary Pyle describes the exile in Yeats's painting as a 'high-minded patriot'.[110] However, this description suits Hannay's story, rather than Yeats's painting.

There is a different kind of narrative in *The Exile from Erin* to that of many images of women readers as the figure is located not in the domestic setting of a study, for instance, but in the public space of an office. The male figure sits beside a prominent, uncurtained office window. The outside world is visible, but does not beckon, where the view is of a bleak and treeless urban scene. The picture's title suggests that the figure is somewhere removed from his home country and estranged from his present circumstance. The flat-roofed architecture through the window indicates perhaps some part of America: his father, John B. Yeats, had emigrated to New York a few years earlier. For Yeats, Hannay's chapter heading, 'The Exile from Erin', conjures a man confined in a grey environment. A noticeboard behind containing letters, which stands out in red-brown colour, may symbolise the world outside. The figure sitting by the window looks at a newspaper, with other papers scattered over the desk. He has a finger between the pages, as if reading or scanning the paper quickly. The papers may be from his home country, or part of his job perhaps as a journalist. He may be indulging in nostalgia or occupied in professional work, but unlike the various images of women readers who focus carefully on, or momentarily glance up from, a book, he is not engaged in reading for the purpose of study or pleasure. He wears a jacket and tie and his close-cropped dark hair is office style; otherwise he might resemble the proud and swarthy dark-haired figures from Yeats's early graphic repertoire of pirates and island men. However, the figure does not have an air of pride but an unhappy expression. Instead of commanding an expansive environment, the figure is physically confined by the wall behind and his desk. The chair itself confines him with its narrow arms and the external wall beyond the window is heavy stone. He is also restricted by the window, although at the same time through the large expanse of modern glass, he is exposed to the bleak scene outside.

Yeats attached importance to his titles. *Exile from Erin* refers to this bleak office scene with its colourless view onto treeless rows of houses. The concept of the exile, and the naming of *Erin*, evokes an alternative space which is the home of the exile. The letters inserted on a noticeboard behind him may be from home, again suggesting the absent place. The name *Erin* derives both from the Gaelic *Éirinn* (Ireland) and from *Ériu*, in pre-Christian Gaelic mythology, Goddess of Ireland. *Erin* has long had connotations of rurality, greenness and independence, the proud 'Emerald Isle', as William Drennan, an influential nationalist from Belfast, christened it in his poem *When Erin First Rose* of 1795. The picture and title together therefore have both an immediate referent, the displaced worker in his foreign office, and an implied referent, a longed-for romantic Ireland. The window and its drab and natureless outlook conjures an idea of exile in contrast to the absent homeland. In Pierre Macherey's terms, *The Exile from Erin* contains a stated text and a more eloquent silence.[111] Yeats's image, therefore, for all its greyness, evokes a colourful, Romantic, absent Ireland. The figure's functional reading forms part of the unpleasurable experience of his current foreign setting.

In summary, pictures that portray men with books at this time tend to use the book to indicate a social status, whether political, religious or scholarly, rather than focusing on the subject as a reader. Jack Yeats's figure and his occupation have a more complex signification. Again the main emphasis is not on the figure as a reader, at least not a voluntary reader. The reading matter, which is ephemeral, constitutes part of the empty and alien condition of exile, which is opposed to the literary and visual allusions of Erin.

The unmanly reader

The men who read books such as novels for pleasure and intellectual stimulus did not easily conform to the attributes of imperial man, nor to those of heroic nationalist mythology. Such engagement would be contrary to the worlds of practical knowledge and sporting and military activities. It would fail to heed the advice on men's reading offered by popular guides and by nationalist writers.

There are images in contemporary Irish literature, however, of a less action-driven and more introverted masculinity. This type tended to be reserved for Protestant protagonists, but not in conformity to the normative Anglo-Irish imperial man. For example, in William Carleton's story *Father Butler*, published in Dublin in 1829, book reading is associated with a man of intelligence. The story's narrator, a Protestant landlord, describes the protagonist, James Butler, when he first sees him by a Churchyard as 'a young man whose appearance was not only respectable but genteel […] his countenance expressive and intelligent […] he had a book in his hand'.[112] The young man is distressed and flings the book to the ground, which, symbolically, turns out to be a Roman Breviary.[113] When the narrator visits James Butler at home, he finds him 'in the parlour, reading' and following him to his study, he finds it 'small, but neat and well furnished with literature'.[114] The narrator too is a reader, observing that on his way home he was 'driving leisurely along, reading a book, as I am in the habit of doing'.[115]

In Somerville and Ross's novel *The Real Charlotte* of 1894, the character Christopher Dysart, a member of the Protestant Ascendancy, schooled at

Winchester and Oxford, presents an example of the 'unmanly' man. Dysart is described as

> a young man of a reflective turn, and […] artistic aspirations […] not smart and aggressive enough for the soldiering type, nor sporting enough for the country gentleman […] his lack of interest in the majority of manly occupations, from hunting to music halls, has small claim to respect.[116]

In the eyes of a more 'manly' character, Roderick Lambert, Dysart's hair 'grew rather long, with a wave in it that was […] the height of effeminacy'.[117] Hiding from the company at a picnic, 'the invertebrateness of his character seemed to be expressed in his attitude, as he lay, supine, under the birch trees'.[118]

Recreational reading

Informal portraits of male subjects reading sometimes showed them with a newspaper, likely to contain reports of local and international news and generally designed for a male readership. Their posture, however, was not always the masculine one of readiness for action. A pencil drawing of Sir Joscelyn Coghill, 4th Bart, by his niece, the Anglo-Irish artist Edith Somerville, executed in Düsseldorf in 1881 (Figure 8), shows him absorbed in a newspaper. Coghill was a wealthy member of the Ascendancy although in some ways not a typical Ascendancy figure, being interested in modern art and a well-known promoter of Art Photography in Dublin.[119] His reading matter may be the County Cork newspaper, the pro-British *Skibbereen Eagle* which was read by the family.[120] In her diary of 8 April 1881, Somerville noted that a copy of the *Eagle* had arrived, containing family news.[121] Somerville depicts Coghill in an almost recumbent position, sunk into a *canapé à confidante* with his shod foot on the upholstered cushion of a supplementary chair.[122] She conveys her subject's relaxation in a number of fluid curves, of the chair-arm, and chair-leg, the back of his body, the newspaper itself.[123] The figure does not project a man of action but a man comfortably reading.

An unsigned and undated oil portrait of the artist Roderic O'Conor by the 'Irish School', or possibly a self-portrait, shows him recumbent on a blanket on the grass reading a newspaper in luminous sunlight.[124] The picture might have been executed in France, where O'Conor worked. In the portrait, O'Conor wears a three-piece suit, albeit with one trouser leg rolled above a sockless ankle, but it was not uncommon in nineteenth-century France for male artists to dress quite formally. The figure is depicted half sitting up to look down on the paper, a grassy bank tilted up behind and a little glimpse of blue, perhaps

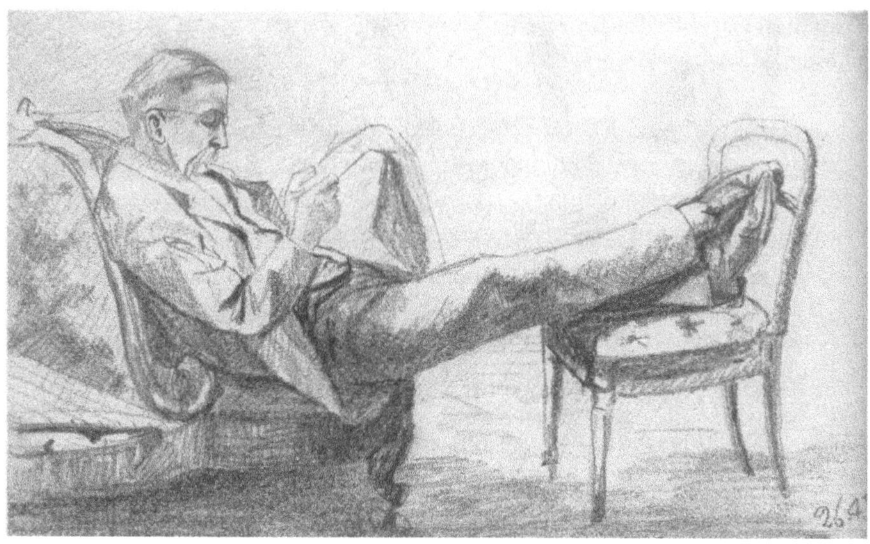

Figure 8 Edith Somerville, Sir J. J. Coghill, Pencil drawing, Dusseldorf 26 April 1881. Edith Œ. Somerville Sketchbook Collection, 1881–c. 1912 (Private Collection). Photo courtesy of Julie Anne Stevens.

the sea, in one corner. This composition focuses the viewer's attention on the reading figure and his concentration on a newspaper and on the act of reading, although the paper itself is painted as a blank. O'Conor is shown in an absorbed and careless pose, not presented as a disciplined man of action, nor does he face or acknowledge the viewer.

In *Marsh's Library, Dublin* of 1898 (oil on panel, Hugh Lane Gallery, Dublin) by Walter Osborne, four men are depicted reading and note-taking.[125] The main collections of the library were theological, scientific and informational texts, so the reading undertaken might be assumed to follow the general pattern of men's reading, but the library also contained plays and poetry. The setting is intimate, and simply furnished with solid wooden chairs. Only a bright green tablecloth stands out from the dark tones of the background. Apart from a scarlet necktie worn by one reader, their clothes are muted in colour. The window shutters are mostly closed, enhancing an air of concentration among the men, cut off from the outside world. The men's quiet focus on their books is emphasised by an absence of eye contact with one another, or with the viewer. Light is thrown on the pages of the book held by the right-hand reader and on the books and papers on the table, as well as on the faces of readers. This emphasises the reading and writing materials, and the men's absorbed or contemplative expressions, conveying an air of study. A vague bust on top of one of the bookcases offers a generalised historical reference, but there is no element here of a status-enhancing public painting.

A bibliophile and nationalist: Seumas O'Sullivan

Seumas O' Sullivan, born James Sullivan Starkey, was an Irish nationalist and a 'passionate bibliophile'.[126] He was the partner and later husband of the artist Estella Solomons. Solomons, also an active nationalist, attended Alexandra College and Dublin Metropolitan School of Art, and her drawings and paintings often featured O'Sullivan busy reading.[127] When Solomons and O'Sullivan moved house in 1938, they transported 10,000 books.[128] Speaking at a P.E.N. celebration after his award of an honorary doctorate by Trinity College, O'Sullivan described creeping around bookstalls at Aston Quay as a schoolboy and worshipping from afar 'those great bookmen – mostly professors of Trinity – who also bent above the books'.[129] O'Sullivan read constantly and throughout his life, and Solomons did many sketches of him reading.[130] A torn sheet in one of her sketchbooks, placed near a related sketch, has an ink drawing of a bookplate inscribed 'Ex libris: James Sullivan Starkey', illustrated for some reason by the Greek mythological figure of Pan sitting in a street window alcove, reading a book.[131] As reader, collector, poet and nationalist, O'Sullivan was an important figure in recuperating Irish literature. O'Sullivan's grand-father, Rev. James Sullivan, a Wesleyan clergyman, had written 'certain small books in the Gaelic language' with his name on the title page given as Seumas O'Sullivan.[132] O'Sullivan clearly admired his grandfather, whom he described as 'sincere and hardworking' and whose Irish name he adopted. Among mis-cellaneous papers of Seumas O'Sullivan are various nationalist newspapers, and a printed sheet from Arthur Griffith, 17 Fownes Street, Dublin, promoting his paper, the *United Irishman*, which had been founded 'to sustain the policy of uncompromising Irish Nationalism'.[133] O'Sullivan's little poem *Dublin (1916)* commemorated the leaders of the Rising.

However, as a nationalist O'Sullivan clearly did not subscribe to the militant and practical aspects of nationalist manhood. O'Sullivan was a poet and he remarked later that 'I have always known, that to exchange the imagination for the reality is only "a spendthrift policy"'.[134] One of Solomons's sketches shows O'Sullivan sitting on a deckchair, reading as usual. Wearing sandals, with body turned sideways to cross his legs, smoking his pipe and holding his book, O'Sullivan looks extremely comfortable and well-provided for, but not in a position such as to jump into action.[135] He is depicted without any attempt at aggrandisement or status-marking, unlike, for example, Spilsbury's curious portrait of Henry Grattan in his study, indicating a tome of Irish history (Figure 3). Indeed, there is no landscape or setting provided.[136] This neglect

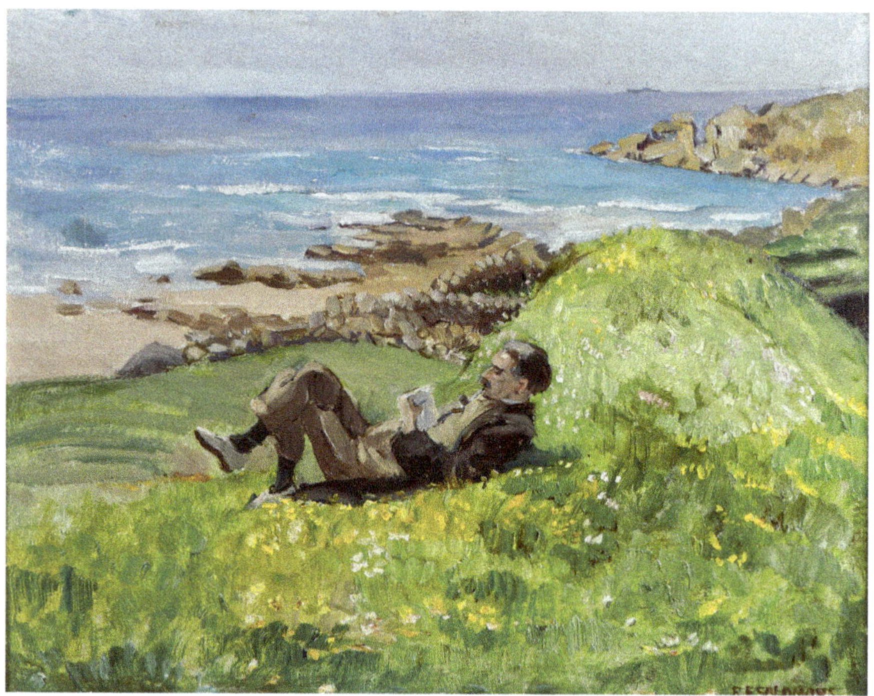

Figure 9 Estella Solomons, *Seumas Reading by the Coast*, oil on board, 31.75 × 40 cm, n.d. © The Trustees of the Estate of Estella Solomons. Photo courtesy of Adam's Auctioneers.

of status-marking seems to have been in character, although as his friend A. J. Leventhal recalled, O'Sullivan was 'always prepared to fight his way into a stiff shirt when I invited him to a College Term dinner'.[137]

Solomons's painting *Seumas Reading by the Coast* (oil on board, n.d., Figure 9) shows O'Sullivan in an informal pose, lost in his book, among sand dunes covered in grass and wild flowers, probably located in north Donegal near Marble Hill, a place of quiet and solitude. Ensconced against a flowery hillock, O'Sullivan is again abstracted from the usual signs of property and power. In a supine position and given the apparent passivity of his occupation, O'Sullivan represents the polar opposite of the man of action. Indeed, his attitude recalls the unmanly 'invertebrateness' ascribed to Christopher Dysart in *The Real Charlotte*.[138]

James Conlon observed with reference to Monet's *Springtime* (oil on canvas, 1872, Walters Art Museum, Baltimore) that 'The female reader at the centre of some luminous summer scene is a familiar cliché of nineteenth-century painting. By placing the woman amid the gentle beneficence of nature, the artist hopes to domesticate the wild act that reading can be.'[139] *Springtime* shows a young woman sitting reading on the grass, dappled in sunlight, her elaborate pale pink dress billowing around her. It is a female portrait designed primarily for an admiring gaze. *Seumas Reading by the Coast* depicts a man similarly located at the centre of a luminous summer scene, engrossed in reading amid grasses and wildflowers. Estella Solomons's sketchily shaped male figure with his book and the act of reading itself are made part of the vibrant summery scene. However, this is the work of a different kind of artist – female and related to the subject – but also implies another kind of model and a different viewer. If *Springtime* shows a delightful but conventional image of a woman reader, *Seumas Reading by the Coast* depicts a male figure reading in an attitude that does not project a typical image of masculine action. O'Sullivan is shown recumbent in a non-dominant and apparently oblivious attitude, the image of a man quietly reading for pleasure wherever he can. Speaking on Radio Éireann following O'Sullivan's death, Leventhal described,

> his sympathy for all that was good in literature and the arts […] his known expertness in the rare occupation of bibliophile […] his knowledge of the habits of birds and his passion for natural science […] apart from all this, he was a rare companion. The last representative, perhaps, of an age that rated dignity and good manners as a curb to impulsive action.[140]

This is an informative eulogy for O'Sullivan, as it depicts a man whose knowledge and interests were in complete opposition to the manly hunting and shooting ethos of the Irish Ascendancy, yet who possessed that important gentlemanly attribute of manliness, namely the ability to control any inclination to act impulsively.

Conclusion

Two dominant conceptions of manliness were current in Ireland at this time. The Anglo-Irish Ascendancy adhered to a manliness formed by their elite status and loyalty to empire, by Protestantism and a belief in Muscular Christianity, the physical strength and moral character supposedly produced by team games. Ancient epics added exemplars of manly valour. Such manliness valued an aggressiveness moderated by gentlemanly self-control. Nationalists produced their own version of manliness, Muscular Catholicism, but with parallels to that of imperial man. They too had their character-forming games, the GAA, and their mythic exemplars, Gaelic heroic tales. Radical republicans valued physical strength and the manly attributes of tempered aggressiveness. None of the dominant forms of manliness was compatible with reading for imaginative or intellectual pleasure. Guides to men's reading derided fiction as suitable only for the lesser intellects of women. This manly rejection of imaginative reading or reading for pleasure was reinforced in visual art, which avoided displaying men as readers. Men are infrequently portrayed reading or even with a book, and when they are, the book generally symbolises their status or profession. There were men who read, and portrayals of such subjects tend to represent them supine with a clear absence of manly assertiveness. However, Yeats's unhappy exile at his desk is an unusual and complex combination of the mythic nationalist man of the West and the modern diasporic office worker.

Chapter 2

'CREATURES OF A DIFFERENT BREED': WOMEN READERS AND PATRIARCHAL DISCOURSE

Women who aspired to intellectual or creative work in this period, whether as independent readers, artists or novelists, were subject to the constraints of the powerful gender discourses common to Ireland, Britain and elsewhere. Art participated in the array of dominant discourses that tended to undermine women's physical and intellectual abilities. This chapter discusses the nature and prevalence of patriarchal ideology in relation to the representation of women readers. Many European and American images of a woman reader, generally by male artists, do not focus on a woman engaged in reading but on a female figure designed for the purpose of pleasing a male gaze. This chapter examines paintings of women readers from Britain, France and elsewhere in which books function as accessories to displays of the female form, whether semi-clothed or elaborately garbed. These images are compared to similar but less ostentatious Irish depictions of women readers, for instance, by John Lavery.[1] This examination presents a standard against which the distinctiveness of the Irish portraits of women readers, mostly by women artists, might be measured.

'Creatures of a different breed'

The French philosopher Michel Foucault argued that sexuality in the Victorian period was a constant focus of discourse.[2] The dominant view was that as a result of their peculiar biology, women were inherently weak, psychologically unstable and unable to engage in intellectual work. This ideology was promulgated through a wide range of contributory discourses and outlets – medical, religious, evolutionary, literary and artistic – that largely emanated from male-dominated institutions and publications. As Foucault commented, 'sex was not something one simply judged; it was a thing one administered [...] it called for management procedures'.[3]

In medical discourse, for instance, women were characterised as frail, their female functions liable to disturbance by serious intellectual work.[4] Foucault spoke of 'a hysterization' of women's bodies [...] the Mother, with her negative image of "nervous woman" constituted the most visible form of this hysterization'.[5] Women have been commonly stereotyped in patriarchal ideology as over-emotional, while men have been characterised as rational. This had far-reaching consequences for women's status because as R. W. Connell suggests, 'hegemonic masculinity establishes its hegemony partly by its claim to embody the power of reason, and thus represent the interests of the whole society'.[6] Reversing this dichotomy, the Anglo-Irish suffragist Frances Power Cobbe observed in 1870 that women had been fighting with logical arguments, but 'it is Sentiment [of men] we have to contend against, not Reason; Feeling and Prepossession, not intellectual Conviction'.[7]

The notion of women's incapacity for rational thought was taken up in many popular communications, with the added claim that women's reading was characteristically lightweight. For example, the English writer William Rathbone Greg asserted in his essay, 'False Morality of Lady Novelists', first published in 1859, that

> novels constitute a principal part of the reading of women, who are always impressionable, in whom at all times the emotional element is more awake and more powerful than the critical, whose feelings are more easily aroused and whose estimates are more easily influenced than ours, while at the same time the correctness of their feelings and the justice of their estimates are matters of the most special and preeminent concern.[8]

Greg not only characterises women readers as lacking in critical judgement but also suggests that this is a matter of particular concern to him, that is, he assumes he and other men have responsibility for women, whose feelings and estimates are incorrect. Greg suggested that novel reading exercised considerable influence 'on the young of both sexes, and on the female sex at every age'.[9] His comment implies that the tastes and abilities of women readers did not develop much beyond childhood. Addressing young men of the Christian Brothers School later, in the 1870s, Judge Richard Carton also observed that 'The novel and the magazine form the only reading of most ladies. The [...] volumes bearing the labels of Greene, or Eason [...] are common objects in every drawing-room.'[10] However, as noted in the previous chapter, Carton took a more favourable view of novels than Greg.

Greg also attacked female novelists, commenting that it was 'impossible that productions of such a character, from such a source [...] should not be radically and inherently defective'.[11] Women were therefore not trusted to make sound or independent judgements about reading matter, nor to respond to their reading in a rational manner, let alone compose novels. In another essay 'Why Are Women Redundant?' Greg pompously observed, 'WOMAN is the subject which for some time back our benevolence has been disposed to take in hand.'[12] Greg noted a surplus of single women in England, especially among the middle and upper classes, 'who, not having the natural duties and labours of wives and mothers [...] in place of completing, sweetening, and embellishing the existence of others, are compelled to lead an independent and incomplete existence of their own'.[13] The role of women was to service and ornament the lives of others, not to seek intellectual or creative independence.

Some women writers, perhaps in the light of a false consciousness derived from the dominant ideology, advocated their own submission. For example, in a series of popular books addressed to 'the middle ranks of society in Great Britain',[14] Sarah Stickney Ellis asserted that 'as women [...] the first thing of importance is to be content to be inferior to men – inferior in mental power, in the same proportion that you are inferior in bodily strength'.[15] Ellis invokes religion in support of her contention, assuming that her reader 'as a Christian woman, has made the decision not to live for herself, so much as for others'.[16] The Church indeed discouraged such independent female pursuits as novel reading. Carton noted, 'the denunciations against novels and romances, which are to be found in the works of all the great spiritual writers of our Church'.[17]

Reading by women provoked dire cautionary tales. Indiscriminate reading had debilitating and fatal effects: 'Tasteless and thoughtless reading [led to] senseless extravagance, insurmountable reluctance to undertake any effort, boundless love of luxury, suppression of the voice of conscience, becoming tired of life, and an early death.'[18] Belinda Jack has observed that 'women readers have long been associated with sexual illicitness and moral degeneration, and male readers with power and authority'.[19] Reading was deemed injurious both to women's health and their moral values, and novel reading in particular was condemned as 'one of the most pernicious habits to which a young lady can become devoted [...] The novel-devotee is as much a slave as the opium-eater or the inebriate'.[20]

Patriarchal discourses in various fields reinforced one another and in turn influenced different domains of social life. For example, arguments relating to women's physical fragility, psychological instability and moral insufficiency, articulated in similar language, were made in relation to the increasingly popular habit in Ireland of tea drinking.[21] Women were regarded as peculiarly susceptible to the addictive properties of tea, such that their health and their families suffered. In a paper read before the Medical Society of the College of Physicians in Ireland, Thomas More Madden, MRIA, noted that tea had been observed to provoke hallucinations: 'I am acquainted with a lady who, if she takes tea in the evening [...] when she falls asleep, is thrown by it into a state of horrible dreaming, from which she always awakes up suddenly, under the illusion that a number of shadowy figures are sitting crouched up on every chair in her room.'[22]

Some authors countered the many critiques of women and their reading habits. An anonymous writer in the Catholic literary magazine *Irish Monthly* in 1886 observed, 'There is one class of the community which is, I think, very unfairly judged and, in fact, slandered – namely, the novel-reading public. Novel-reading ladies are generally denounced as indolent idlers.'[23] Charlotte O'Conor Eccles, an Irish author and journalist, observed in *Irish Monthly* in 1904 that 'the attitude of the world towards women is largely that of Englishmen toward Irishmen. In each case the former thinks the latter to be queer, unaccountable, irrational creatures, who want no one knows what.'[24] Writing under a *nom de guerre* Eccles had observed different critical judgements applied to herself as a woman or as 'the supposed "rising young man" [...] [o]nce a thing is known to be by a woman, it is in a sense discredited'.[25] Eccles observed that women were regarded and treated in business 'as beings fundamentally unreasonable, beings entirely different from [men] in their intelligence, ideas of honour, uprightness, truth, public spirit, and mutual kindliness'.[26] Eccles concluded that 'there really is no such thing as an equal chance in life for men and women'.[27] Eccles herself laid the blame for this common view of women as 'creatures of a different breed to men, whose chief good qualities are youth and beauty' at the door of 'largely, women themselves, comfortable, narrow-minded women',[28] and she noted that 'those who work with pen, or brush [...] are set up as a target for the arrows of misrepresentation and slander. "How can she do it?" says Mrs. So-and-so. "I never could. I'd die first" '.[29]

Novel reading and creative work on women's part thus provoked discouraging and derogatory arguments from professional and lay commentators, based on assumptions of women's physical and intellectual weakness, their supposed emotionality and their attributed duty to embellish others' lives instead of having an independent existence. Virginia Woolf observed that 'women have served all these centuries as looking glasses possessing the magic and delicious power of reflecting the figure of man at twice its natural size'.[30] Despite the growing number of portrayals of women reading, it is clear that a variety of strong voices were raised against women's engagement in any intellectual activity, and that women were regarded as incapable of serious reading. If they attempted it, or over-indulged a passion for novels, they apparently put their physical and mental health at risk. This was the patriarchal context in which many portrayals of women readers did not focus on the intellectual act of reading but on their bodily attributes.

Readers under the male gaze

European portraits of women from the late eighteenth into the early nineteenth centuries do not always picture them smiling at the artist/viewer, for example, works by the Spanish artist Francisco José de Goya y Lucientes, like his portrait of the actress Doña Antonia Zárate (oil on canvas, 1805, National Gallery of Ireland). There is little attempt to please a putative male gaze. However, over the nineteenth century and with the establishment of art galleries and exhibitions, many pictures of women were designed for an admiring male viewer, and this was often achieved by displaying an idealised female body. The French artist Alexandre Cabanel's *Birth of Venus* (oil on canvas, 1863, Musée d'Orsay, Paris) typifies the mythologised and idealised portrayals of women in much nineteenth-century art.

Anglo-Irish women who travelled to Paris for art training in the late nineteenth century encountered new ideas about art and writing, but they also found that 'more often than not, the female was placed in front of the canvas rather than behind it'.[31] For many male artists, patriarchal ideology encouraged the notion that a woman's function in art was to be pictured either in a domestic setting or as an object of allure or desire. In some European images a woman reader presents a demure figure enclosed in a domestic interior. Many more depictions of the woman reader do not actually focus on a woman engaged in reading but on her body and/or her dress.

Sometimes a female figure is shown reading but viewed as if secretly through a keyhole, for instance, in her boudoir or another private space and in déshabillé. In Gustave Courbet's *A Young Woman Reading* (oil on canvas, c. 1866–68, National Gallery of Art, Washington, DC) the figure, partly secluded among shrubbery, wears loose undergarments that hang off her shoulder to show her bosom. Jamie Camplin and Maria Ranauro comment on this picture that 'Its subject is so lost in the unreal world of her book that she is wholly unselfconscious of her appearance.'[32] However, the incongruity of the woman's location and her semi-undressed state suggest that the point of Courbet's depiction is rather that a fictive male viewer is offered a secret sight of the young woman in déshabillé. *Reading* (c. 1890) by the French painter Joseph Marius Jean Avy depicts a young woman reading a newspaper with her morning tea or coffee at a small round table facing a window, where net curtains filter a translucent light.[33] In this private space, the reader is viewed from the back, her negligee falling off her shoulders showing smooth rounded flesh, and her flushed cheek. Beside the table is a shelf or sideboard bearing a round ceramic teapot and coffee pot and a large bouquet of pink flowers. These accessories contribute to presenting an image that can be read as one of conventional soft rounded femininity.

Pierre-Auguste Renoir executed many paintings of girls or women reading, in various attitudes and states of dress or undress. *Femme lisant* ('Woman Reading', oil on canvas, 1891, Private Collection) depicts a young woman intently focused on a paper, her face in profile, but her body slightly turned to the viewer.[34] She is shown in déshabillé, with bare rounded shoulders and half-covered bosom. Her rosy cheeks and orange-red lips match the large orange flowers floating on the wallpaper behind. In Renoir's *Young Girl Reading* (oil on canvas, c. 1891–1895), the figure is shown engaged in a book, but again as if in private, wearing a thin negligee that hangs off at the shoulder, again partly revealing her bosom.[35] Renoir's *Woman Reading* (oil on canvas, c. 1895, Figure 10) depicts a woman seated casually sideways on a chair by the window, wearing only a thin undergarment that once again falls off her shoulder. Her face is in profile, with her hair swept up to uncover an expanse of neck and shoulder, while her upper body is turned towards the viewer, allowing a sight of her bosom. In this instance, the figure's focused reading allows the viewer to scrutinise her body in her private space, as if unseen.

By contrast, some portraits of women readers present them in elaborate dresses conforming to what Linda Doherty dubbed a 'material' visual type of woman reader and drawing attention to the woman's sartorial interests, rather than her intellectual engagement.[36] For example, *Girl Reading* (1856) by the Belgian artist Alfred Émile Stevens depicts a young woman seated in a red velvet chair, one dainty foot on a velvet cushion.[37] She wears a voluminous dress in layers of white chiffon and beside her is a small table carrying an arrangement of pink flowers, a common metaphoric accompaniment to femininity. The English painter John Morgan's *The Afternoon Rest* (oil on canvas, n.d., nineteenth century) shows a young woman in an elaborate pink dress with short puffed sleeves and low neckline leaning back against a cobalt blue velvet cushion.[38] Her neck and arms are smooth and unblemished and her attitude one of lassitude, rather than interest in her book.

Some depictions of female readers show them wreathed in flowers, perhaps standing amid a floral garden, or seated beside enormous bouquets. In the English artist Edmund Blair Leighton's painting *Sweet Solitude* (oil on canvas, 1919), a young woman in an elaborate white and blue summer dress and blue-ribboned hat stands reading in a highly cultivated garden amid roses, agapanthus and snapdragons, a trellis wreathed in deep pink roses rising above her.[39] The garden is bordered by a neat but unbroken hedge, suggesting that the woman and flowers are safely and naturally contained.

Among other outdoor scenes, the English artist Alfred Chantrey Corbould's *A Girl Reading in a Sailing Boat* (oil on canvas, 1869) depicts an engaged reader, but the image focuses also on her soft rounded face, an immaculate coiffure topped with a cap edged in blue fur, and her semi-transparent dress decorated

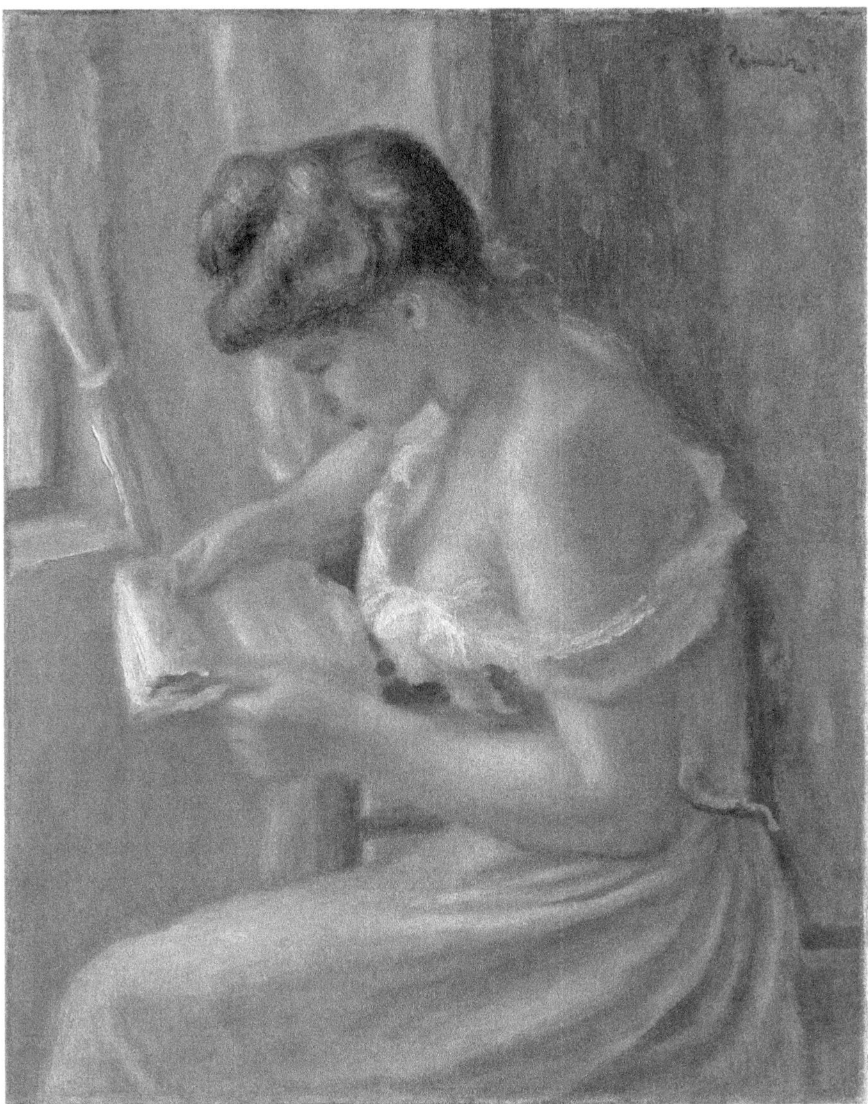

Figure 10 Pierre-Auguste Renoir, *Woman Reading*, oil on canvas, 41.6 × 32.7 cm, c. 1895. © 2010 The Sterling and Francine Clark Art Institute Williamstown, Massachusetts. Photo credit: Michael Agee.

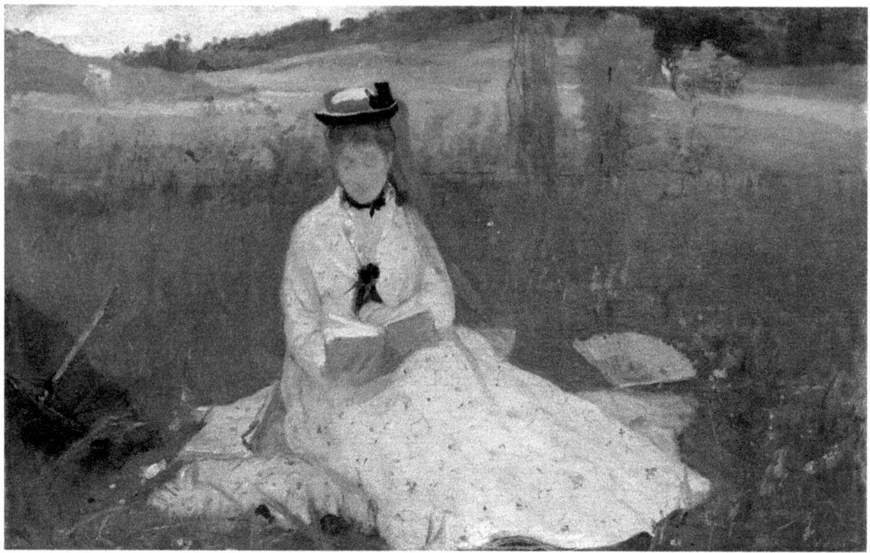

Figure 11 Berthe Morisot, *Reading*, oil on fabric, 46 × 71.8 cm, 1873. 1950.89. Public domain: Open Access Courtesy of The Cleveland Museum of Art.

with blue embroidery and a gilt brooch.[40] A painting by the American Childe Hassam, *Summer Sunlight (Isles of Shoals)* (oil on canvas, 1892, The Israel Museum, Jerusalem), depicts a woman reading sitting on rocks by the sea. However, the wild setting is counteracted by the model's voluminous chiffony dress decorated with flowers and the absence of features in her face and therefore of any reaction to her surroundings. The face, like those of many female models in modernist art, is a de-individualised blank.

Morisot and Manet

Not all images of women reading by modern European artists conformed to these stereotypes. The French painter Berthe Morisot produced a number of portraits of women readers that focus on the occupation of reading, such as *The Mother and Sister of the Artist* (oil on canvas, 1869–70, National Gallery of Art, Washington, DC). This depicts the two figures sitting on a sofa quietly dressed in white/cream and black respectively, Morisot's mother absorbed in reading a book, while her sister looks on with a thoughtful expression.[41] Morisot's *Reading* (oil on fabric, 1873, Figure 11) depicts a summery scene with her sister Edma Pontillon sitting on the grass reading, her legs folded comfortably under her long dress. There is an adumbrated fence, and a view of gentle hills and vegetation beyond. Kathryn Brown describes the location as 'an extravagantly open field'.[42] However, Camplin and Ranauro place the scene in 'Edma's considerable garden at Maurecourt, Île de France', that is, a private domestic space.[43] Edma, shown frontally, wears a modest summer dress decorated with sprigs of leaves and flowers and a hat with a trailing green organza ribbon, the motifs and colours linking her to the surrounding nature. The focus of the picture, however, is Edma's engagement in her book as she looks down at it, her hand poised to turn a page. In the seriousness of their occupation and an absence of feminine display, such paintings by Morisot can be compared with the work by women artists in Ireland to be discussed later.

Édouard Manet's *The Railway* (oil on canvas, 1873, National Gallery of Art, Washington, DC) provides another European example of an untypical representation of a woman reader. *The Railway* depicts a woman sitting on a low wall in front of the Gare Saint-Lazare, Paris, while a little girl beside her, seen from the back, watches the trains. The reader was posed by Manet's model, Victorine Meurent, and the little girl by a daughter of his friend, Alphonse Hirsch, an artist.[44] This is a complex urban scene, the dangers of the city hinted at by the thick railings securing the pair that dominate the composition. Yet the woman is shown to be unperturbed and thoughtful as she glances up from her open book, her fingers keeping the page. Her gaze meets the viewer's on equal terms. The figure is placed a little precariously at the edge of the picture, which gives a sense of her being almost passed by, especially as she leans in from the edge, as if to catch the viewer who looks at her. The woman is soberly clothed in dark blue, but the little girl is dressed up as if for a party, in a white dress with an enormous blue bow, drawing the viewer's eye. However, it is the woman's enquiring eyes to which the viewer's gaze reverts, while the book on her lap announces her current preoccupation. Manet's *The Railway* depicts an independent urban reader, the New Woman in Paris.

Before examining the concept of the New Woman and the Irish portraits that help to construct the New Woman as a reader, in Chapters 3 and 4, the following section considers some Irish examples of women readers that do not emphasise the female body itself but do not focus on the woman as a reader either.

Elegant women: Lavery, Osborne and Orpen

There are few examples of bodily display among Irish representations of woman readers at this time, although there are various examples where the figure's dress is the salient feature of the portrait. One exception is *A Girl Reading* (white marble, 1838) by Patrick McDowell, originally from Belfast but working in London. The figure stands reading a book, garbed in a diaphanous dress or robe, making this effectively a nude portrayal. It was commissioned by a private client, Mr W. T. Beaumont, MP for Northamptonshire.

The Irish artist John Lavery executed paintings of women readers in which the occupation of reading seems subsidiary to other narratives. Lavery, a Catholic, was born in Belfast and trained in Glasgow and Paris before moving to London, although he retained connections with Ireland and later returned there.

Lavery's *The Letter* (oil on millboard, 1908, National Museum Wales) shows a woman reading a letter as she sits, elegantly coiffed, in her negligee on a bed hung with dainty net curtains. The theme of a half-clothed woman in her boudoir seems less salient, however, than the hint of a story, as the figure looks thoughtfully, even sadly at the letter in her hand and a large blue shadow of her head and shoulder is cast onto the bed frame and wall behind her.

In *Girl in a Red Dress Reading by a Swimming Pool* (oil on canvas, 1887, Private Collection), Lavery depicts a woman reading a book near an outdoor pool.[45] The figure is turned from the viewer who has a back view without sight of her face. She is using both of a pair of chairs, leaning an arm on the second chair to support her head, introducing a narrative element with a slight mystery to the picture: Is she discouraging company or waiting for someone to occupy the spare chair? The woman is bent over her book in an attitude of concentration. However, encouraged by the picture's title, the viewer's attention is drawn to her red dress, a startling scarlet with matching hat, and a gold necklace; the dress as if caught by the sun falls over the chair beside her in thick brilliant strokes of red and orange. The theme of a woman reading is subsidiary to an elegant appearance. Lavery's *Mary Auras: The Red Book* (oil on canvas, c. 1892, Private Collection) also focuses on the staged elegance of the figure and her dress, the red book becoming a fashion accessory. The picture was shown in Dublin at the Irish International Exhibition in 1907 and then in an exhibition series of 'Fair Women' at the International Society of Sculptors, Painters and Gravers in London in 1908. *Mary Auras: The Red Book* depicts a young woman in profile, carefully coiffed and garbed in an elaborate white dress decorated with satin ribbons.[46] She holds up a little red book to read, while turned a little awkwardly in an armchair. The picture title, *Mary Auras: The Red Book*, emphasises the colour of the cover rather than the content of the book. Her red lipsticked lips, slightly parted, match the red book cover, highlighting both.

In Lavery's portrait *Mary Black-Hawkins Reading* (oil on canvas-board, c. 1901–7, Private Collection) Black-Hawkins is depicted in a long black dress, decorated with a thin gold necklace, sitting at one end of a straight-backed sofa.[47] She is placed at an uncomfortable angle to an inlaid table and to a large illustrated book open upon it, towards which she is turned, at the same time twisting around to hold the viewer's eye. Her modern red lipstick

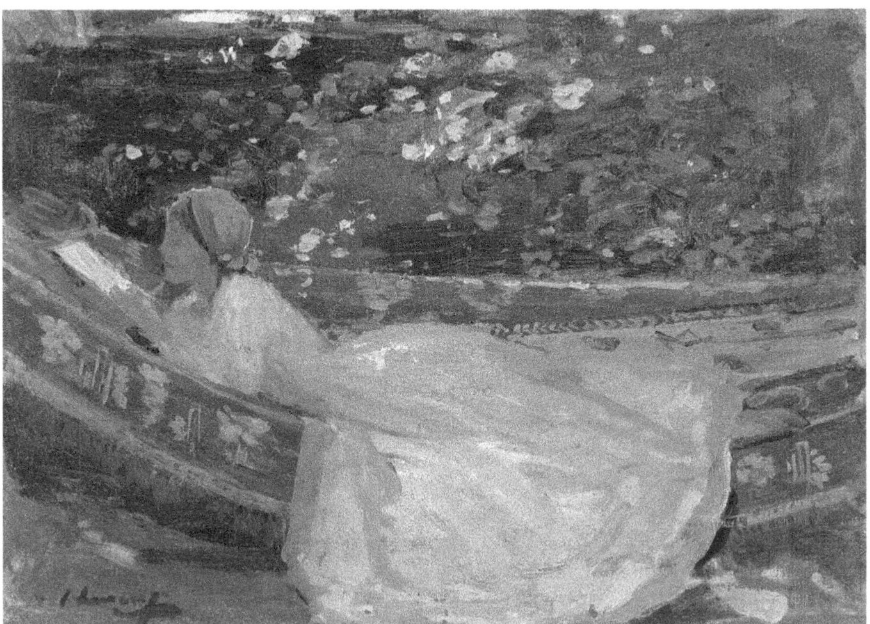

Figure 12 Sir John Lavery, *The Green Hammock*, oil on canvas board, 26 × 36.6 cm, c. 1905. © 13.12.2012. Christie's Images Limited.

is matched by a vase of carefully arranged scarlet flowers, perhaps gladioli, as light falls on her face, and a small handbag dangles from her hands. Black-Hawkins's garb and assured engagement with the viewer suggest feminine elegance rather than a representation of a woman reading, or credibly interrupted from reading. Lavery's portrait presents, perhaps, the fashionable aspect of the New Woman, with the added cultural capital of perusing an illustrated book of art.

The Green Hammock (oil on canvas-board, c. 1910, Figure 12) by Lavery depicts a young woman lying on her stomach on a hammock, one calf outstretched, reading, a splash of orange suggesting an art book, or perhaps a magazine.[48] The hammock, made of a green-patterned and fringed fabric, hangs against a background of thick green foliage. The woman wears lipstick and a long white dress tinged with blue shadows that falls over the curve of her body, emphasising her figure. The floral green hammock and sweeping brushstrokes create a harmony with the surrounding foliage. The merging of figure and flora in an impressionistic natural scene eclipses the subject of a woman reading. Despite its inventive modernist style, the picture reworks an older convention of aligning women with nature, allowing men to assume the superior role of defining culture.[49]

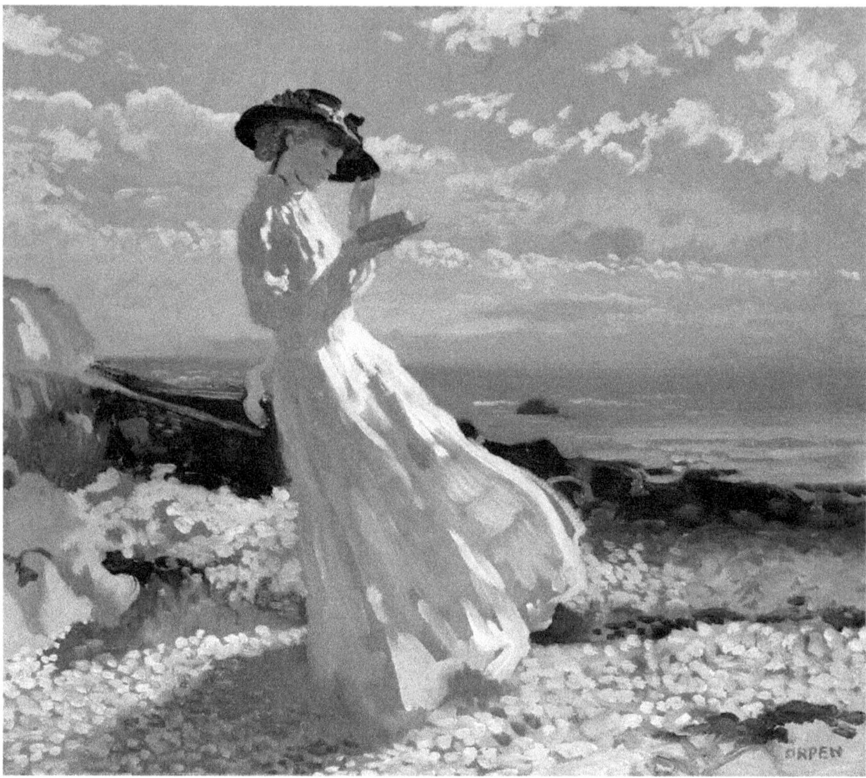

Figure 13 Sir William Orpen, *Grace Reading at Howth Bay*, oil on canvas, 45.8 × 50.8 cm, early 20c. Private Collection.

In *Mrs Noel Guinness and Her Daughter Margaret* (oil on canvas, 1898, Hunt Museum, Limerick) by Walter Osborne, a mother reads with her child and their faces are carefully studied as they look at the little book.[50] Osborne, from a well-off Protestant family, was acquainted with Mrs Mary Guinness and this large picture was a commissioned work, for which Osborne prepared an oil sketch. In the finished portrait, the viewer's eye is drawn particularly to the lustrous, tactile satin fabric of Mrs Guinness's dress, decorated with sprigs of tulip or rose, and beneath which her toes are encased in dainty silver shoes. This is a recognisable portrait, but also one in which the sitter's dress is a dominant element and in which the pattern and texture of her garb is on show in a way that it is not in contemporary portraits of male readers.[51]

William Orpen's *Grace Reading at Howth Bay* (oil on canvas, n.d., Figure 13) depicts his wife Grace standing reading against a backdrop of sea and large sky as the wind blows her dress and her hat which she secures with one hand, holding a book in the other. Orpen rented a summer house at Howth Head, Co. Dublin with Grace and their two children. This picture could be interpreted as one of Grace holding firmly onto her book, determined to read against the elements. However, Orpen's *On the Cliff, Dublin Bay, Morning* (oil on canvas, n.d., Private Collection), which similarly depicts Grace in an elaborate long white dress and bottle green hat with the addition of a long cream jacket but without a book, diminishes the significance of the book in *Grace Reading at Howth Bay*.[52] Especially when considered together, the emphasis in both pictures seems to be on the elegance of the female figure and the magnificence of the view. In *On the Cliff, Dublin Bay, Morning*, the figure's white and cream garb tones with the sky and in *Grace Reading at Howth Bay*, her long white dress matches the pebbly ground and billows in harmony with the clouds above. In each painting, the female figure becomes a decorative object set against a fine sky and an integral part of the natural scene.

Conclusion

In many paintings of women readers by male artists in various European countries and in the United States, the focus is not on a woman reading so much as on the reader as an attractive, generally young woman in a state of fine dress, or undress, and a setting that confirms her femininity. There are exceptions. Manet's painting *The Railway*, as well as Morisot's depictions of her mother and sister quietly reading depict independent women who are not primarily presented for display to an admiring spectator. In Ireland, there are few portrayals of women readers in which the figure's body is on display, although there are examples where the figure's garb appears to be the dominant feature.

There were many associations between Irish and French artists, especially among those Anglo-Irish women able to study abroad. Sarah Purser owned a watercolour by Morisot.[53] Like Anglo-Irish artists in Dublin such as Purser and Solomons, Morisot was well-off and well-connected in Parisian society, and like them she gained contemporary recognition for her work, although histories of impressionism long overlooked her by contrast with her male colleagues. In Ireland, the practice of focusing on a woman reader's body was perhaps less marked because a number of the portraits of women readers were produced by Solomons, Purser and other women artists whose work collectively challenged the patriarchy with a new kind of female representation.

Chapter 3

THE SHAPING OF THE NEW WOMAN IN IRELAND

The emergence and naming of the New Woman took place concurrently with movements in Ireland, England and elsewhere to establish women's civil rights. Dublin in the latter nineteenth and early twentieth centuries seems to have been a space of relative independence and creativity for women, at least for those in the more privileged generally Anglo-Irish sectors of society. This was a period of political and cultural ferment in Ireland, stirred by ideas of Irish nationalism and women's rights to suffrage and higher education. A number of women became politically active as suffragists or nationalists while others – or often the same women – were successful as writers and artists and patronised the arts. These confident creative and social interventions drew on and contributed to the constitution of the 'New Woman'.

This chapter examines the idea of the New Woman in relation to the campaigns for women's suffrage and access to higher education in Ireland and their links with parallel movements in England. It argues that like these campaigns, the emergence of the New Woman was a transnational and trans-atlantic phenomenon. The close association between the Anglo-Irish and England, as well as the ability of Anglo-Irish women to travel and undertake art training in France and other European countries resulted in exchanges of ideas about women's rights, as well as cultural exchanges including lit-erary and visual representations of the New Woman. Such transnational and cosmopolitan cultural sharing was in contrast to the ideology of Irish-Irelanders who turned geographically and symbolically to the west of Ireland for the authentic roots of a desired de-Anglicised Irishness and looked back in time to a heroic Gaelic culture.

The New Woman in Ireland was often Anglo-Irish and commonly a reader. As well as serving as some compensation for restricted educational opportunities even among otherwise privileged women, reading was regarded as an attribute of the intelligent, cultivated woman. Literary sources from various countries, including Irish writings, helped to create the concept of the New Woman. It was also shaped by visual imagery from England where *Punch* magazine parodied it.

This chapter focuses on the historical, political and literary contexts in which the concept of the New Woman emerged. In Ireland, the idea of the New Woman was expanded and enriched by the distinctive portraits of women readers which are examined in detail in the following chapters.

Irish suffrage societies and cross-channel collaboration

Suffrage societies in Ireland began to formalise agitation for women's suffrage, better education and other rights for women from the 1860s. The Quaker reformers Anna and Thomas Haslam promoted women's suffrage in Ireland from 1860. Thomas Haslam was in contact with the Anglo-Scottish philosopher John Stuart Mill, after Mill's parliamentary petition in London for women's votes in 1866.[1] A public meeting in Dublin organised in 1870 by Anne Isabella Robertson, a Dublin novelist and suffragist, had as speaker Millicent Fawcett, leader of the suffragist movement in England, and this was fully reported by the *Freeman's Journal*.[2] Isabella Tod founded the first Irish suffrage society for the north of Ireland in 1872 and Anna and Thomas Haslam set up the Dublin Women's Suffrage Association in 1876.[3] Campaigners drew on the Victorian assumption of 'separate spheres' for men and women based on the special competencies and social roles ascribed to them to argue the need for expanding women's public engagement.[4] For instance, Thomas Haslam in 1874 wrote that women

> do not despise their home duties [...] they wish to become more capable wives and mothers than their stunted education has ever yet permitted them to be; but none the less do they desire to take an earnest part in the stirring movements which are going on around them.[5]

However, Haslam's arguments may have been pragmatic attempts to promote women's suffrage to a male audience.[6]

The suffrage movements in Ireland and England collaborated again, for example, to organise a visit by Miss Helen Blackburne to Alexandra College Dublin from London. The *Irish Times* reported that Blackburne discussed the suffrage movement and the possibilities for women's entrepreneurship in Ireland in the arts of distilling perfumes and cordials, and growing daffodils for sale in their gardens.[7] The following day, Blackburne addressed a meeting of the Women's Suffrage movement attended by Anna Haslam, the honorary secretary of the Dublin association, and Sir Charles Cameron, who talked of the opening to women of the medical professions and anticipated 'a Lady President of the College of Surgeons'.[8] Cameron, like Thomas Haslam, was among a number of staunch male supporters of the movement.

The Dublin Women's Suffrage Association acquired powers as poor law guardians, becoming the Dublin Women's Suffrage and Poor Law Guardian Association, and the right to be elected as district councillors was marked by another name change to the Dublin Women's Suffrage and Local Government Association.[9] As membership increased in the early twentieth century it became the Irish Women's Suffrage and Local Government Association. A meeting of the Women's Suffrage and Poor Law Guardian Association in Dublin in July 1898 was addressed by Miss Clifford, PLG (Poor Law Guardian), Bristol. Mrs Anna Haslam read the letters of apology, including one from the Earl of Meath, whose mother was ill, who expressed his great interest in the association and regretted his inability to attend.[10] In 1904, the Irish Women's Suffrage and Local Government Association began a series of drawing-room gatherings, the first chaired by Sir Charles Cameron and addressed by Mr Haslam, who effectively demolished arguments against women's enfranchisement. Mrs Haslam urged women to apply for admission to the Bar.[11]

A few years later, the Irish artist Cecilia Harrison executed a fine double portrait of the Haslams, *Thomas and Anna M. Haslam* (oil on canvas, 1908, Figure 14). Harrison herself was a significant figure in turn-of-the-century Dublin. Born into a wealthy family at Holywood House, Co. Down in 1863, Harrison studied at the Slade School of Fine Art in London and travelled on the Continent. In 1889, aged 26, she moved to Dublin and became well-known as a portraitist, executing various paintings of women as readers (see Chapter 4). She was a committee member of the Irish Women's Suffrage Association established by Anna and Thomas Haslam, a nationalist and a social reformer. Harrison became the first woman councillor for Dublin Corporation in January 1912, elected to represent the South City with a majority of 149 votes over the Unionist candidate.[12] She took on vested interests to argue for improved conditions for the poor and for women.[13] She supported Hugh Lane in establishing the Municipal Gallery of Modern Art in Dublin, and when the gallery produced its first catalogue in 1908, Harrison provided biographical notes.[14] Harrison embodied the emerging concept of a New Woman whose creative work, public engagement and political activism enhanced Dublin's cultural and political life at this time.

In Harrison's portrait, the Haslams are depicted smiling quietly and in close proximity, their modest black clothing merging together. Thomas holds a paper, the importance of which Anna, slightly turned towards him, shares. This double portrait and a self-portrait were hung in Dublin's new Gallery of Modern Art in 1908. They were praised by Thomas Bodkin, later director of the National Gallery of Ireland, as 'portraits of which Holbein himself need not have been ashamed'.[15] However, for Harrison, as for the Haslams, the portrait clearly functioned to celebrate and publicise the Haslams' work for

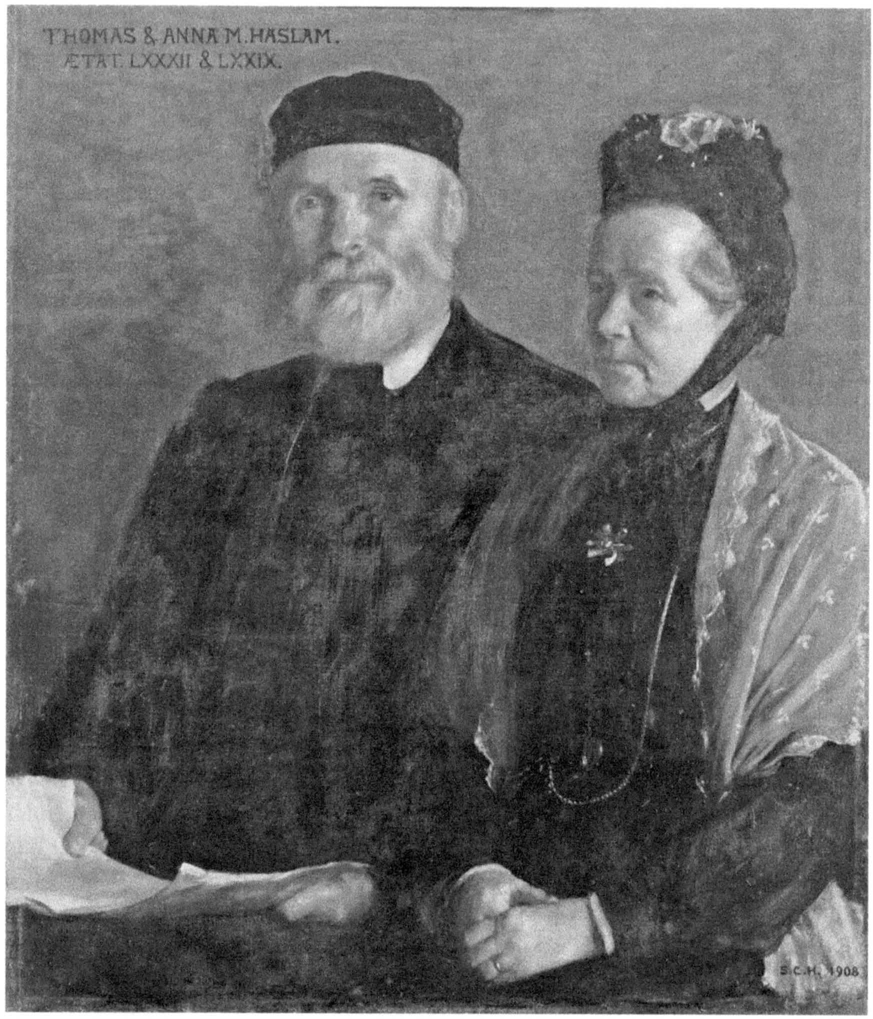

Figure 14 Sarah Cecilia Harrison, *Thomas and Anna M. Haslam*, oil on canvas, 91.5 × 78.8 cm, 1908. Collection and image © Hugh Lane Gallery (Reg. No. 57).

female suffrage and the document they hold is likely to be meaningful in this context.

There was much opposition to female suffrage in Ireland, however. Disapproval came not only from men protecting their power and privilege but also from women's groups. The Catholic Church was especially condemnatory. For example, David Barry STL (Licentiate of Sacred Theology) in 1909 cited 'the passive virtues of humility, patience, meekness, forbearance, and self-repression' regarded by the Church as 'the special prerogative and endowment of the female soul'.[16] Some women's groups adhered firmly to the principle of separate spheres, such as the Women's National Anti-Suffrage League founded in London in 1908, which opened a branch in Dublin the following year. The women's nationalist paper *Bean na hÉireann* (Woman of Ireland) in 1909 put nationalist dogma above women's claims when it concluded that 'to accept enfranchisement by a "hostile Parliament" would only be "humiliating", undermining all the work that had been achieved by nationalist groups in developing a spirit of nationhood'.[17]

In May 1912, a new paper, the *Irish Citizen*, was founded by Francis Sheehy Skeffington and James Cousins in order to promote the cause of women's suffrage and provide a forum for feminist debate. It was established because the press ignored suffrage events.[18] The two editors were associate members of the Irish Women's Franchise League, a more militant body than previous suffrage organisations which had been set up by Hanna Sheehy Skeffington and Margaret Cousins in 1908. Most of its writers were middle class, but with a wide spectrum of views represented, for instance, over whether all women or only those of property should have the vote.[19]

In summary, despite opposition from the Catholic Church and from various women's groups, Irish suffrage societies were active from the later nineteenth and into the twentieth centuries, and in contact with similar organisations in England. The Quaker couple, Anna and Thomas Haslam, were prominent in this work throughout the period, and they were celebrated in a portrait by the artist Cecilia Harrison, herself an active suffragist and exemplar of the New Woman.

'What poor delusiveness is all this "higher education of women"'

The Anglo-Irish novelist Sarah Grand remarked in 1894 that 'Man deprived us of all proper education, and then jeered at us because we had no knowledge.'[20] Catholic and Protestant spokespersons alike publicly deplored the idea of independent well-educated women.[21] Even the term 'woman' in the nineteenth century was subject to criticism and unfavourably opposed to the term 'lady', the former obliged to work but the latter not expected to do so, with contrasting modes of appearance and behaviour.[22] A plethora of handbooks on etiquette, mainly for 'ladies', and a few for gentlemen, were produced and published in London and also in Dublin. Such guides, which frequently ran into many editions, were a prime means of establishing and maintaining correct social practices for the upper and aspiring middle classes, particularly women, and they tended to reinforce women's unsuitability for intellectual work or public activities.

Samuel Orchart Beeton in his *Etiquette for Ladies* of 1876, for example, advised, 'let her refrain from controversy and argument on [political or financial] topics, as the grasp of the female mind is seldom capable of seizing or retaining'.[23] A common patriarchal view of the result of women entering higher education is exemplified in comments by the Anglo-Irish poet William Butler Yeats when his sister Elizabeth Corbet Yeats, known as Lolly, was taking her examinations to qualify as a teacher: 'What poor delusiveness is all this "higher education of women" [...] They come out with no repose, no peacefulness, and their minds no longer quiet gardens full of secluded paths and umbrage-circled nooks, but loud as chattering market places.'[24]

Anglo-Irish society traditionally determined that young women were tutored at home, while their male relatives were sent to university. Edith Somerville, brought up in Castletownsend, Co. Cork, in a family associated with prominent Anglo-Irish landowners, as a girl still typically had only 'a patchy home education with assorted short-stay governesses and one term at Alexandra'.[25] Yet without stating her gender Somerville is said to have tried and passed the entrance exam paper for Trinity College Dublin.[26] Among the elite classes, 'leisure was a way of life' but women were expected to spend their time managing the household and the domestic practice of leisure.[27] Keeping the house and housework were women's responsibilities at all levels of society. Writing in the nationalist weekly publication the *Irish Homestead* in 1903, Susan L. Mitchell critiqued women's role in maintaining a tidy house, which she regarded as an obsession springing from the English, and leading to 'armies of sweeping, dusting, "settling" women, who act as if they believe that life was simply a perpetual struggle against dirt [...] and disorder'.[28] Henrietta Lynch's undated watercolour, *A Busy Housewife*, exhibited at her address in Merrion Square Dublin, depicts a woman literally blocked in by the objects of her daily chores. Sitting by a tea-table and gazing anxiously towards a viewless window, the figure is hemmed in by the table and dominated by the frame of a spinning wheel.

Debate about women's intellectual potential and their right to further and higher education had a long history in Ireland, as in Britain. Arthur Houston, professor of political economy at Trinity College Dublin, in a lecture on 'The Emancipation of Women' in 1862 argued that even when women were financially secure, it did not benefit either themselves or the national economy for them to be confined to the home, 'passing their lives, as at present they do, in a process as nearly allied as possible to vegetation'.[29] Houston's was a minority view and one for which he was mocked in the *Dublin Review*, a Catholic periodical, which asked if he proposed that women take up arms like the Amazons.[30]

However, in 1866 Anne Jellicoe, a Quaker, founded Alexandra College Dublin to offer further education to women over the age of 15, which was 'soon frequented by the élite of Dublin girlhood', most of whom were members of the Church of Ireland.[31] Later, under an Act of 1879, the Royal University of Ireland, a degree-awarding body located at St Stephen's Green Dublin, opened degrees to women in Ireland for the first time.[32] Yet although students could sit examinations and gain degrees at the Royal University of Ireland, it was a non-teaching institution and the existing men's colleges, apart from the Royal College of Surgeons, did not allow women to attend lectures. Queen's College Cork allowed women to attend classes in 1886, followed by Galway in 1888.[33] The Provost of Trinity College Dublin between 1888 and 1904, George Salmon, opposed women's access to classes or degree awards. In 1892, a petition requesting admission to Trinity College signed by 10,560 women was rejected.[34] Neither were women permitted to read in Trinity College library. When Mary Hayden, a student of the Royal University of Ireland in 1897, requested to read in the university library she was refused on grounds that there were no conveniences for ladies.[35]

Trinity's University Board in 1903 eventually resolved to grant women access to lectures, examinations and degrees 'in arts and the Medical School, but not to fellowships or scholarships' and women were admitted on this still discriminatory basis in 1904.[36] That year, several women were among those who were awarded an honorary degree, and other degrees, which were 'conferred on ladies for the first time in the history of the University'.[37] By comparison, the University of London had also allowed women to receive degrees from 1879.[38] At the University of Oxford, although women could attend lectures and even take the university examinations, they were not allowed to gain degrees and women were not admitted as members of the university until 1920. Girton College, Cambridge was established for women in 1869, but the University of Cambridge did not permit any women to graduate until the late 1940s. Between 1904 and 1907, Trinity College Dublin awarded *ad eundem* degrees (allowed to alumni of equivalent institutions) to women who had succeeded in the Oxbridge exams and who travelled to Dublin for this purpose, becoming known as the 'Steamboat Ladies'. In 1904, five such degrees were awarded to women from Cambridge.[39] These moves in Dublin to open access to degrees for women suggest that in this period there was some recognition of women's intellectual potential and independence, although this was limited and hard-won.

Women art students were disadvantaged compared to men. The Royal Dublin Society School of Drawing was established for male students in 1746. In the mid-nineteenth century, it began to focus on design. In 1849 when Henry McManus (the painter of *Reading 'The Nation'*, Figure 2, discussed earlier) became headmaster of the Dublin Society School, he introduced classes for women and it was reported that 'they have made progress beyond his expectations'.[40] However, the school was not then designed to train artists and while the women mostly planned to teach afterwards, the male students mainly used the school to learn technical drawing in support of other professional studies.[41] From 1877, the Royal Dublin Society School became the Dublin Metropolitan School of Art, offering basic drawing classes, and continued to admit women. However, women were denied entry to the Royal Hibernian Academy (RHA) which with its life class provided an education in fine art. Furthermore, RHA membership carried prestige, 'to be an R.H.A. was to be virtually a public figure, a prestigious person comparable to a Fellow of Trinity'.[42]

Nonetheless, Anglo-Irish women of means were able to travel and to train in the international ateliers in Paris and elsewhere which were open to women. For instance, money and independence enabled Somerville to travel and study in London, Düsseldorf and Paris. Women were admitted to the RHA schools only in 1893, and the RHA did not elect its first female member, Sarah Purser, until 1924.[43] Interestingly, the enrolment figures for the RHA schools for 1895–1905 show an average annual attendance of 17 women and 6 men.[44] This further indicates the significance of this period for women as one of creative, intellectual and public engagement.

Women's contributions to artistic and political life in Dublin therefore took place in the face of continuing restrictions on their independence and education, even for women from affluent and well-connected families. The Anglo-Irish institutions of Trinity College Dublin and the RHA blocked women's access to higher education and fine art training until around the turn of the century, although the Royal Dublin Society's design school admitted women earlier and Alexandra College provided some educational opportunities for young women.

The idea of the New Woman

In her book *The Irish New Woman* (2013), Tina O'Toole suggests that Ireland has been absent from histories of the 'New Woman'.[45] This seems to have been generally the case. One explanation for such omission may be because the New Woman in Ireland in many ways was a creation of the Anglo-Irish. In post-independence Ireland, the Anglo-Irish for some decades were 'forgotten' by a dominant nationalist narrative which represented Irish history in and beyond Ireland.[46] The history of the New Woman in Ireland may have been elided in the same process, especially as women's autonomy was repressed by both Church and State following independence.

In parallel with the campaigns for women's suffrage and access to higher education, the idea of the New Woman was taking root in later nineteenth-century Ireland, England and elsewhere. The 'New Woman' was, and remains, a fluid term which came to encompass a range of female attitudes and behaviours based on a common factor of rebelling against women's subservience to patriarchal ideology by subverting norms of femininity in some way, whether through political activism, independent work, sexual choice or matters of dress and propriety. As well as being an oppositional term, the idea of the New Woman connoted positive, independent action on women's part, for example, as campaigners, artists or writers.

It has sometimes been proposed that the New Woman was a discursive construction without any referent. However, the New Woman had a history. There were calls from both women writers and men prior to Mary Wollstonecraft's famous text of 1792, *A Vindication of the Rights of Woman*, as well as subsequently, for women to be given opportunities similar to men's for their intellectual development.[47] The eighteenth-century English society dubbed the Blue-Stockings and led by Elizabeth Montague and an Irish woman, Elizabeth Vesey, held salons where educated women and men could converse.[48] The concept of the New Woman had a long gestation and involved many strands of feminist, artistic, literary, political and pragmatic thought and practice. In England by the 1850s, a new type of woman active in the public sphere was becoming known and being mocked, following the introduction of women's trousers, dubbed 'Bloomers' after the American suffragist and temperance campaigner Amelia Bloomer, who advocated and demonstrated their wear. Subsequently, the New Woman was variously shaped by literary and visual art, while writers, artists and political activists embodied versions of the New Woman.

The Ladies' Land League

O'Toole argues that in Ireland the creation of the nationalist Ladies' Land League in 1881 constituted 'a paradigm shift: the moment when "New" possibilities for Irish women begin to emerge'.[49] The emergence of the New Woman is not generally associated with Irish nationalism, which tended to be a masculine sphere (as discussed in Chapter 1). The Ladies' Land League came into existence by default because the male Land Leaguers were unavailable. The Irish National Land League was founded by Michael Davitt, a member of the Fenian (Irish Republican) Brotherhood in 1879, and headed by Charles Stewart Parnell, from a Protestant landowning family and leader of the Irish Home Rule Party, which sought separate government for Ireland within the UK. The League aimed to reform the landlord system and fight for tenants' rights. The Ladies' Land League was created after the leaders of the Land League were arrested and Davitt suggested that women could stand in for the men.

The Ladies' Land League, an all-female body, was led by Charles Stewart Parnell's sister, Anna Parnell, a prototypical New Woman. Under her leadership, the Ladies' Land League worked hard and successfully to assist evicted families and provide for prisoners and dependants, as well as campaigning for land reform. It expanded to 321 branches across Ireland. Patriarchal responses included condemnation by Archbishop McCabe of Dublin who issued a pastoral letter to be proclaimed in every church in his archdiocese, accusing the women of the Ladies' Land League of forgetting

> the modesty of their sex and the high dignity of their womanhood [...] Very Rev. dear fathers [...] do not tolerate in your societies the woman who so far disavows her birthright [...] as to parade herself before the public gaze in a character so unworthy as a Child of Mary.[50]

The *Times* newspaper commented that 'when treason is reduced to fighting behind petticoats and pinafores it is not likely to do much mischief'.[51] The Ladies' Land League suffered a 'strategic termination' when it was dissolved by Anna Parnell's brother, Charles Stewart Parnell. Valente argues that this action was in order 'to reclaim the gendered authority of Irish men vis-à-vis Irish women'.[52] However, the Ladies' Land League had been active countrywide. It had demonstrated women's courage, autonomy and organisational ability, serving as a model for women's activism and potential and contributing to the emergence of the independent and active New Woman.

Anglo-Ireland, England and the construction of the New Woman

Anglo-Irish connections with England remained strong, and the notion of the New Woman developed across both countries. For example, when Lolly and Lily Yeats lived in Bedford Park London from 1879, before returning to Ireland, Lily worked as an embroiderer for William Morris, and Lolly worked as a teacher and then, after training at Bedford Froebel College (1888–92), a lecturer at the Froebel Institute in London.[53] Working women themselves, they came into contact with the idea and the embodiment of the New Woman.[54] Lolly and Lily were habitual readers, and May Morris lent them books such as *Anna Karenina* which 'both pleased and shocked Lolly'.[55] They met New Women such as Florence Farr Emery, a feminist who had successfully undertaken the Oxford Women's Examination.[56] William Morris, who was keenly interested in Ireland, visited Dublin in 1885–86 to address the newly founded Contemporary Club, one of a number of meeting places for Dublin's 'considerable intelligentsia'.[57]

No doubt encouraged by this ferment of ideas in London and Dublin, on returning to Ireland in 1902, Lolly and Lily Yeats together with Evelyn Gleeson established the Dun Emer Guild in Dublin, a women's craft cooperative, drawing on the social and aesthetic ideals of the English Arts and Crafts movement. Lolly became the first woman to take charge of a private art press, Cuala, in 1908. She published modern Irish literature, including works by her brothers, Jack and W. B. Yeats, and gained international recognition.[58] The Yeats sisters, back in Ireland, had themselves become New Women. Other cross-national contacts brought further exchanges of ideas and practice associated with the New Woman. For instance, studying art in Germany in 1882, Somerville drew from life models and smoked as an independent 'New Woman'. In 1904, back in Ireland, she was cycling, 'the New Woman's sport'.[59]

A rather different conception of the New Woman to that embraced here by Somerville is presented in several contemporary women's periodicals published in London in the late nineteenth century. Michelle Tusan in her article, 'Inventing the New Woman: Print Culture and Identity Politics during the Fin-de-Siecle' (1998), argues that these periodicals set out to construct an ambitious new type of woman. They endeavoured 'to create a respectable image for political women through the invention of the identity of the New Woman [...] They called her the New Woman as it was on her shoulders [...] that the future of civilized society rested.'[60] One of these publications, *The Woman's Herald* (London, 1888–93), issued a piece entitled 'The Social Standing of the New Woman' in August 1893, which 'marked the first time that the term New Woman with the imposing capital letters first appeared in a periodical'.[61] Another of these periodicals was *Shafts: A Magazine of Progressive Thought* (London, 1892–1900), edited by Margaret Sibthorp, who announced that 'Our object is to encourage thought.'[62] In these publications, the New Woman was represented as 'a reasonable and thoughtful woman'.[63] *The Woman's Herald, Shafts* and similar papers promoted one another and were passed around among women readers, so that their content was 'not limited to a small number of writers and readers'.[64] Ireland at this time relied on magazines published in London (as discussed in the introduction), and it is quite likely that these women's papers would be read by progressive women in Ireland, or that Anglo-Irish visitors to London would find them.

O'Toole and other writers such as Carolyn Nelson in *A New Woman Reader* (2001) state that the term 'New Woman' made its first appearance in an essay by the Anglo-Irish writer Sarah Grand in March 1894 entitled 'The New Aspect of the Woman Question'.[65] Ann Heilmann in her book *New Woman Strategies* (2004) also argues that Sarah Grand, together with Olive Schreiner, an Englishwoman born in South Africa, and Mona Caird who was Anglo-Scottish could 'be credited with implanting the New Woman on the *fin-de-siècle* cultural landscape'.[66] However, Grand's use of the term post-dated its first appearance in *The Woman's Herald*.

Nonetheless, Grand's writings and the controversy her essay of 1894 sparked were important in publicising the term New Woman. Grand, a novelist and suffragist, was born Frances Elizabeth Bellenden Clark in Co. Down in 1854, but her family moved to England after her father died when she was 7, where she spent most of her life.[67] Grand's essay, 'The New Aspect of the Woman Question', published in the *North American Review* mentions the phrase 'new woman' just once and uncapitalised.[68] A savage attack on Grand's essay in the same journal, the *North American Review* two months later was entitled 'The New Woman', and drew further attention to the term 'New Woman' by repeating it, capitalised, 14 times in the course of the essay.[69]

In her essay, Grand identifies as a counterpart to the 'Shrieking Sisterhood' a 'Bawling Brotherhood' which either regards women as its domestic cattle or consorts with what Grand dismisses as 'the scum of our sex':

> Both the cow-woman and the scum-woman are well within range of the comprehension of the Bawling Brotherhood, but the new woman is a little above him, and he never even thought of looking up to where she has been sitting apart in silent contemplation all these years, thinking and thinking, until at last she [...] proclaimed for herself what was wrong with Home-is-the-Woman's-Sphere.[70]

Grand's notion of the 'new woman', albeit one that most likely takes the privileged woman of leisure as its template, corresponds to that of the editors and writers of *The Woman's Herald* and *Shaft*, in that it emphasises constructive thought and contemplation as a basis for women's revolt.

The author of the opposing essay to Grand's, Ouida (Mary Louise de la Ramée) was an English novelist and in many ways a New Woman herself, who insisted on staying in the room with men when they lit up their pipes and cigars.[71] However, Ouida considered it more important that a woman should be able to gesticulate gracefully and 'learn to dress, instead of clamouring for a franchise'.[72] Ouida added that 'Public life is already overcrowded, verbose, incompetent, fussy, and foolish enough without the addition of her in her sealskin coat with the dead humming bird on her hat.'[73]

The sobriquet New Woman was quickly picked up, for example, in an unsympathetic comedy in 1894 by the English playwright Sydney Grundy entitled 'The New Woman' which was 'immensely successful'.[74] For this, the Irish illustrator Albert Morrow designed a poster showing the New Woman writer George Egerton (Mary Chavelita Dunne Bright) in which 'we should note the pince-nez, the plain dress, the mass of books and papers and the cigarette'.[75] In September 1894, a paragraph in the *British Medical Journal* headed 'A New Light on the "New Woman"' proclaimed, 'She is as puzzling to the philosopher as she is startling to ordinary mortals.'[76] A stereotype of the New Woman was imagined: 'She was educated at Girton College, Cambridge, rode a bicycle, insisted on rational dress, and smoked in public.'[77]

Some Irish women rejected the concept of the New Woman as foreign to Ireland and Irish nationalism. For example, Mary E. L. Butler, a writer from a Catholic landowning family, was a fervent advocate of the Irish language and active in the Gaelic League. In an essay published as a pamphlet by the Gaelic League in 1900, Butler argues that women's historical role was to be an unassuming homemaker and a teacher of Irish to her children:

> The women of our race are dignified and decorous [...] this language war [...] is warfare of an especial kind [...] which can best be waged not by shrieking viragoes of [sic] aggressive amazons, but by gentle, low-voiced women who teach little children their first prayers, and, seated at the hearth-side, make those around them realise the difference between a home and a dwelling [...] Their mission is to make the homes of Ireland Irish.[78]

Butler claims that 'in Ireland we are all of the old school – the new woman has not made her appearance amongst us'.[79] Nonetheless Butler's urgent defence of 'gentle, low-voiced women', her hyperbolic critique of 'amazons' and her determination to deny the presence of the New Woman in Ireland at this time suggest the opposite.

The New Woman was therefore a complex term, developed over a long period in different countries and contexts. One of its origins was women's agitation and arguments for the right to suffrage and access to higher education, and in Ireland also women's involvement in the political struggles of the Land League. The New Woman in Ireland was particularly associated with the Anglo-Irish, whose close connections with England fostered transnational exchanges of ideas about women's rights and independence. The editors and writers of a group of women's periodicals produced in London in the early 1890s invented an ideal New Woman who as a progressive thinker would create a civilised future society, and Grand's essay envisaged a similarly thoughtful New Woman. However, there was opposition in Ireland towards women who failed to maintain the traditional and Catholic womanly role of meek piety. The term 'New Woman' was quickly disseminated and frequently satirised but also offered women a model of resistance to patriarchal dominance.

Literary formations of the New Woman

Fictional characters provided early models of women who acquired admirable moral and intellectual qualities through wide reading. For instance, in Jane Austen's novel *Pride and Prejudice* (1813), Mr Darcy, asked for his opinion on women's merits, chooses 'the improvement of her mind by extensive reading'.[80] Edmund in *Mansfield Park* (1814) comments on his cousin Fanny, 'He knew her to be clever, to have a quick apprehension as well as good sense, and a fondness for reading, which, properly directed, must be an education in itself.'[81] George Eliot's narrator in *Adam Bede* (1859) remarks of its tragic female character Hetty Sorrel: 'Hetty had never read a novel; if she had ever seen one […] how then could she find a shape for her expectations?'[82]

Women prominent in arts or politics were frequently avid readers. Amy Cruse in *The Victorians and Their Reading* (1935) concludes that 'the pioneers of the Woman's Movement […] read widely and eagerly […] Through their influence, books whose reading required real intellectual exertion became familiar to a wide circle of women readers'.[83] For example, Frances Power Cobbe, who addressed women in the 1870s to argue the rationale for female suffrage, devoured philosophical and scientific books from her father's and other libraries and was also 'a great lover of novels'.[84] Lily Yeats owned a variety of books, for instance, selections from Maria Edgeworth's writings, British poetry and Esmé Stuart Lennox Robinson's nationalist work *Patriots: A Play in Three Acts* (1912) presented to her by the playwright.[85] Edith Somerville's reading included Henry James's *Portrait of a Lady* and later novels by Sarah Grand and others with a New Woman as protagonist.[86]

Influential popular guides for women encouraged them to read. Charlotte Eliza Humphry, an author born in Londonderry and educated in Dublin, produced *A Word to Women* (1898) in which she blamed a 'vacuous ideal of femininity' for dissuading many women from engaging in intellectual activity. She identified 'the purse-proud and the vulgar' as those who sought to raise their daughters as 'fine ladies', in fact, 'the idlest and most empty-minded'.[87] Humphry warns women against focusing only on practical domestic skills since 'many an intellectual life has been killed by intemperate sewing'.[88] Although Humphry doubted the benefits of certain pursuits of the nascent New Woman, such as bicycling, which she regarded as liable to risk promiscuous encounters, she urged women and girls to take up reading.[89]

> We owe an enormous debt to the writers of books, and especially to biographers of interesting lives, to novelists, travellers who write of what they have seen […] poets […] and those photographic storytellers who delineate for us the workers of our world.[90]

Humphry extolled fiction as 'the most delightful recreation' for women readers, in contrast to the popular guides to men's reading that dismissed fiction in favour of informational texts.[91]

The New Woman in European, American and Irish fiction

The concept of the New Woman was formed partly through literary sources. In Gustave Flaubert's *Madame Bovary* (1857) and Leo Tolstoy's *Anna Karenina* (1878), the protagonists wish to enact an interesting life, such as those they read about in novels.[92] These works, as well as Henry James's *Portrait of a Lady* (1881), offered powerful prototypes of women aspiring to independence of thought and action, even though the consequences might be tragic and admonitory. Although the authors of these novels were men, there is an attempt to present the individual reflections of a female protagonist. James's *Portrait of a Lady*, for example, follows the life experiences of a young woman, Isabel Archer. Henry James explains that his starting point was the image of a young lady, complex, intelligent, engaging. She is to be made interesting by focusing on her life from her point of view, that is, from the place of her own thoughts.[93] Isabel Archer represents a New Woman not merely through her role as a significant female character but through James's decision to make her the conscious protagonist of the story.

In Ireland too, the New Woman emerged in literary fiction. Anna Parnell, leader of the Ladies' Land League, became the model for a fictional New Woman in *The Prince of the Glades* (1891), a novel by Hannah Lynch, herself a nationalist and secretary for the Ladies' Land League.[94] Books were part of Lynch's upbringing, and this was also the case for her heroine Camilla Knoys in *The Prince of the Glades*, as for Parnell herself, 'books and reading are central to her intellectual and ethical formation'.[95] Lynch's novel is based around the Fenian rising of 1867.[96] Knoys astounds her male companions with her physical and moral courage, for instance, when she gallops 60 miles alone at night to warn them of imminent arrest, although she is also portrayed like a medieval damsel 'her head bent sideways over her shoulder, revealing a white profile that justified a sane youth's conclusion that the picture was born of imagination's mists'.[97]

A short story, 'The Undefinable', by the Irish writer Sarah Grand was published in the American magazine *The Cosmopolitan* in October 1894. It recounts the tale of a mysterious woman who arrives at the studio door of an artist whose work seems to him lifeless. The stranger appears to him unattractive, and neglectful of his superior status, 'the direct look of her eyes into mine was positively distasteful'.[98] Examining her features, he notes 'the mocking eyes of that creature most abhorrent to the soul of man, a woman who […] does not care to please'.[99] However, he is induced to accept her as a model and he becomes entranced by her as she advises him on his art: 'The mere outer husk of me is nothing […] you must reveal the beyond of that […] I mean, all resplendent within.'[100] When she leaves, and his manservant is struck by the picture so far, the artist reflects, 'I recognized her now – a free woman, a new creature, a source of inspiration the like of which no man hitherto has ever imagined in art or literature.'[101] Grand's story represents a New Woman who breaks through the veil of female appearance to convince her interlocutor, the male artist with traditional views of women's place, to acknowledge her independent thoughts and feelings.

In Somerville and Ross's *The Real Charlotte*, also published in 1894, the key figure, Charlotte Mullen, was based on a relative of Somerville's, Emily Herbert, whom she called 'an awful drunkard'.[102] Mullen is an unprepossessing, wily and intolerant but independent and well-read exemplar of the New Woman. Mullen runs an estate and also has 'one or two sources of income which few people knew of […] two or three householders […] paid rent to her, and […] others […] had money dealings with her of a complicated kind'.[103] She is found absorbed in a pamphlet on the unladylike topic of stall feeding (keeping an animal in a stall to fatten it for slaughter), and she possesses 'a gentlemanlike capacity for liquor'.[104] In addition to her employment, financial independence and masculine drinking capacity, Mullen diverges from the feminine norm in appearance and dress: 'She was under no delusion as to her appearance, and, early recognising its hopeless character, she had abandoned all superfluities of decoration [with a] habit of costume so defiantly simple as to border on eccentricity.'[105] Typical of the new type of independent woman, Mullen reads voraciously and widely from literary classics to French novels and English newspapers. She has even built her own bookcase. Mullen is

> a great and insatiable reader, surprisingly well acquainted with the classics of literature, and unexpectedly lavish in the purchase of books. Her neighbours never forgot to mention […] the awe-inspiring fact that she 'took in the English *Times* and the *Saturday Review*, and read every word of them', but it was hinted that the bookshelves that her own capable hands had put up in her bedroom held a large proportion of works of fiction of a startlingly advanced kind, 'and', it was generally added in tones of mystery, 'many of them French'.[106]

As well as these stories with strong independent female protagonists, the idea of the New Woman was infiltrating mainstream women's reading. For instance, *Lady of the House*, the first women's magazine produced in Ireland and launched in 1890, aimed to focus on the 'Beautifying of the Home and

Person', giving an Irish context to 'women's concerns' current in English ladies magazines, such as fashion. The editor, Henry Crawford Hartnell, belonged to an advertising agency for Findlaters, an upmarket wine and grocery business that regularly featured in the magazine. The readers were 'women who were predominantly Protestant, middle-class (but not always very wealthy) and mainly if not entirely concentrated around Dublin'.[107] *Lady of the House* in addition to approving women's cycling, a venture closely identified with the New Woman, also developed a surprisingly progressive agenda for women's education and employment.[108]

In summary, the New Woman was a transnational phenomenon in nineteenth-century fiction, found and shared in novels and stories from Ireland, Europe and the United States. The concept of a new kind of independently minded woman was formally christened the New Woman in a group of women's periodicals published in London in the early 1890s and developed through the work of authors like the Anglo-Irish writer Sarah Grand. The New Woman infiltrated popular literature in the form of the first women's magazine produced in Ireland from 1890.

Visual art and the New Woman

As well as the verbal pictures conveyed through novels, visual art in various modes was crucial in representing and helping to shape the New Woman. The painting of modern life that became a feature of avant-garde Parisian art in the second half of the nineteenth century included depictions of modern women, such as the reader in Manet's *The Railway* of 1873 discussed in Chapter 2. Mary Cassatt's *At the Opera* (oil on canvas, 1878, Museum of Fine Arts, Boston) depicts a fashionable young woman deploying binoculars from an opera box, her binoculars trained towards other boxes, while more conventionally a man trains his binoculars on her. Griselda Pollock observes that the figure, seen in profile, 'looks across the viewer's line of vision in a determined action. Her looking elsewhere adamantly ignores the viewer's gaze'.[109] The figure also ignores that of the observing male figure. In this way, she refuses objectification by either the man depicted watching her or by the viewer. These pictures, publicly exhibited in Paris and elsewhere, arguably provided exemplars of the independent New Woman.

Smoking, a men's habit, was adopted by some New Women as an obvious sign of social contravention, and a woman smoking in a public place was a theme of visual art in France and elsewhere, sometimes with parallels to images of the New Woman as reader. For instance, Louise Lavrut's pastel *La fille de Montmartre* (*Young Woman of Montmartre*) of c. 1900 shows a young woman at a café with a cigarette and a beer.[110] Her dress is chic and expensive, a black, fur-edged coat and matching hat with high-necked cream blouse and lipstick, and her clear complexion as well as her dress identify her as middle class. The woman is depicted in profile in solitary thoughtfulness, one hand holding the cigarette, the other on her hip, elbow towards the viewer. Not only is she not looking at the fictive viewer but her body language holds the viewer at a distance. There was a belief in the nineteenth century that smoking stimulated fantasies and memories, and therefore creativity, so that her thoughtfulness might be seen as constructive.[111] Such a representation of a woman thinking and undistracted, like the reading figure in Irish art discussed in the following chapters, helped to define the New Woman as independent, assured and with her own thoughts.[112]

Kathryn Brown describes the New Woman in France by the turn of the century as 'easily recognizable […] [w]ith her comfortable, sometimes masculine clothing, athletic physique, and desire for recognition in political, professional, and artistic circles'.[113] However, this characterisation partly resonates with the many caricatures of the New Woman which played on such signs of revolt as masculine clothing and powerful build. The English magazine *Punch or The London Charivari*, even from the 1870s, made the New Woman (not yet named) a constant feature of its cartoons, introducing 'The Manly Maiden' in 1890, and first using the term 'New Woman' in September 1894.[114] The New Woman as depicted in fiction in the 1890s sometimes played on the idea of gender role reversal.[115] This notion was frequently pilloried in *Punch*, for example, in its caricatures of women bicyclists in 'Bloomers'. Tracy Collins points out that *Punch* imagery characterised the New Woman as an athletic type wearing practical clothes, which Collins believes accurately represented the New Woman: '*Punch* constructed an image of a female body (often quite sturdy) clothed in an athletic costume. The costume was a choice the New Woman embraced […] *Punch*'s captioning text was the distortion.'[116] The figure's costume is not always quite accurate, however. For instance, in *Nosce Teipsum* (*Punch*, 4 June 1898) a woman bicyclist wears huge baggy trousers as she mocks a Dutchman in the same, a cartoon that attacks two *Punch* targets, the New Woman and foreigners.[117] Using the trope of the bicycle costume, the New Woman's logic is also brought into question by *Punch*, as in *Gertrude and Jesse* (12 January 1895). Gertrude asks Jesse why she wears a bicycling costume when she has not got a bicycle. Jesse explains 'no, but I've got a sewing machine'. Between the mid-1880s and 1899 the topic of the Manly or New Woman received 200 iterations, so that '*Punch* had burned the stereotypical portrait of the New Woman into the public imagination'.[118] For all *Punch*'s ridicule, this constant image was one of an independent and mobile woman, and women did increasingly take up the liberating activity of cycling.

Punch was circulated throughout the British Empire, and Ireland anyway shared English magazines.[119] The magazine was therefore available in Ireland bearing those bicycling images of female independence and mobility. Women cyclists became a feature in Ireland, and by the 1890s the New Woman was receiving a welcome in Dublin, being admired for her practical clothing and even taking a lead in teaching the skill of cycling. For instance, in early 1895, when the Cycle Show was being held at the Rotunda, Dublin, it was reported that 'not the least prominent of the attractions are the ladies in rational dress, and who are to show the men how to ride [...] Everyone who saw them [...] was delighted with the neat appearance of the costume.'[120]

This fresh impulse in Dublin towards women's independence from patriarchal constraints was also manifested in new kinds of representation of the New Woman that were emerging in Ireland. Women artists were producing portraits of women as absorbed independent readers. Their depictions, as we shall see, had much in common with the 'thoughtful' New Woman imagined and anticipated in women's periodicals and represented in Sarah Grand's writing in the early 1890s.

Conclusion

The New Woman was publicly visible in late nineteenth-century Dublin wearing rational dress and adept at the new and liberating skill of cycling. This was the activity and garb that *Punch* cartoons associated with the New Woman and repeatedly mocked. However, the phenomenon of the New Woman was not confined to bicycling. Women challenged patriarchal boundaries in Ireland through campaigns for suffrage and access to higher education. The Ladies' Land League also set an example of female activism. Anglo-Irish women were prominent in such campaigns. The efforts to achieve women's suffrage were part of an international movement, and the multifaceted concept of the New Woman similarly was a transnational one. By contrast, the focus of the Irish Irelanders was inwards, towards the west of Ireland and looking to an imagined Gaelic history and culture, which entailed a rejection of both the English and the Anglo-Irish. The New Woman was given shape in the works of European and Irish literature that created exemplars of female protagonists with minds of their own. Such imaginative reading was important to the New Woman as a means of education and of liberation. As we shall see in Chapters 4 and 5, Irish portraits of the woman reader subtly presented the reader as an autonomous, reflective individual, the New Woman as thinker.

Chapter 4

THE SILENT READER AND THE FICTIVE VIEWER

A number of Irish portraits executed during the long nineteenth century depict a single reader, usually a woman, silently absorbed in a book, such as Sarah Purser's *The Afternoon Read* (oil on canvas board, n.d., Figure 15), or sometimes momentarily interrupted from it, as in Estella Solomons's *Portrait of a Woman* (oil on canvas, n.d., Figure 16). These portraits, largely by women artists, were produced in the context of the movements towards greater independence and better educational opportunities for women. Embodying new habits of reading, they show women occupied in independent intellectual and imaginative activity. Chapter 4 argues that such depictions of solitary engagement in a text by a female figure and the implied practice of silent reading helped to constitute a typology of the New Woman as literate, focused and reflective.

The chapter has five sections, each of which analyses a particular aspect of these portraits, with reference to examples. The first section, 'Silent Reading and Space for Interiority', explores the concept of silent reading. It explains how silent reading was related to the development and proliferation of the novel, when reading also became subject to literary judgements and issues of taste. Reading therefore became a complex activity, and one in which women readers would become intimately engaged. The second section, 'Absorption and the Reading Figure', examines the concept of 'absorption' in art, showing its particular application to the reading figure. The notion of the absorbed reader is intimately connected to the idea of the imagined viewer of an artwork, and the concept of the 'fictive viewer' is explored. The 'absorbed' reading figure had a counterpoise in the 'interrupted' reader, and this embodiment is discussed in section three, 'The Interrupted Reader'.

'The Style of the Reader', section four, considers the overall style(s) of the portraits and their use of traditional or modernist techniques, especially the use of colour. It also explores the potential symbolism of the reader's bodily attitude. Section five, 'A Private Space', concerns the reader's habitat. This section examines the domestic settings depicted in some of these portraits

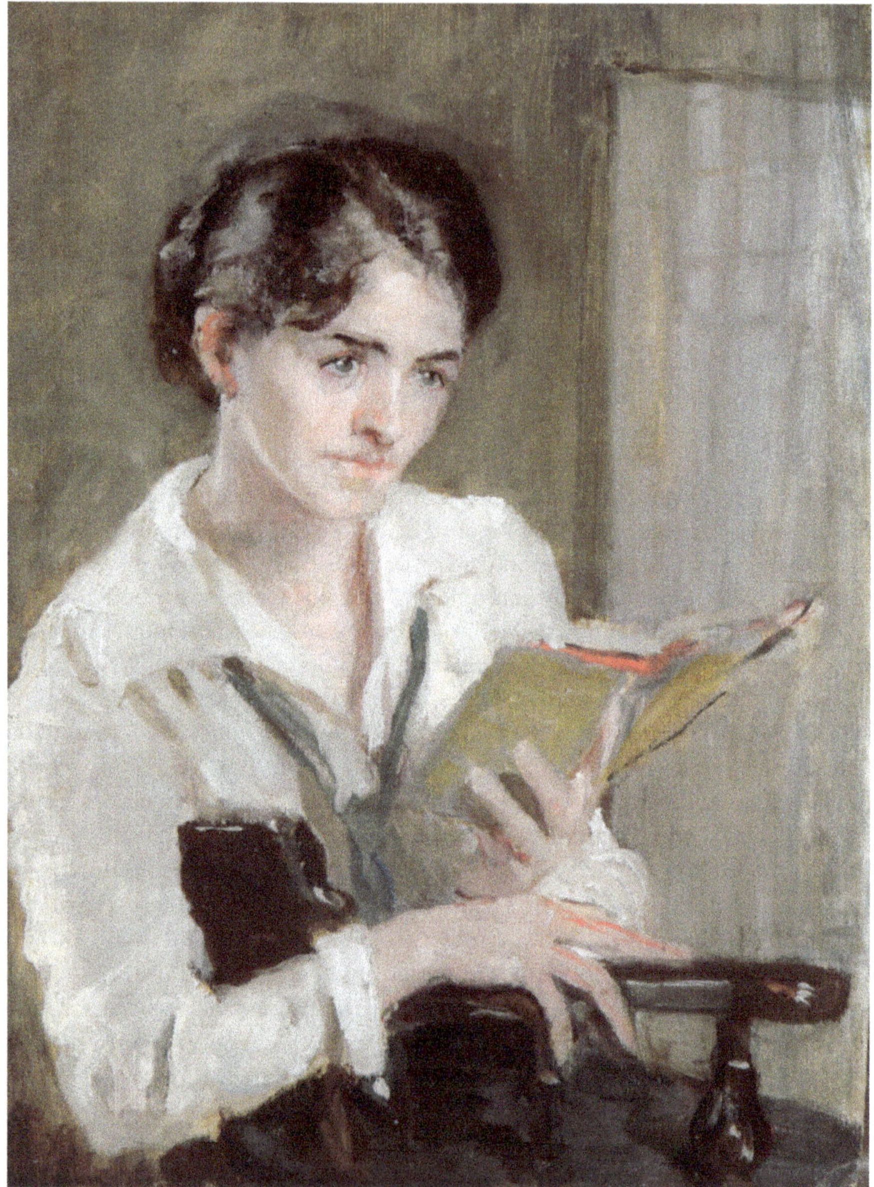

Figure 15 Sarah Purser, *The Afternoon Read*, oil on canvas board, 35 × 25 cm, n.d. Courtesy of Michael Purser. Private Collection. Photo Courtesy of Adam's Auctioneers.

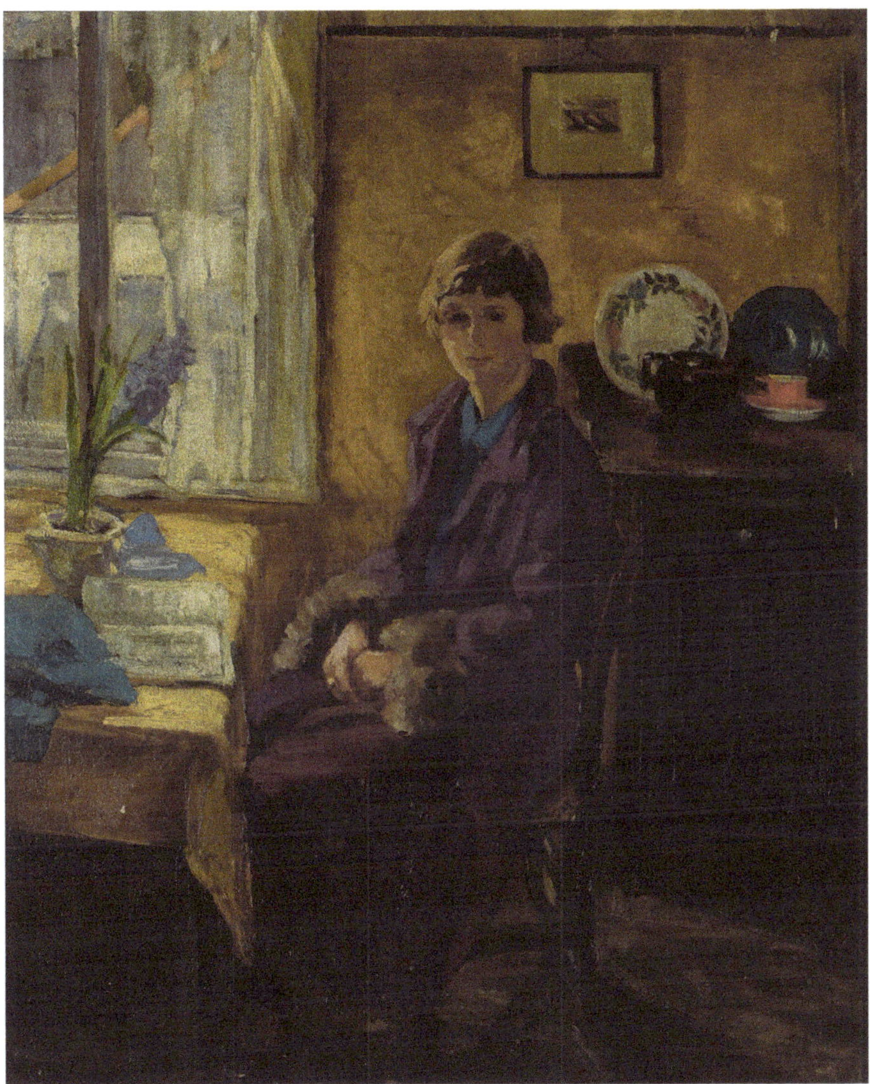

Figure 16 Estella Solomons, *Portrait of a Woman*, oil on canvas, 39 × 48.5 cm, n.d. © The Trustees of the Estate of Estella Solomons. Estella Solomons HRHA (1882– 1968), *Portrait of a Woman*, N.D., oil on canvas, 39 × 48.5 cm, Bequest of Ms Kathleen Goodfellow, 1980, Courtesy of The Model, Home of The Niland Collection.

which invoke a private space within which a woman could undertake her own study and creative work.

Silent reading and space for interiority

This section examines the concept of silent reading, together with the associated development of the novel, and suggests how readers in this period could establish a solitary and private relation to a text, with important implications for women's intellectual independence. The surprisingly recent practice of silent reading offered many more opportunities and contexts for reading apart from the didactic readings aloud performed in educative, religious and other public or communal settings, which tended to be selected and performed by men.

Silent reading, like reading for pleasure, was not an immediate corollary of the activity of reading. Silent reading had existed among monastic scribes but did not become a common practice in the West until later when it spread to the upper classes and the universities, then gradually to a wider population.[1] It became prevalent between 1750 and 1850, although reading aloud in a group continued to be common in nineteenth-century Ireland, particularly among the less affluent.[2] Newspapers were read aloud by speakers who visited the cottages of those unable to read or to buy a paper. *Reading the News* (oil on canvas, 1871) by the Irish artist Richard Staunton Cahill represents a man reading out his newspaper to an attentive family group in a simple stone-flagged Irish cottage. Reading aloud implied a sociable but often patriarchal reading, especially of a Bible, for instance, a head of household reading to his assembled family which was a common scene in Victorian painting and illustration.

The growth of silent reading has been associated with the existence in the late seventeenth and eighteenth centuries of a critical mass of potential readers and the consequent publication of texts amenable to silent reading.[3] The emergence of silent reading from the mid-eighteenth century brought new concepts of both writer and reader, as well as changes to prose style. Reading aloud involved a reader who embodied a speaker and addressed hearers also present. The 'embodied reader' could perform the text using appropriate expressions and gestures. Silent reading did not mean simply not reading out loud. Texts intended for silent reading implied 'a silent reader who conceives of himself or herself as the hearer of an internal voice, that of the notional writer'.[4] In silent reading, the writer became a disembodied or fictive narrator, and the reader was no longer a speaker but a hearer. This also changed the way texts were written. The absence of embodied speech meant that prose itself had to be adapted to make it comprehensible, for instance, through greater use of connecting words and phrases and a more conversational style. The new way of writing and of reading incorporated a fictive writer and a fictive listener. One of the outcomes of this new way of writing and of reading was the novel.[5]

Silent reading, evoking 'space for interiority', resonates with the focus of novelists such as Henry James on the inner thoughts of characters. In his preface to the Penguin edition of *The Portrait of a Lady* (1881) with its protagonist of a young woman, Isabel Archer, James recounts telling himself to 'place the centre of the subject in the young woman's own consciousness'.[6] James saw similarities between portraits drawn in literature and in art, and he believed that 'there is no greater work of art than a great portrait'.[7] James considered that 'the perceptive artist transforms the portrait into an illustration of, and an entrée *into*, character'.[8] In *Portrait of a Lady*, the novelist imagined the invisible emotional life of his character and incorporated it into his writing. Reflecting on *Portrait of a Lady*, James finds the best part of the book for him is a long meditative passage in which his female subject realises a life-changing moment, and during this reflection, she never rises from her chair:

> I might show what an 'exciting' inward life may do for the person leading it even while it remains perfectly normal. And I cannot think of a more consistent application of that ideal unless it be in the long statement, just beyond the middle of the book, of my young woman's extraordinary meditative vigil on the occasion that was to become for her such a landmark [...] It was designed to have all the vivacity of incident and all the economy of a picture. She sits up, by her dying fire, far into the night [...] It is a representation simply of her motionlessly *seeing* [...] [and] it all goes on [...] without her leaving her chair.[9]

For James, this episode possessed 'all the economy of a picture'. It offers a strong visual image of the young woman sitting thinking in the night by the embers of her fire, her lively 'inward life' unhampered by her sedentary situation. Portraits of the woman reader similarly may convey an idea of the character thinking and experiencing an exciting inward life while she sits silently reading. In the visual image, however, her thoughts remain opaque to the viewer.

Despite the reader's active involvement in silent reading, the fact that the reading subject was normally still and seated offered apparent evidence of mental passivity. Reading was therefore criticised as an incapacitating and addictive pastime that must result in bodily and mental passivity. Such criticism was no doubt reinforced by the fact that women were the main consumers of novels and patriarchal critics such as William Rathbone Greg accordingly characterised novels as lightweight fare suited to women, deemed incapable of serious intellectual application (as discussed in Chapter 2). Greg characterised novel reading as a passive and unintellectual activity, unworthy of men's full attention: '[Novels] are the reading of most men in their idler and more impressionable hours, when the fatigued mind requires rest and recreation; when the brain, therefore, is comparatively passive.'[10]

A contrary theory to the claims of passivity also arose that reading, while apparently passive, could promote mental activity and alertness, 'the discourse of reading as invisible movement, as edifying mental activity, develops'.[11] The German philosopher, Johann Adam Bergk, argued that the effects of reading depended not on the influence of reading per se but on the reader's approach and disposition. A bad reader received passively what they read, and their bodily inactivity would be matched by a passive mind. A good reader might appear passive, but their mind would be 'in motion', fully active and independent.[12]

Silent reading was especially important for women readers who thereby acquired an inner world that could be impenetrable to conventional masculine oversight, and the images that represent women reading celebrate this independence. Silent reading is not a sociable pursuit, and the occupied reader is not available to engage with an onlooker. Unlike many visual representations of women at this time, portraits of the engaged reading figure are not designed for an admiring male gaze. Silent reading enabled women to read privately and widely without restriction. By contrast with the claims that novels demanded little thought, and that women adopted them on this basis, the images of the reading subject discussed in this chapter demonstrate a view of the woman reader as independent, absorbed and alert and their reading matter as worthy of sustained attention.

'Books began to acquire a devotional aura'

Reading fiction depended on a notion of reading for pleasure, a concept that Stefan Bollman dates to the seventeenth, but especially the eighteenth century, when there was a great interest in reading.[13] The novels which proliferated in the nineteenth century offered the reader an inner life of adventure, and the reader's experience was potentially transformed as an expanding range of fiction offered new imagined worlds of places, characters and stories. Joep Leerssen argues that the middle classes looked to literature disconnected from their lives: 'It is the condition of nineteenth-century middle-class readers that their books are about everything they are not: outlaws, bandits, rakes, adventurers [...] honest cottage-dwelling peasants.'[14] However, the idea of literary taste became current in Europe from the mid-eighteenth century, in tandem with a burgeoning cult of 'sensibility', and this resulted in the establishment of a literary canon.

Deirdre Lynch examines how English literature, or literariness, came to embody an affective element. Across various forms of writing over the eighteenth and nineteenth centuries, literature became differentiated from other kinds of writing.[15] It did not fit neatly into earlier categories of informative writing nor evidently into the public sphere. Reading also came to involve 'taste'. While the literary canon was not a matter for individual judgement, a reader could experience a personal and emotive relation to canonical works and their authors. Subsequently as Joshua Rothman observed, writing in the *New Yorker*,

> Being a reader becomes an identity unto itself. A reader is unsatisfied with the present and yearns for something more. She finds it by cultivating intimate relationships with kindred spirits from another time [...] Books began to acquire a devotional aura [...] They entered into the home's most private spaces.[16]

A new aesthetic definition of literature again disturbed the use of texts in the public – and masculine – sphere as 'instruments of social power'.[17] There are many examples of women readers in Ireland in this period reading personally and widely, from 'the classics' to a range of other texts. For example, Lady Charlotte Stopford, from an aristocratic Anglo-Irish family, is pictured reading in an undated photograph (Figure 17). Stopford borrowed from libraries in Dublin and London, completing 'at least thirty books' in 1869, over half of which were fiction. These included classics such as Austen's *Mansfield Park*, which with its subplot of a play rehearsal while the patriarch Sir Thomas is absent may have encouraged her in a visit backstage at the Gaiety Theatre, Dublin, scandalising her family.[18] Stopford also consumed adventure stories such as *Cast Up by the Sea* aimed at male readers, as well as books on history, heraldry, ethics, etiquette and religion and English and Irish newspapers, including the nationalist paper *The Freeman's Journal*.[19]

If women were reading alone, it is likely that the realisation that they shared this habit, and even read many of the same books, might contribute to a shared sense of identity.[20] Such a shared identity was reinforced by portraits that depicted women readers.

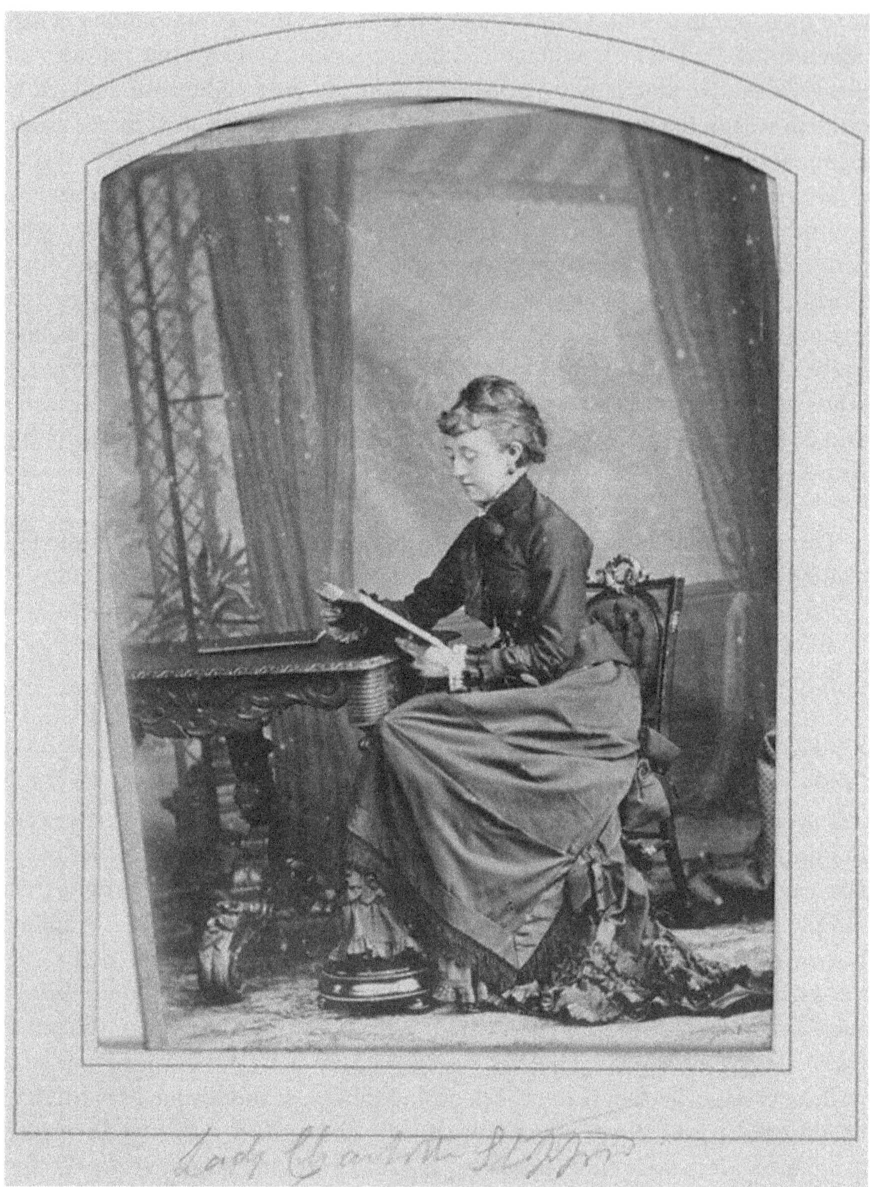

Figure 17 Lady Charlotte Stopford, photograph, n.d. MS 11412/1_14. Courtesy of The Board of Trinity College Dublin.

Absorption and the reading figure

In a study of French painting and criticism from the 1750s to the 1780s, Michael Fried analyses what he calls the 'absorption' of depicted figures. This refers to figures that focus intently on an activity to the exclusion of any distraction, whether by other figures located in the painting or the gaze of the fictive viewer. Fried notes that such works can also appear to indicate the time taken by the depicted activity, for instance, by suggesting a pause, or an incipient movement on the part of the absorbed figure.[21] Some of the most convincing of Fried's examples involve readers, such as Jean-Baptiste-Siméon Chardin's *Un Philosophe occupé de sa lecture* (A Philosopher Busy Reading) (oil on canvas, 1734, Louvre, Paris), in which a man reads and thinks, lost to the world, as a contemporary critic observed,

> On voit un home […] appuyé sur une table, & lisant très-attentivement un gros volume […] Le Peintre lui a donné un air d'esprit, de rêverie & de negligence […] il semble qu'on auroit peine à le distraire.[22]
>
> [We see a man leaning on a table and reading a large volume very attentively. The painter has given him an air of intelligence, reverie and obliviousness. One would have a hard time distracting him.]

The philosopher turns up the page as he reads, perhaps to look back in the book, a potential movement that extends the moment. Fried's analysis of 'absorption' is relevant to a number of Irish portraits of women readers, as we shall see.

The fictive viewer

The notion of absorption is closely linked to the role of the fictive viewer. A painting has an implied or 'fictive viewer' just as a novel has an 'implied reader'. The 'implied reader' commonly had two aspects, the author's intended reader(s) and the reader who was interpellated or addressed by the text. The fictive viewer similarly might be regarded in these two aspects, that is, as the artist's intended viewer(s) and as a viewer who is attracted by the image. The intended fictive viewer may be a composite of possibilities. For instance, the viewer imagined for a commissioned portrait might include its subject, as well as perhaps the curator and the critic. The viewers who actually see the portrait may be different and even unforeseen by the artist. For example, a portrait that depicts a serious female reader, focusing on an apparently passive and opaque activity, might interpellate other readers, perhaps especially other women readers. A portrait therefore constitutes an amalgam of conceptual and aesthetic possibilities and constraints and might be seen by a fictive viewer in various guises.

In his book *Techniques of the Observer: On Vision and Modernity in the Nineteenth Century*, Jonathan Crary discusses his concept of the fictive viewer. Crary distinguishes between the 'spectator', whom he identifies as a passive consumer, for instance, in an art gallery, and his preferred term, the 'observer', which he believes has overtones of observance of or compliance with rules. Crary notes a common assumption that while art changes over time, the observer stays the same, and he argues that the observer changes over time too, particularly with the onset of modernisation in the nineteenth century. For Crary, the observer is understood to be both enmeshed in and constitutive of a historical network of social conventions and possibilities, which answer to a disciplinary function maintained by those in power:

> [A]n observer is […] one who sees within a prescribed set of possibilities, one who is embedded in a system of conventions and limitations […]. Vision and its effects are always inseparable from the possibilities of an observing subject who is both the historical product *and* the site of certain practices, techniques, institutions, and procedures of subjectification […] For Foucault, nineteenth-century modernity is inseparable from the way in which dispersed mechanisms of power coincide with new modes of subjectivity.[23]

The observer will certainly be influenced by dominant historical and visual conventions. However, Crary does not note that the disciplinary 'mechanisms of power' were different for men and women at this time, a point on which Foucault is clear.[24]

In the light of Crary's comments, it might be asked whether the fictive viewer in Ireland changed over the course of the long nineteenth century, and what constraints applied to the viewer. While Crary places his observer in shifting time and space, he overlooks the differential statuses of women and men at the same time and in the same place. It is notable that *Techniques of the Observer* has 32 iterations of the words man/men, but only three of the words woman/women and none of 'female' or 'gender'.

The fictive viewer in any particular historical instance is likely to already be an amalgam of different interests and also constitutive of different orders of power. Women in Ireland and elsewhere were especially subject to disciplinary procedures, which included the denigration of their abilities and the withholding of higher and art education from them. The visual texts of the paintings themselves, especially portrayals of serious women readers, might interpellate female viewers who were themselves readers. However, the curator or critic with the ability to pass public judgements was generally a male viewer, although he too was changing and to some degree offering greater credence to women's art.[25] By the turn of the century, rapid social change and the burgeoning idea of the New Woman began to slightly alter the balance of power in favour of women, especially those of the Anglo-Irish middle classes.

How the viewer engages imaginatively with the subject of a picture might to some extent be predetermined by the character of the image. The role of the fictive viewer is important in Fried's terms in relation to the depicted reader's absorption. A number of Irish portraits in this period depict female figures solitarily absorbed in the act of reading as if no observer is present. Not only are there no other figures in the picture, but there is no acknowledgement of nor room for a fictive viewer who might occupy an imagined place in the depicted scene. For instance, an image might exclude the fictive viewer by such devices as denying the viewer an imaginary foothold in the depicted scene. In terms of Fried's analysis, the absorption of a figure may have the effect of ignoring the possibility of a viewer or, in Fried's terminology, the beholder. Paradoxically, as Fried suggests, the absorption of the figure is mirrored by the viewer, who is drawn in to concentrate on the activity shown. The conditions of the viewer's apparent absence – the depicted figure's preoccupation and obliviousness – ensure the beholder's attentiveness to the painting: 'Only by establishing the fiction of his absence or nonexistence could his actual placement before and enthrallment by the painting be secured.'[26] A number of Irish portraits represent absorbed women readers, while excluding the fictive viewer.

The absorbed reader

For example, Sarah Purser's *The Afternoon Read* (oil on canvas board, n.d., Figure 15) depicts a solitary young woman silently engrossed in a book. The definite article in the painting's title, *The Afternoon Read*, suggests a habit. The book, with its dull yellow cover, would be recognisable to a contemporary audience as a 'yellowback' or 'mustard plaster', which were novels reprinted in yellow paper boards, instead of leather or buckram (a stiff cotton cloth). Initially produced from 1849 for the new railway bookstalls, they included not only sensation novels by Mrs Henry Wood and Wilkie Collins but also classic works by Jane Austen and Anthony Trollope.[27] The young woman's eyes are fixed on the book, in which she appears to be deeply involved. The figure is turned around a little in her chair with an arm hooked over the back, as if she has shifted position to focus even more intently on the novel. This pose tilts the figure towards the viewer, her elbow and forearm almost in the viewer's space, yet the reader remains oblivious to any other presence. The viewer is effectively occluded. Visible above the yellow cover of her book are the edges of some inner leaves of scarlet, which attract the viewer's attention among the predominantly muted colours of the painting. The red is picked up in a streak along the reader's finger, which has the effect of attaching her physically to the book and reinforcing the intentness of her gaze. The fictive viewer is completely excluded from this intimate scene, and yet paradoxically drawn to it by the reader's concentration, in the way that Fried proposed.

In Estella Solomons's *A Woman Reading at a Desk by the Window* (oil on canvas, n.d., Figure 18), the viewer's gaze follows the movement of the figure as she

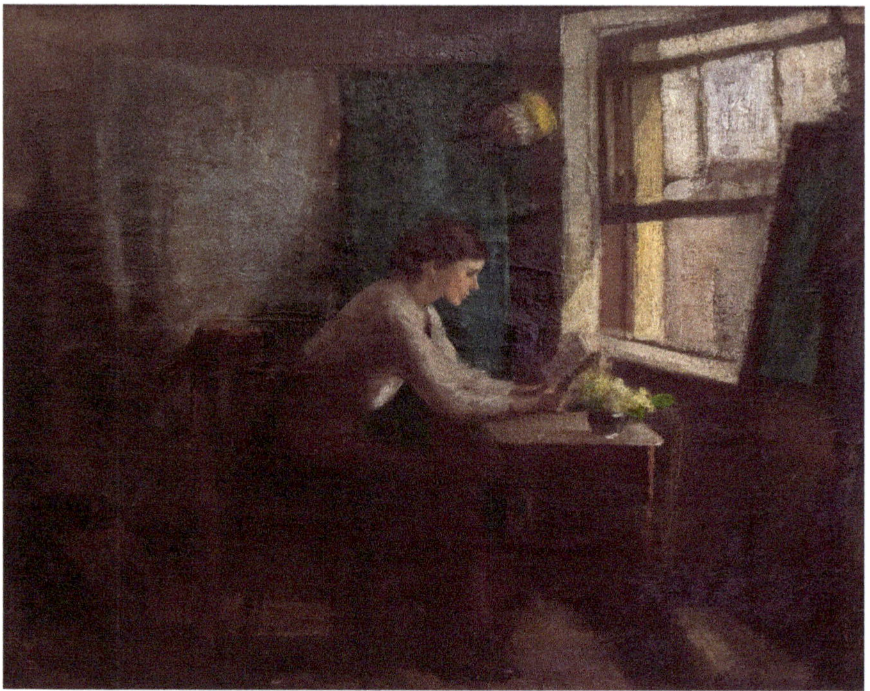

Figure 18 Estella Solomons. *A Woman Reading at a Desk by a Window*, oil on canvas, 42 × 52cm, n.d. © The Trustees of the Estate of Estella Solomons. Photo courtesy of Adam's Auctioneers.

leans forward, both arms firmly on the desk holding her book on which her whole attention is concentrated. The reader is comfortably, not dressily attired, her hair drawn back, workmanlike, from her face. This stance, her focused attention and her environment convey an image of an independent, thinking woman in her own space. There are few clues about the kind of book she is reading, although her serious expression and her posture, supporting her arms on a small table or desk, and leaning in towards the book, suggest this is a work that requires intellectual effort rather than a light romance. This is again a portrait of an absorbed reader and in this quiet studious scene, the fictive viewer becomes an interloper.

John B. Yeats executed various sketches of his daughters, Lolly and Lily, focused on reading. *Lolly Reading* (pencil, n.d., Figure 19), drawn in grey-brown pencil on buff-coloured paper, presents a softer image than might be shown in a black-and-white reproduction.[28] The tone and colouring suggest an evening light, while the figure's close focus on her substantial book suggests an effort to see it properly, as well as the concentration and imperviousness to distraction

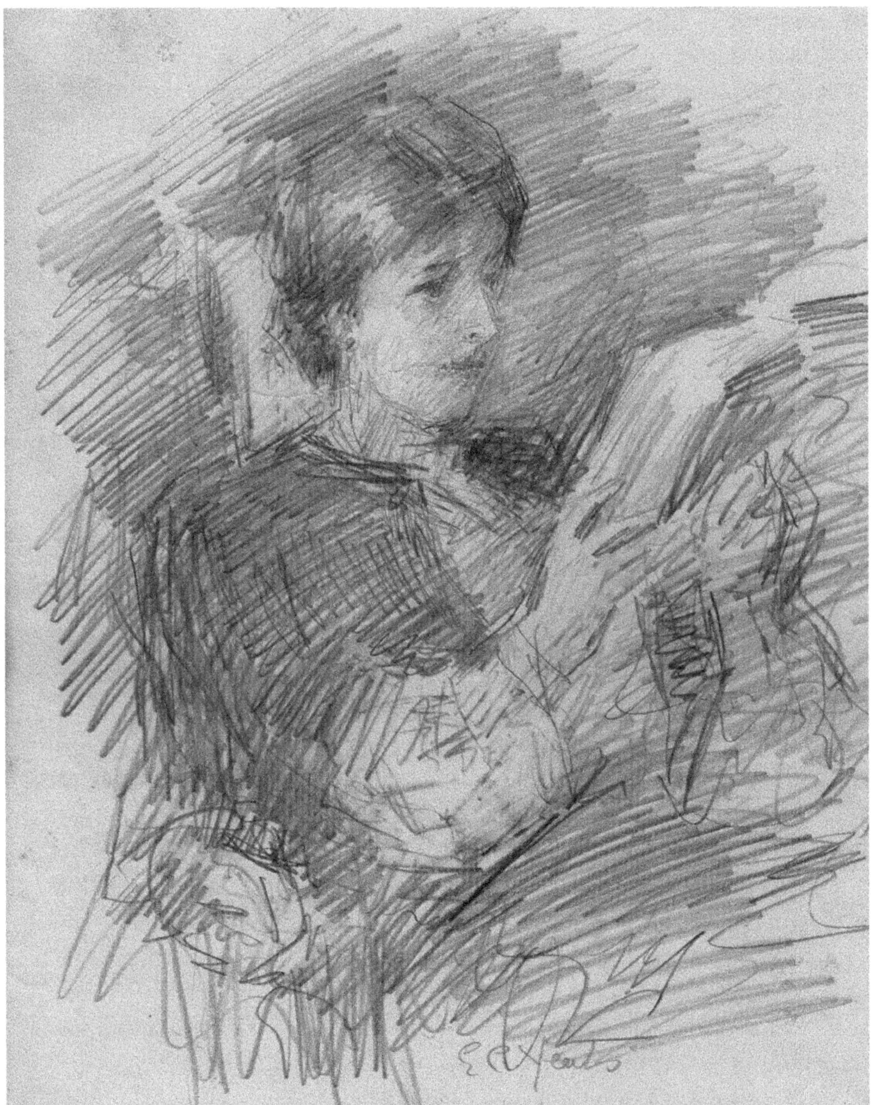

Figure 19 John Butler Yeats, *Lolly Reading*, pencil, 24.13 × 18.42 cm, n.d. Private Collection, image courtesy Whytes.com.

that Fried characterises as absorption. The pencil shading and shaping with rough hatching constructs a figure that emerges out of and yet is an organic part of her environment. The transparency of execution represented by the pencil marks could be compared to the unconcealed strokes of the paint brush characteristic of modernist painting that challenge the viewer to recognise the artifice while believing in the subject created. The merging of the figure with her environment in *Lolly Reading* (Figure 19) also has the effect of completely excluding the fictive viewer, who must remain external to the scene, even while, as Fried proposed, the reader's absorption attracts the viewer.

The interrupted reader

A trope that has often been employed in portraits of readers is that of the 'interrupted reader', which in the case of a solitary figure may signal the presence, rather than imply the absence, of a fictive viewer. The figure is not currently reading, but may hold an open book, often with a hand or finger marking the page. Readers are interrupted from engaging with various reading materials from novels to Bibles. The trope of the interrupted reader can have various functions. The pose enables a figure to be depicted with head raised, allowing the face to be fully visible and perhaps permitting the figure to engage with a fictive viewer. Portraits of the interrupted reader may also convey social, political or religious messages. For example, a portrait may place the viewer in the company of a genial preacher with his Bible, as in Maria Spilsbury's portrait of *The Revd. B.W. Mathias, AM.* (Figure 4) discussed in Chapter 1.

In a study of women readers in American art from the early seventeenth to the early twentieth centuries, Linda Docherty postulates eight pictorial types which she characterises as: conjugal, venerable, material, cerebral, isolated, cultivated, worldly and interrupted. Her article focuses mostly on male artists and sitters in New England.[29] Given differences of geography, culture and often of chronology, Docherty's categories are not generally applicable to depictions of women readers in Ireland in the long nineteenth century. However, her characterisation of the interrupted reader is worth mentioning as it differs markedly from that considered here. Her type of the interrupted reader is one 'whose engagement with books is limited by social responsibility', for example, a mother who puts her book aside to play with her child.[30] For Docherty, 'the interrupted reader's character was expressed by what she does for others'.[31]

Catherine Golden, in a study of the woman reader as illustrated in Victorian fiction in Britain and America, similarly concludes that 'The interrupted reader, who puts aside her book to attend to her child or visitor, chooses social responsibility over personal pleasure and represents an ideal vision.'[32] This ideal vision was one that celebrated the maternal and domestic duties of women. Golden discusses a range of book illustrations in which a woman is depicted with an open, unattended book while she addresses her attention instead to a child, or to a visitor or other interlocutor.[33] Golden argues that these depictions exemplify the Victorian ideology of domesticity to which women are shown to conform by prioritising domestic concerns over reading. Although illustrators used the accessory of a book to indicate women's education and refinement, their images demonstrated that the book would readily be put aside to attend to domestic duties.

In contemporary Irish visual images of women readers, the trope of the 'interrupted reader' has rather different connotations to those examples of women readers interrupted by children or by household duties, with their pervading ideology of dutiful domesticity. The women reading are not depicted as defined or circumscribed by some well-established domestic role. Instead, their primary identity is as readers, with their attention only temporarily removed from an application to reading. Indeed, the presentation of the interrupted reader paradoxically demonstrates the power of reading to absorb attention and to sustain it over time, as the reader is shown as only momentarily distracted while the book is open or held with a place kept, waiting to be continued. This holding or keeping of a place in the book also tends to indicate a stretch of time taken for the activity, extending the moment in the way that Fried suggests.

For example, Estella Solomon's *Portrait of a Woman* (Figure 16) depicts a woman in her own space unencumbered by household duties or family calls, a New Woman free to read and write. The figure pauses to acknowledge a viewer, but her pose, only partly turned from the book resting open in front of her, represents the exchange as a passing interruption to her occupation of reading. Solomons's portrait *The Writer* (oil on canvas, n.d., Private Collection) depicts a grey-haired woman seated by a table glancing up from an open book she holds, while more books and a paper lie on the table.[34] The title of the portrait, with the books and paper depicted nearby, represents another woman busily occupied in creative intellectual work.

In *Mrs Charles Hughes* (oil on canvas, 1901, Figure 20) by William Orpen, the figure holds a book, keeping her place as she turns towards an unseen window. The figure wears a full-length dress of dark turquoise with a high neckline and long sleeves, elaborately designed although unostentatious, and exposing only her face and hands. Her dress forms a brilliant element of the picture, but there is as much emphasis on the figure's face and on the book she holds which are illuminated as she turns to the hidden window. The viewer's focus is on the woman and especially on her face, her hands and on her book. The figure's brilliant red hair, picked up in the reddish-brown wall or screen beside her, is complemented by the green dress and surround, adding a glow to her face. There is some other detail in the image, a patterned green-hued carpet, an indeterminate picture on the wall, some flowers and a vase, but all are shadowed or tinted blue-green, as if subsumed by the brilliance of the figure's

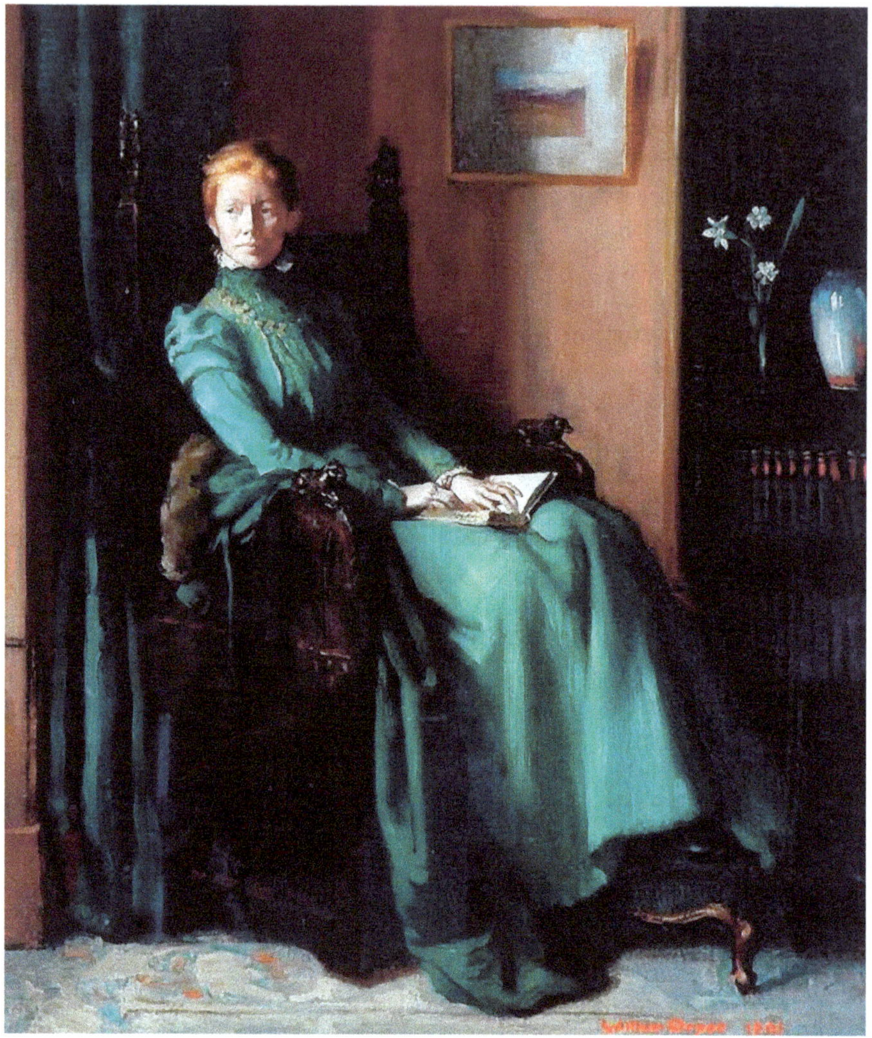

Figure 20 William Orpen, *Mrs Charles Hughes,* oil on canvas, 59.5 × 49.9 cm, 1901. Photo courtesy of Priory Studios, www.sirwilliamorpen.com.

garb. Yet her dress is not what draws the viewer so much as the woman's face in the light, and her serious abstracted expression. The presence of the book matches and enables the representation of this abstracted air, releasing the figure from conventional requirements to display her finery, or to acknowledge the viewer.

In Henry Walter Barnett's photograph of Georgina Hariot, Marchioness of the barony of Dufferin in County Down, Ireland, and Vicereine of India

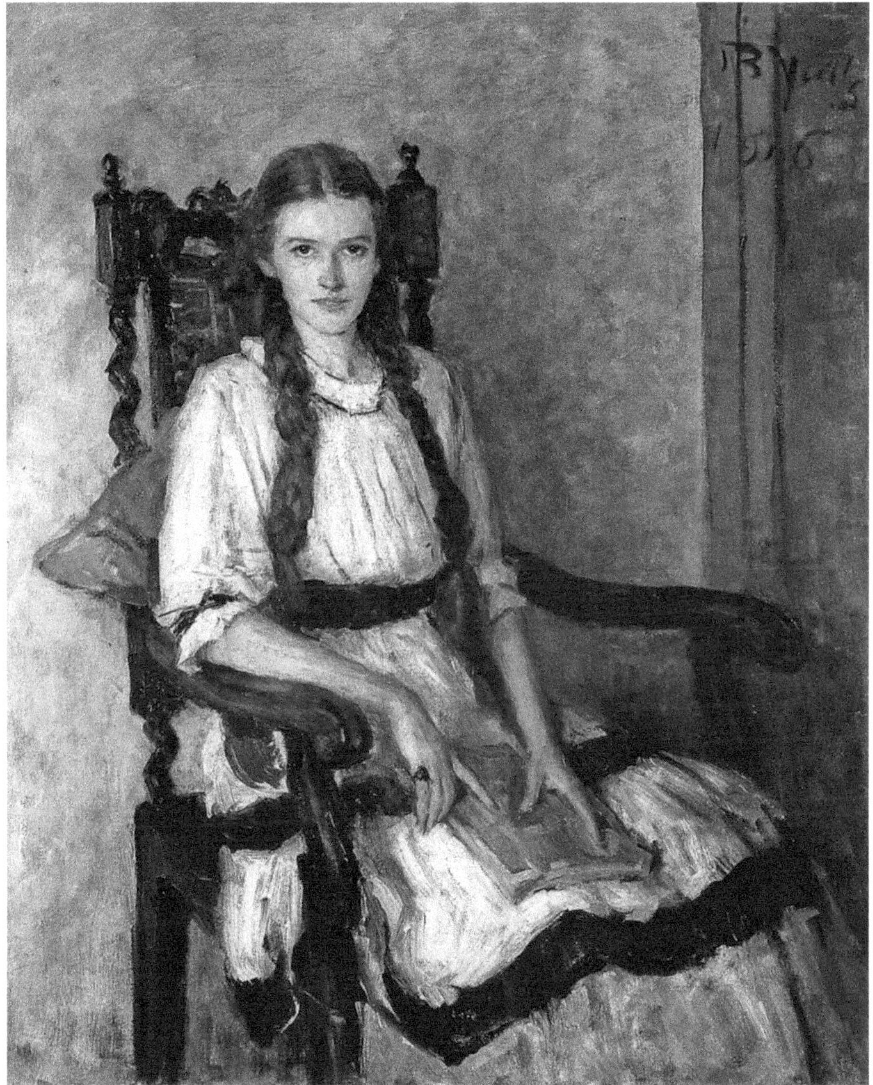

Figure 21 John Butler Yeats, *Portrait of Mary Lapsley Guest (née Caughey)*, oil on canvas, 105 × 84 cm, 1916. NGI.1821. Photo © National Gallery of Ireland.

(c. 1900, National Portrait Gallery, London), Hariot sits book in hand in a drawing room, stately windows suggested by a large expanse of curtain.[35] With curtains closed, there is no view outwards, focusing the viewer's attention on Hariot's central figure. Her dress is formal and elaborate, conveying her rank. Accompanying her husband to various imperial appointments abroad, Hariot

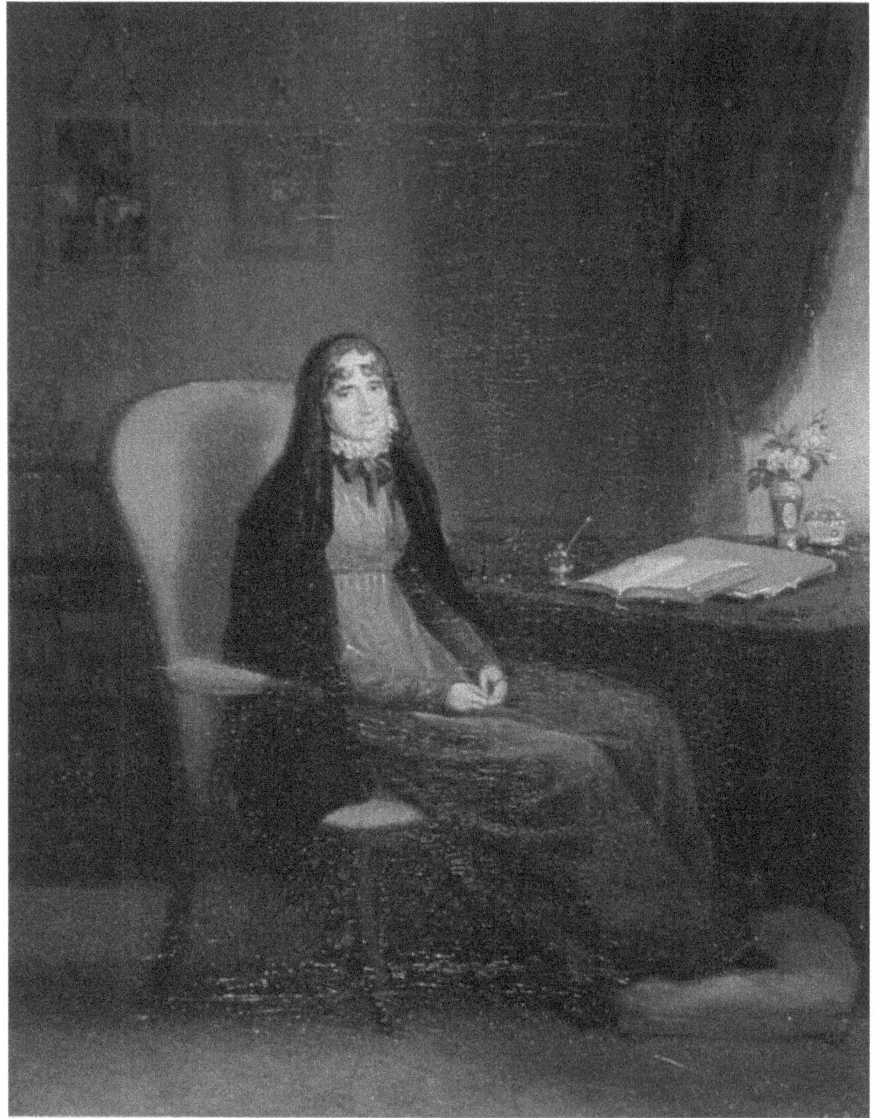

Figure 22 Maria Spilsbury, *Mrs Henry Grattan*, oil on canvas, 43 × 34 cm, c. 1814–19.
NGI.567. Photo © National Gallery of Ireland.

herself undertook diplomatic activities. For example, at the request of Queen
Victoria she successfully improved women's medical care in British India
by enlisting the support of local Maharajahs. She later wrote her memoirs.
In the image, holding her book, she gazes reflectively to one side. Several

more books of mixed sizes rest prominently on a small table in front of her including a larger book with a place marked and another in a dustcover, perhaps a novel, suggesting varied reading. The significance given here to books and the indications that she is presently busy reading them, as well as her own writing and adventurous biography suggest that Hariot was an active and studious woman. Despite her conservative status, she embodied many attributes of the New Woman.

John B. Yeats's *Portrait of Mary Lapsley Guest (née Caughey)* (oil on canvas, 1916, Figure 21) was executed after he moved to the United States.[36] Mary Tower Lapsley Caughey invited him to lecture in her home in Pennsylvania, and Yeats painted family members including Mary, then 15. AE (George William Russell) observed of John Yeats that 'few artists [...] found it more easy to be interested in the people they [...] painted. All his portraits, whether of men or women, seem touched with affection.'[37] In Yeats's portrait, Mary Lapsley Caughey looks out trustingly at the artist/viewer. She has a well-used book on her lap, which she touches gently with her fingers, as something to be cared for, so that her identity is represented here as that of a content and independent young reader.

Some representations of the interrupted reader, while not designed to please a male gaze, do not either embody or prefigure the New Woman. In Spilsbury's portrait of Henrietta Grattan, *Mrs Henry Grattan* (oil on canvas, c. 1814–19, Figure 22), the figure sits beside a table bearing an open Bible. The figure wears a black mantilla, a sign of her married status.[38] The figure is slightly hunched, as she sits near the table bearing the Bible, her feet resting comfortably on a footstool and holding her spectacles in readiness to continue reading. Her posture is relaxed, but Henrietta Grattan suffered poor health and in the portrait her face expresses sadness and resignation. The corner of a window is just visible and beside it a heavy fringed drape which casts a large shadow over the wall behind, as another shadow of Henrietta Grattan herself is cast on the back of her chair. The light from the window illuminates her face and hands, her Bible and a small vase of pink roses, and falls on parts of the red chair, and onto a red file supporting the Bible. However, her surroundings convey an oppressive gloom. In this portrait, the subject's central position and her acknowledgement of the spectator, the lack of an outside view and the fall of light restrict the viewer's gaze to the figure of Mrs Grattan, especially her face, and to the open Bible, emphasising her sad, contemplative gaze and a dominant religiosity.

Sarah Purser's portrait of her mother, *Anne Mallet (Mrs B. Purser)* (oil on canvas, 1886, Figure 23), shows her seated in three-quarters view, slightly turned from the viewer, with a book open on her lap, as she keeps the page.[39] Curiously, the figure is unfinished, especially her right hand, compared to the

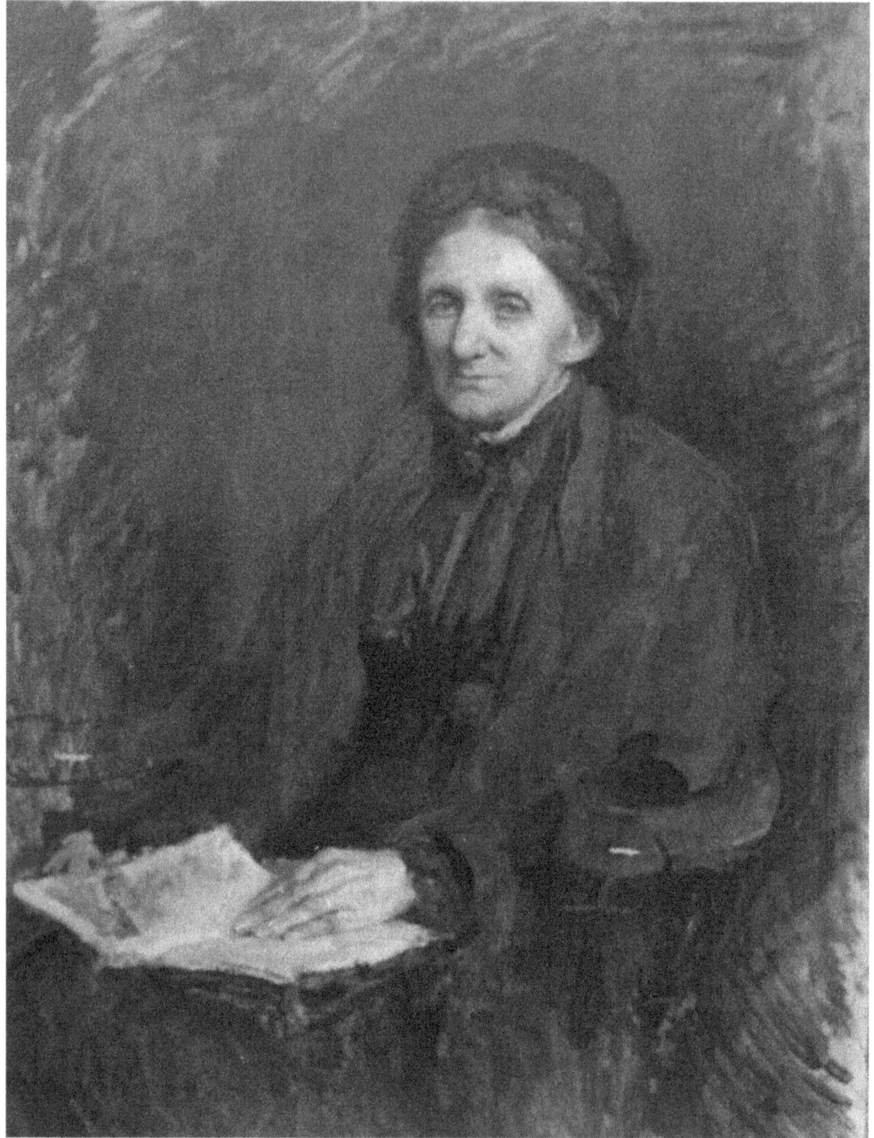

Figure 23 Sarah Purser, *Anne Mallet (Mrs B. Purser)*, oil on canvas, 91.5 × 71 cm, 1886. Courtesy of Michael Purser. Private Collection.

left. Sarah Purser's nephew, Michael Purser, states that the hand was unfinished because 'mother and daughter are said to have fallen out over the picture'.[40] Mrs Purser is not shown as poised to put her book aside to look after or even engage with others. In sharp contrast to Purser's portrait of Jane Barlow (discussed in Chapter 5), her mother looks out with a joyless and forbidding expression. In this image, there is no evident embrace of reading as an expression of independent study or pleasure.

The trope of the interrupted reader subtly complicates the act of reading. The interrupted reader in all these portraits appears to have paused on behalf of an interlocutor or spectator. The reader may gaze to one side, or look up deliberately to engage with the fictive viewer. The viewer is no longer excluded from the reader's space, but the book held still symbolises a private world. The figure's attitude generally suggests that reading may be temporarily paused but remains an absorbing activity that waits to be continued, although not all portraits of the interrupted reader contained this promise.

The style of the reader

The bodily attitude of a depicted figure contributes to his, or more commonly her, identity as a reader. Indeed, 'identity formation, frequently seen as an exclusively cognitive process – a mental category for labelling self and others – is also a bodily one'.[41] Portraiture traditionally attempted to show a recognisable likeness, displaying a frontal or three-quarter aspect of the subject. However, portraits of an engaged reader often fail to show the subject's face clearly in favour of an attitude showing a figure's absorption in reading, so characterising the figure as a reader. An extreme example of this is *The Newspaper* (oil on cardboard, 1896–98, The Phillips Collection, Washington, DC) by the French artist Edouard Vuillard which portrays his mother reading a spread newspaper that entirely conceals her face from the viewer. Despite the picture containing much visual interest, its focus remains the newspaper and the mystery of the unseen figure, glimpsed in black, behind it. John Lavery's *Girl in a Red Dress Reading by a Swimming Pool* (1887) discussed in Chapter 2 unusually presents the back view of a reader. Paradoxically, this may allow a fictive viewer to be present, not occluded but unseen.

Whether a figure is depicted full-face or in profile may convey particular symbolic values, as well as having implications for the relation of viewer to subject. A profile view of a figure tends to evade the fictive viewer's engagement with the subject. Meyer Schapiro characterises the profile as the grammatical equivalent of the third person:

> The profile face is detached from the viewer […] It is […] like the grammatical form of the third person, the impersonal 'he' or 'she' […] while the face turned outwards is credited with intentness, a latent or potential

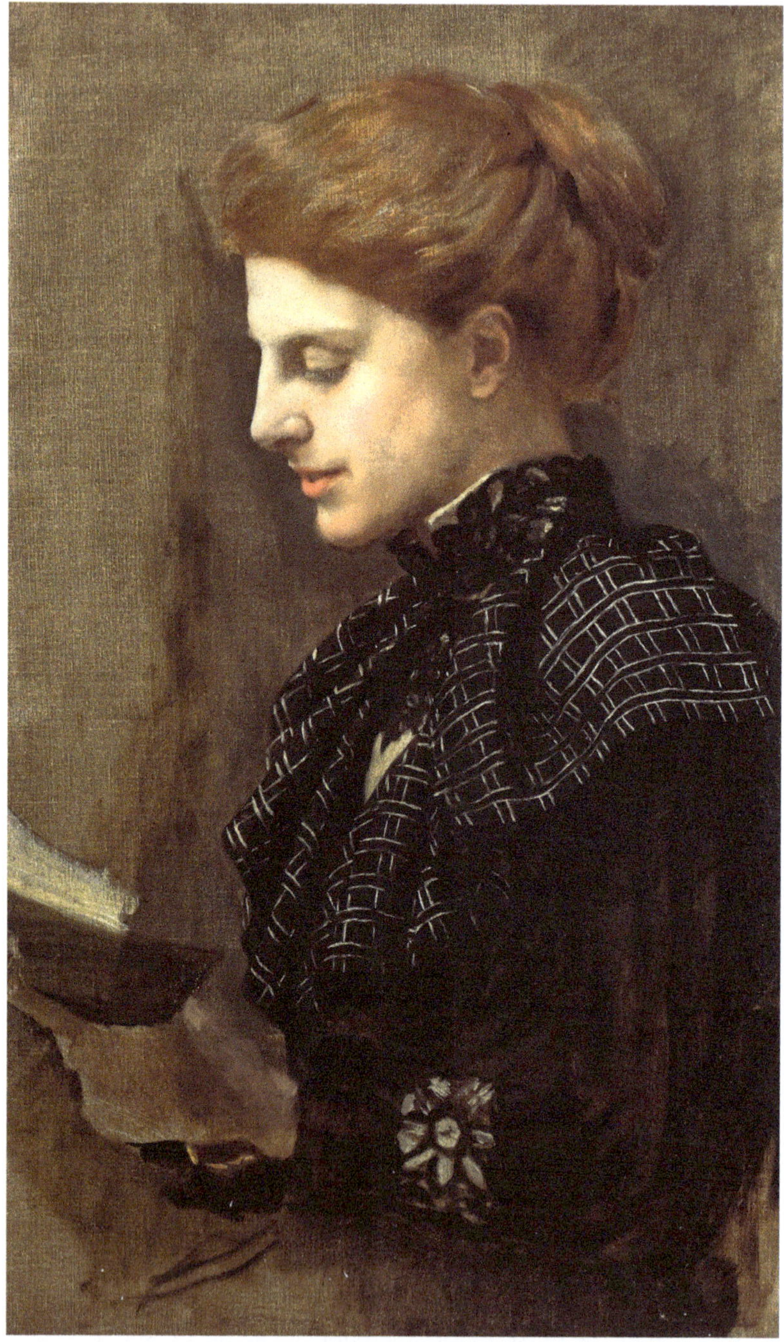

Figure 24 Sarah Cecilia Harrison, *Portrait of a Young Lady Reading*, oil on canvas, 76.20 × 45.72 cm, n.d. Private Collection. Image Courtesy Whytes.com.

glance directed to the observer, and corresponds to the role of 'I' in speech, with its complementary 'you'.[42]

Schapiro comments that the profile, unlike a full-face, is asymmetrical and displays more character: 'While the full-face has an ideal closure and roundness – smooth, regular and symmetrical – the profile is indented and asymmetrical and shows a less complete but more sharply characterized face.'[43] The profile view can be more arresting than a full-face view and can be studied at leisure by the unnoticed onlooker. While the profile view lessens or even occludes the impression of a viewer's presence at the depicted scene, conversely there may be an enhanced sense of unauthorised observation. A face seen frontally, on the other hand, is assumed to be directed towards the viewer as 'we are inclined to see whatever faces us as looking at us'.[44]

In Solomons's *Portrait of a Woman* (Figure 16) depicting her friend Kathleen Goodfellow, the figure, interrupted from reading, turns a 'full face' to the viewer. Her features are identifiable and her gaze is directed at the viewer. Other Irish portraits of absorbed readers make use of the profile view discussed by Schapiro. For example, in a sketch by Sarah Purser of her mother Anne Mallet, the figure is seen in profile engrossed in reading a large book, the family dog in back view with its chin towards her knee.[45] Everything in the sketch points to a focus on the book, the figure bent over it, even the dog's orientation. In such images, the reading figure is again shown to be oblivious to the presence of a viewer.

Cecilia Harrison's *Portrait of a Young Lady Reading* (oil on canvas, n.d., Private Collection, Figure 24) and her *Study of a Young French Woman* (oil on canvas, n.d., Private Collection) are both profile views of readers.[46] *Portrait of a Young Lady Reading* is a carefully observed portrait of an absorbed reader. The reverse of the painting is reported to be inscribed with 'Miss Connolly' and the artist's name, with an indistinct date.[47] The figure is elaborately but modestly garbed in a sort of ruffled short shawl over a dark long-sleeved dress, her hair carefully coiffed. The reader's lips, highlighted with lipstick, are slightly parted. In Victorian art, faces often assumed social and moral values gleaned from their features and expression. For instance, parted lips but with a show of teeth indicated working-class status.[48] The closed mouth in most Irish portraits of women readers is likely to have subtly signified middle- or upper-class status. In Harrison's portrait, the figure's slightly parted lips as she looks down at her book suggests she is reading to herself.[49] The figure does not engage with a viewer and the careful dress is not displayed for a viewer's benefit. There is no implied viewer here at all, insofar as the profile view as well as the figure's absorption in reading deny the possibility of an interlocutor.

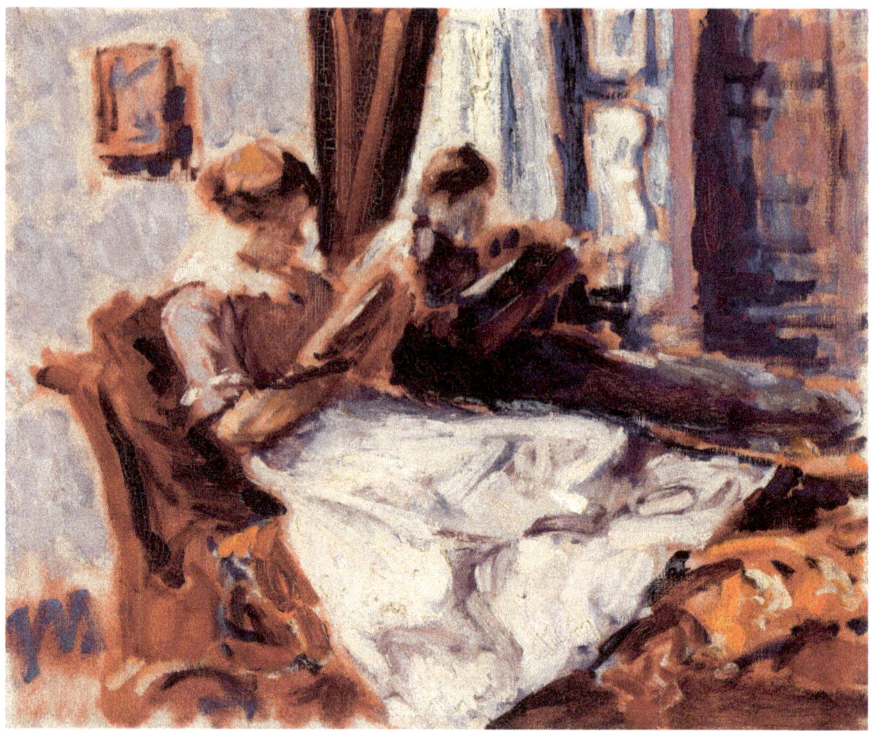

Figure 25 Roderic O'Conor, *A Quiet Read*. oil on canvas, 46 × 55.5 cm. c. 1907–8. Photo © National Gallery of Ireland. NGI.1806.

Apart from an unusual use of profile views, Irish portrayals of solitary women readers, although not strictly academic in style, tend to be painted in a relatively traditional mode. Prior even to the invention of photography, painters employed what might be termed 'snapshot' techniques, depicting figures as if spontaneously caught in informal or even awkward poses. For example, *Kitchen Maid with the Supper at Emmaus* (oil on canvas, c. 1617–18, National Gallery of Ireland) by the Spanish artist Diego Velázquez depicts a maid bent towards a table, which is cut by the frame so that the viewer of the scene logically would be placed upon the table. The maid's awkward and preoccupied stance and the mixed objects on the table, including a metal bowl on its side, remain puzzling, like an unplanned sighting of a private moment, presenting the fictive viewer with a puzzle to solve. By contrast, the Irish portraits offer quiet scenes of contemplative activity.

Rosa Mulholland in 1889 criticised the dark tones of Irish art: 'Whether it be due to the scantiness of our sunshine, and the coldness of our atmosphere [...] too many brushes seem to have learned a trick of moderating the hues

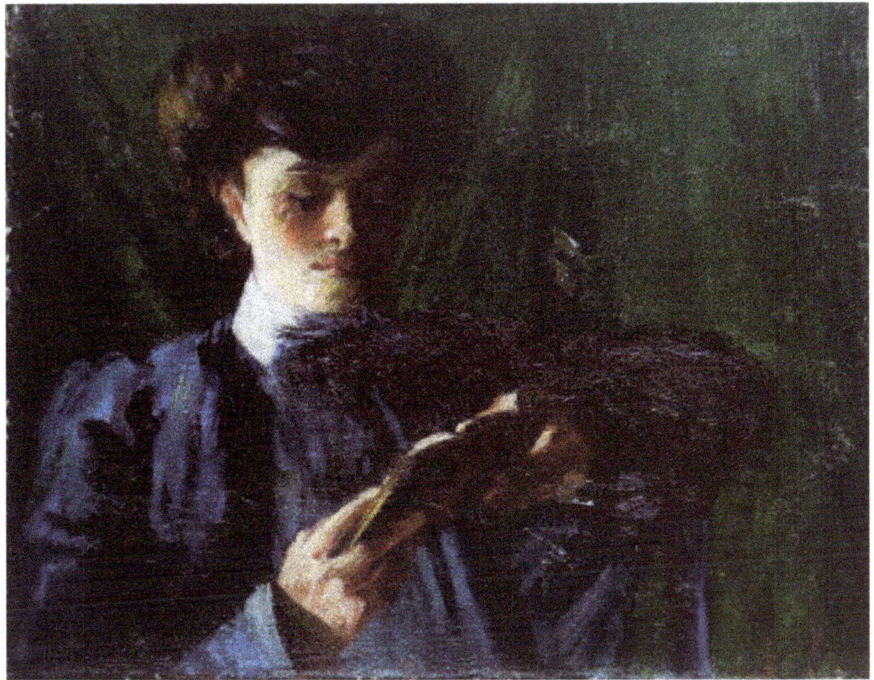

Figure 26 Katherine McCausland, *Ellen Helleu lisant*, oil on canvas, 52.5 × 41.2 cm, c. 1905. Collection and image © Hugh Lane Gallery (Reg. No. 2057).

of the prism with an infusion of soot.'[50] Impressionism, with its 'momentary' glimpses of scenes and figures, and the brilliant colours of modernist art would be well-known to Anglo-Irish artists, who were familiar with continental European practices, or in some cases had moved to France. However, instead of the bright colour that characterises much modernist art at this time, the Irish images of readers often have muted colours. For example, in Harrison's *Portrait of a Young Lady Reading* (Figure 24), the figure's red-brown hair and black dress are set against a brown background. Purser's *The Afternoon Read* (Figure 15) is again muted in colour, almost to monochrome. The figure wears a cream blouse and a dark skirt. She has brown hair and sits in a chair of dark brown varnished wood against a wall of mustard-brown, which tones with the mustard cover of her book. Solomons's *A Woman Reading by a Desk at a Window* (Figure 18), with its many tones of brown, is quite a dark picture. In John B. Yeats's *Portrait of Mary Lapsley Guest* (Figure 21), the dominant colours are again browns. The earth colours that characterise a number of Irish representations of women readers invoke a long tradition of realist painting, and the sombre tones are effective as a way of conveying a serious and undemonstrative occupation. Furthermore, the quiet dress of these women readers signals a new type of woman, carefully and individually garbed, yet uninterested in an ostentatious sartorial display of conventional femininity.

However, some Irish portraits depict the woman reader in a modernist style, or with some modernist use of colour, for example, *A Quiet Read* (oil on canvas, c. 1907–8, Figure 25) by Roderic O'Conor, *Ellen Helleu lisant* (Ellen Helleu reading, oil on canvas, c. 1905, Figure 26) by Katherine McCausland and Solomons's *Portrait of a Woman* (Figure 16).[51]

In O'Conor's *Girl Reading* and *A Quiet Read* (Figure 25), a blaze of complementary colours draw the eye to the figure at the heart of the picture, a young woman, self-possessed and relaxed with legs outstretched on a comfortable chair, or on a chaise longue, her attitude indicating attention directed exclusively to her book.[52] O'Conor was born in Milltown, Co. Roscommon, and trained at the Metropolitan School of Art, Dublin and the Royal Hibernian Academy School, but with independent means he moved to live and work in France.[53] In Paris, O'Conor painted various female nudes doing little but posing. However, he also painted women reading. Modernist facture could de-individualise its subjects by erasing facial features. It has been argued, for instance by Crary, that modernism, with its reliance on surface effects, rejects 'interiority'.[54] Yet O'Conor's images of women reading are structured in ways that draw attention to their absorptive occupation. *A Quiet Read* (Figure 25) has a double focus on the reading figure by means of a large mirror depicted next to her chaise longue. As well as the reader's reflection, this shows a window that provides a light source from the left, given substance in the mirror by a dark red curtain tied back next to it. The setting may have been O'Conor's studio in Paris. Nonetheless, the scene is staged to show a woman reading a book in her own space. The vibrancy of the complementary reds and blues, and the repeated image of the reader dramatise the act of reading and emphasise the figure of the absorbed young woman reader at the heart of the picture. However, O'Conor's gestural style eliminates individuality from his female figures, a trademark of much modernist art.

By contrast, in Solomon's *Portrait of a Woman* (Figure 16) the sitter, Kathleen Goodfellow, who faces the viewer has recognisable features. Her figure and the interior are depicted in brilliant and complementary colours. Goodfellow wears a purple coat with fur-trimming at the wrists over a brilliant blue blouse.[55] The purple and blue complement a yellow tablecloth, on which sits a blue hyacinth. The purple of the figure's coat is picked up in a purple teapot on the bookcase, alongside a scarlet cup. The use of colour, with its links to the avant-garde art spreading across Europe, may have determined the choice of outdoor dress for the sitting. The paired and repeated colours unify and vivify

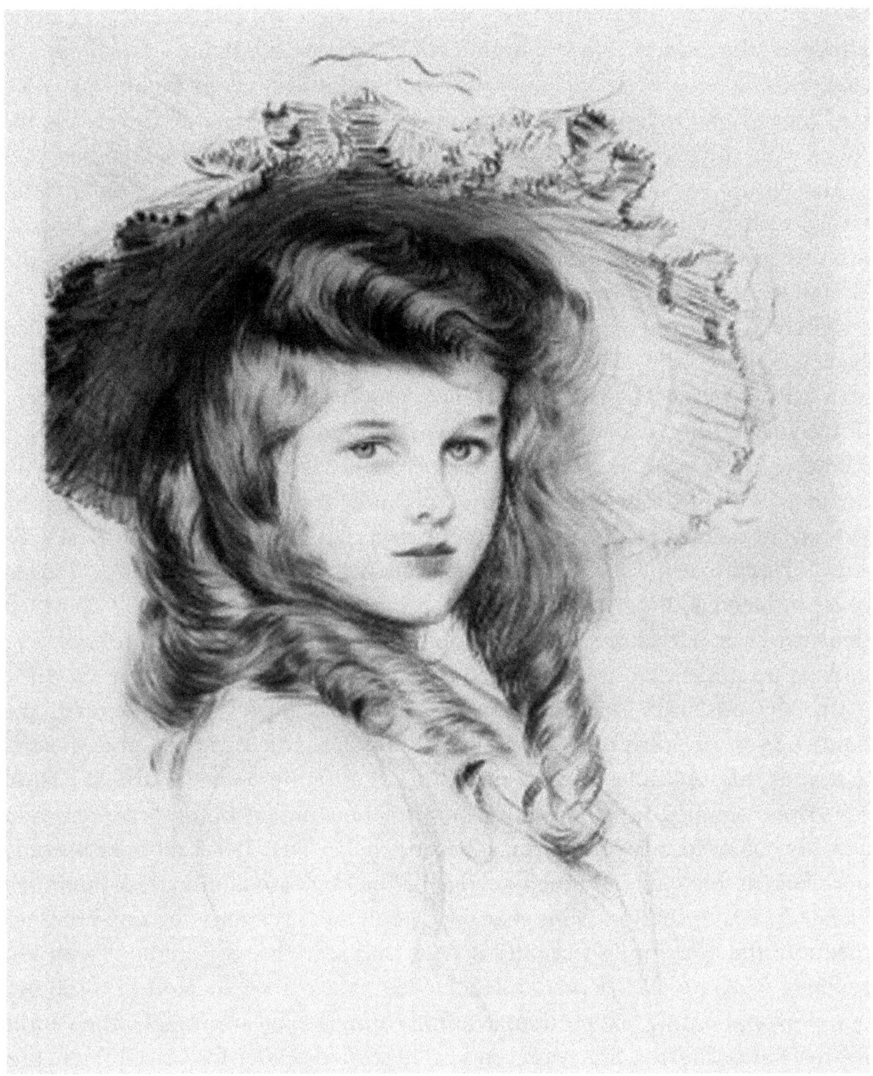

Figure 27 Paul Cesar Helleu, *Ellen Helleu the Artist's Daughter in a Lace-Trimmed Hat,* drypoint on wove paper, 54.5 × 34 cm, c. 1902. Courtesy of Sothebys.

the scene. Unlike the more muted portraits of readers, the scene is bright and colourful, but it still represents an intimate setting for the activity which is to be central to it, reading.

Katherine McCausland's portrait *Ellen Helleu lisant* (Figure 26) depicts a young woman absorbed in her book. The vivid colours are again typical of contemporary modernist art, including work by her friend O'Conor. However, the portrait has enough detail to suggest the figure's facial expression, emphasising her concentration. McCausland, born in Dublin in 1859, had moved to England, then Paris in the 1880s, studying at the Académie Julian and staying in Pont-Aven in the 1890s.[56] Her father was a barrister at the King's Inns, Dublin, and like O'Conor she had independent means, buying a house in south-west France.[57] McCausland's visits back to Ireland are unknown, but her portraiture included Irish politicians and perhaps the Fenian leader John O'Leary.[58]

There is a telling contrast between McCausland's representation of Ellen Helleu reading and a number of portraits of Ellen by her father, another artist, Paul Cesar Helleu. Paul Helleu produced over 600 drypoint prints portraying fashionable women from Paris, London, Rome and New York.[59] Many of his titles refer to details of dress, such as bonnets or bows. Helleu's images of Ellen show her in a range of fancy hats and looking back at the viewer, for instance, *Ellen Helleu* (colour drypoint c. 1900), or *Ellen Helleu, the Artist's Daughter in a Lace-Trimmed Hat* (drypoint, c. 1902, Figure 27).[60] Helleu also produced a lithograph of Ellen reading, *Ellen à la lecture* (c. 1902–3) which depicts her as if reclining while propping herself up over an open book and looking up under elaborately coiffed hair.[61]

In McCausland's portrait *Ellen Helleu lisant* (Figure 26) by contrast, the figure's eyes are lowered, cutting off all contact with a viewer, and she has a serious, almost sulky facial expression. The figure wears a brilliant royal blue dress against the close background of a saturated-bottle-green curtain, a richly coloured, private setting. The side of her face, her forefinger keeping her place in the book, and the top edge of the book are illuminated, but much of her face is in shadow. This shadowing enhances the sense of non-communication: this is a young woman's private and secretive engagement with her reading. McCausland depicts Ellen Helleu as a reader, located in a vibrant and personal setting, rather than a young woman to be admired by the viewer for her hat or hairdo. She represents an absorbed reader for whom the fictive viewer is irrelevant although drawn to explore the opaqueness of the image. The woman reader is no longer an object for the gaze, but a woman occupied with her own study and pleasure in reading, the figure of a New Woman.

A private space

The reader's habitat may help to convey the idea of a figure enclosed in a private world. Insofar as reading may show the denizen of a domestic environment quietly absorbed in her solitary occupation, this might appear to suit a conventional feminine image of compliant domesticity.[62] However, reading was

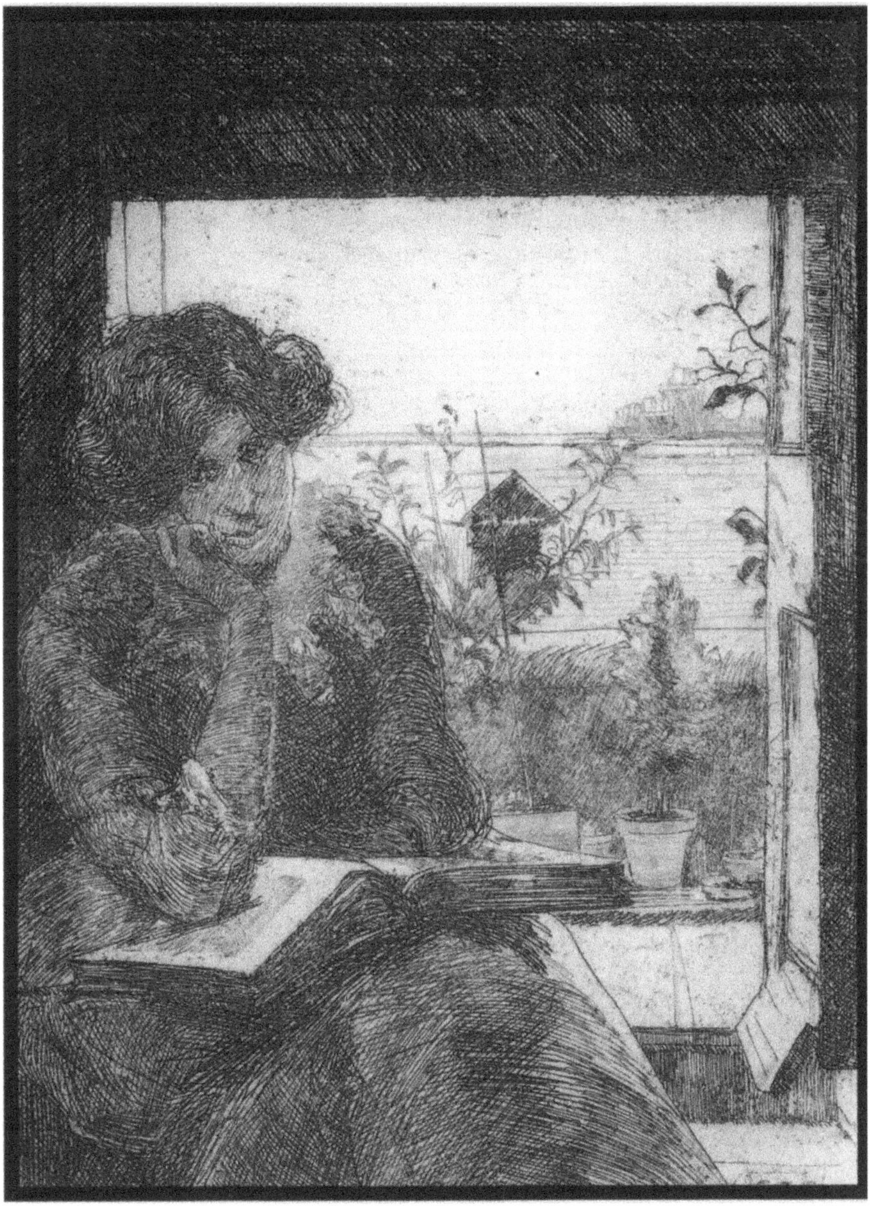

Figure 28 Estella Solomons, *Self Portrait in a Window*, etching, 17.14 × 12.7 cm, c. 1910. Private Collection. © The Trustees of the Estate of Estella Solomons.

not a conventional domestic skill. Nor was the domestic space occupied necessarily one associated with household chores; it might be a study or a space designated as a private domain. Reading figures might be portrayed in a domestic interior, sometimes near a window and perhaps in a study. Placing the reader by a window satisfies the narrative logic of providing light for reading, and a window also offers a rationale for light to enhance a figure or to illuminate a book. Lorenz Eitner, writing in the *Art Bulletin*, refers to the window as both threshold and barrier, suggesting, 'Through it, nature, the world, the active life beckon, but the artist remains imprisoned, not unpleasantly, in domestic snugness […] It contrasts […] the 'poetry of possession' – the intimate interior – with the 'poetry of desire' – the tempting spaces outside.'[63] However, neither an idealised view through the window, nor a plush interior is typical of Irish pictures of readers. The interior space tends to be represented as a simple and pleasant, or neutral refuge for study, while the view outside may sometimes be unattractive, or undisclosed, focusing interest on the reading figure within.

In Solomons's *Self-Portrait in a Window* (etching, c. 1910, Figure 28), the boundary between inside and out is permeable. The window echoes the frame of the painting, offering a kind of double looking into the picture and through the window. Shutters open onto a large uncompromising rectangle of light which forms the background to the reader as she sits with her back to the outside world and a large book open on her knee. She has paused from reading, with an elbow resting on the book and her hand cupped under her chin in an attitude of contemplation. The view outside, onto what seems to be a balcony with a table bearing several potted plants and across to a sloping tiled roof with a dormer window, is suburban and homely. Self-portraits raise the question of how an artist represents her/himself, and here Solomons presents herself as a reader in a pleasant suburb happy to sit and read at the edge of interior and exterior spaces.[64]

Window curtains may emphasise the boundary between a domestic interior and a public exterior. They appeared in the seventeenth century and were common from the eighteenth century, although Alice Barnaby concludes that 'no sustained or detailed work into the cultural significance of early nineteenth-century window drapery exists'.[65] Early nineteenth-century art in Germany, Denmark and France featured swag curtains in translucent, cream or sometimes brightly coloured fabrics serving as a fashionable decorative frame for conversation pieces, or sometimes adorning an empty room.[66] Apart from voluminous long curtains, elaborate curtaining arrangements seem to be absent from Irish portraits of the reader, and sometimes the window is left bare. Curtainless windows also made a statement: they might indicate poverty, or in a different context a disregard for luxury or comfort, or an unadorned studio. Elsewhere a curtain adds rich colour to a reader's environment, not only enhancing the vitality of a figure but also dramatising the act of reading itself as in O'Conor's *A Quiet Read* (Figure 25).

Over the nineteenth century, as the supposed natural link between women and domesticity became enshrined in the ideology and mores of European culture, curtains provided reinforcement to the windows as the boundary between the domestic interior and the world outside.[67] However, in Irish portraits of reading women in the long nineteenth century, although curtains might still hint at the protective boundary between the domestic interior and the outside, the ideological link between women and domesticity is fundamentally disturbed by the woman's absorption in reading, or by the emphasis given to a reader's open book. In Orpen's *Mrs Charles Hughes* (Figure 20) the figure sits enthroned in a Jacobean carved oak chair with an open book on her lap. Behind her is a heavy blue-green curtain which, rather than acting as a barrier to the public space, symbolically serves, together with the substantial chair-back, to secure the figure against intrusion from the outside world.

In the photograph of Lady Charlotte Stopford reading (n.d., Figure 17), mentioned earlier, Stopford is posed informally at a small ornate table. She sits near tall lattice windows with long, decorative curtains that locate her in a drawing room or studio, but probably the former, as the table and window are slightly but unprofessionally tilted. There is an Aspidistra on the window sill, which was popular in well-provided late Victorian households. Stopford wears a dark long-sleeved blouse with high neckline and long skirts with her hair carefully coiffed, but swept away from her face: she is dressed for comfort and private study and neither for show, nor household duties. Slightly angled towards the front, the figure seems, through her expression, conscious of being photographed. However, she is shown absorbed in her book and reads without attending to the viewer. Here the window and the curtain may still function as boundaries, but any sense of confinement is again diminished by the figure's focus on her reading.

The reader's setting may suggest a study, as in Solomons's *Portrait of a Woman* (Figure 16) or *A Woman Reading at a Desk by the Window* (Figure 18). In *Portrait of a Woman* the interior of the room is more salient than a pale urban domestic scene glimpsed through a window. The outside world is not excluded, but it does not beckon. Goodfellow, the subject of the painting, was an author and poet.[68] The partly drawn net curtain on the writer's side of the window might be seen through from the inside, but not from the outside, affording privacy. The figure is screened, but not cut off from the world outside, perhaps a writer's vantage point. The room is simple but well-furnished with pleasing objects, such as a potted hyacinth, a picture on the wall, decorative plates, a teapot and cup and saucer, and, of course, a book open on the table. Solomons's *A Woman Reading at a Desk by the Window* (Figure 18) depicts a woman in a simple study sitting at her desk on a wooden chair facing an open sash window. Another window beside her is screened partly by a translucent material and partly by a deep green curtain. A little pot of primroses decorates her table, its leaves picking up the darker green of the curtain. The view through the open window is urban and undefined and the focus is on the central reading figure. The reader has her hair tied back from her face and wears plain practical clothing. Her environment, together with her dress, stance and focused attention, conveys an image of an independent thinking woman in her own space.

Conclusion

Portraits of the reading subject, while often executed in a relatively traditional style, constitute a significant shift in Irish representations of the female figure at this time, as well as a contrast to the contemporary European images of women readers discussed in Chapter 2. The genesis of silent reading, with its private contents, presented women with new possibilities. An expansion in the production of novels and the development of a concept of literary 'taste', with the potential for personal attachment to canonical works, made the activity of reading both more complex and more embracing.

The Irish portrayals of the woman reader convey her absorption in reading through bodily attitude, facial expression and sometimes a studious setting. The reader is shown focusing on her book to the neglect of a potential onlooker or fictive viewer, or, in the case of the interrupted reader, an application to reading is emphasised by a body language that indicates the temporariness of the pause. The fictive viewer may be excluded from imaginative entry into the depicted scene, enhancing the reader's seclusion and absorption and yet drawing the viewer to examine the reading figure. The 'interrupted reader' may enable an encounter, but this is indicated as a temporary distraction, or else the reader is shown paused from reading without acknowledgement of a viewer.

Silent reading and the fictional inner life it allowed were especially important for women readers who thereby acquired an inner world that could be resistant to conventional masculine oversight. The various Irish examples of women absorbed in solitary silent reading, or temporarily interrupted from it, present a new imagery of women involved in their own imaginative worlds, without any necessary reference to an admiring or judgemental fictive viewer. Portraits of the reader represented more than a sight of a woman with a book; they contributed to a new Irish discourse that affirmed women's individuality and intellectual engagement and the emergence of the New Woman.

Chapter 5

A ROOM OF HER OWN: FOUR NEW WOMEN IN DUBLIN

Virginia Woolf famously stated that 'a woman must have money and a room of her own if she is to write fiction'.[1] To be creative, women needed to possess both money and personal space. Woolf herself worked at the few odd jobs available to women until in 1918 aged 36 she received a legacy of five hundred pounds a year from her aunt:

> That five hundred a year stands for the power to contemplate [and] a lock on the door means the power to think for oneself [...] Intellectual freedom depends upon material things. [...] And women have always been poor [...] Women have had less intellectual freedom than the sons of Athenian slaves.[2]

Woolf in 1929 wrote of her anger when she had attempted to enter a Cambridge library while preparing lectures for Newnham and Girton Colleges and been told that 'ladies are only admitted to the library if accompanied by a Fellow of the College or furnished with a letter of introduction'.[3] Although Woolf had achieved financial independence, she was still subject to patriarchal hegemony. In Ireland a little earlier, as in England, a 'room of her own' in which to write, read or paint was something even upper- or middle-class women often lacked, while men possessed a private study or personal studio. For example, when Lolly and Lily Yeats lived with their family in Bedford Park, London, the house had 'room for only one member of the family to have a separate study and William [their brother, W. B. Yeats] was the fortunate one'.[4] Lolly and Lily Yeats were also brought up amid persistent financial problems.[5] To gain independence, they both found employment, and they passed their earnings home, as well as doing the housekeeping and looking after their mother. Their father John B. Yeats wrote later, 'and all this when quite young girls, and cut off from living like other young ladies of their age and standing. They paid the penalty of having a father who did not earn enough and was besides an Irish landlord.'[6] As middle-class working women, the Yeats sisters might be seen as part of a movement for change that was evident in this period, for instance, in the political campaigns for women's rights. There was a burgeoning of intellectual and creative enterprise among women artists and writers in Ireland with sufficient means. Portraits of women readers, as we have seen, constituted a distinctive visual imagery that was helping to define the New Woman in Ireland.

This chapter focuses on two Dublin artists, Sarah Purser and Estella Solomons, and their portrayals of two readers, Jane Barlow and Alice Milligan. All four were key figures among the successful women artists and writers of this period and each did come to occupy a room of her own. In their creative work, cultural leadership and political engagement, all embodied the idea of an independent and active New Woman. The portraits, *Miss Jane Barlow, D.Litt* (oil on canvas, 1894, Figure 29) and *Portrait of Alice Milligan* (oil on canvas, 1918, Figure 30), each a 'full-face' view of the subject, draw on their personal likenesses, but they also help construct a generalised image of an independent thinking woman, accompanied by the significant accessory of a book.

Productive women

Commenting on women novelists in an interview for the *Irish Women's Writing (1880–1920) Network* in July 2019, John Wilson Foster explains that in his earlier published work he had overlooked

> the very diverse and rich body of popular Irish fiction of the period. (I mean by 'popular' that the fiction sold well and had a broad readership, not that it was never 'serious'.) Some of the women writers were prodigiously productive [...] I discovered that Irish women writers more or less owned popular Irish fiction of the Revival period and that it [...] contradicted the [...] restricted canon of the Irish Literary Revival.[7]

Somerville and Ross regarded themselves as contributing to the Irish Revival, but 'as feminists of the ascendancy class, they were wary of a predominantly male organization that tended to subsume female expression under its wider aims'.[8] However, the number of women writers continued to expand and they were enormously productive. There were over five hundred women authors in nineteenth-century Ireland, many producing multiple volumes.[9]

There was little specialisation of genres, so that it was normal for a woman writer to turn her hand to a variety of writings.[10] Women wrote fiction and non-fiction including scientific texts. For example, Alice Milligan wrote 4 novels,

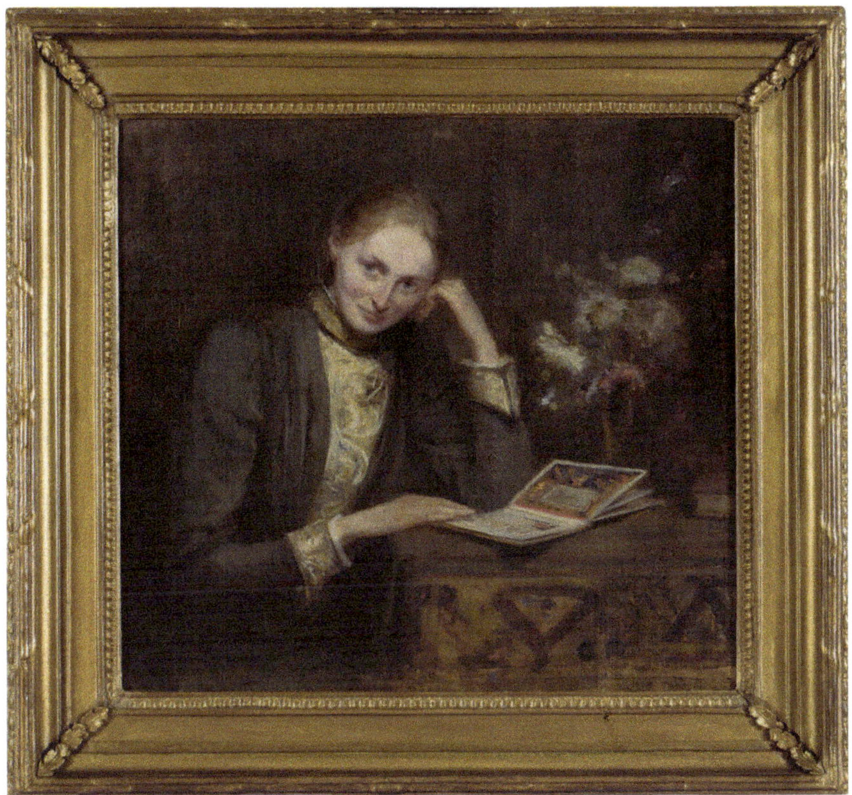

Figure 29 Sarah Purser, *Miss Jane Barlow, D.Litt.*, oil on canvas, 62.2 × 67.4 cm, 1894. Courtesy of Michael Purser. Collection and image © Hugh Lane Gallery (Reg. No. 232).

11 plays, short stories, poems, biography and a travelogue, as well as many articles.[11] Two of her plays were written for the women's nationalist group *Inghinidhe na hÉireann* (Daughters of Erin).[12] Women like Sarah Grand wrote stories with strong female characters who were embryonic New Women (as discussed in Chapter 3). The catalogue for Marsh's Library, Dublin, contains a number of interesting contemporary items by women authors, for example, *Poisoners and Propagandists, or, A Developed Age: A Tale in two vols.* (London, 1856) by Mary Baker, of Bansha, Co. Tipperary, and *Angelica Kauffmann: A Biography* (London, 1892) by Frances A. Gerard (pseud.).[13]

Like Wilson Foster, Brian Fallon notes women's particular productivity at this time and he includes women who were politically active, as well as writers and artists:

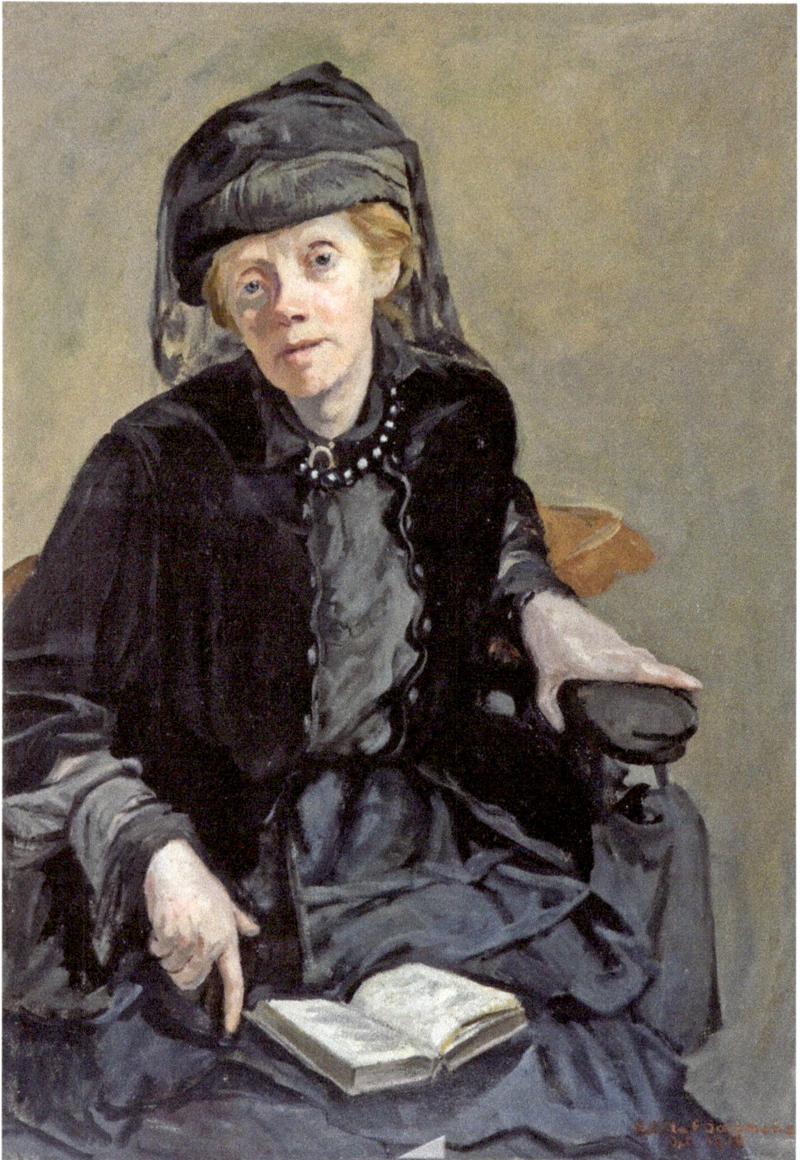

Figure 30 Estella Solomons, *Portrait of Alice Milligan*, oil on canvas, 92 × 71.5 cm, 1918. BELUM.U405. © The Trustees of the Estate of Estella Solomons. Collection Ulster Museum.

The part women played in a whole epoch – Maud Gonne, Countess Marcievicz and many others in politics, Lady Gregory in literature, Louie Bennet in the trade-union movement, Estella Solomons' generation in art – make it clear that an essential element in the ferment that created modern Ireland, was an upsurge of feminine creativity and self-expression.[14]

In visual art, this creativity and independence on the part of women is apparent not only in Solomons's generation but also earlier in the nineteenth century in the work of Sarah Purser. It is notable that Hugh Lane in 1908 envisaged the new Municipal Gallery of Modern Art in Dublin displaying portraits of modern Irish women as well as men.[15]

Sarah Purser and Estella Solomons: Publicity and the press

Although portraits of family or friends might be executed in a domestic setting or private studio, they were opened to public viewing and critical scrutiny through the regular art exhibitions held in Dublin at this time, and the subsequent press reports. The Irish press was occasionally condescending in tone towards women artists. For example, their dress was routinely highlighted. At the opening of the Municipal Gallery of Modern Art in January 1908, it was observed of Cecilia Harrison, who was instrumental in the founding of the gallery, that 'Miss Harrison was entirely in black and she had a large picture hat with long net veil.'[16] Covering the opening of the RHA exhibition in March 1912, the *Irish Times* spent four-fifths of its quite lengthy report describing the attire of women attendees including the artists, where it is reported that 'Miss Sarah Purser had a wine-coloured cloth costume, and black satin hat, with plumes [and] Mrs Orpen wore black velvet.'[17]

However, the press regularly publicised and reviewed women's art shown at the exhibitions of the RHA, and elsewhere. Purser frequently exhibited her work, won prizes and was invariably praised in press reports. Following the annual prize-giving ceremony at the Royal Dublin Society's School of Art in February 1876, the *Irish Times* reported that Sarah Purser was among those who had 'much distinguished themselves [and] greatly contributed to the reputation of the society by their performance'.[18] Prizes were distributed by the Lord Lieutenant. Mr Charles Kelly, Q.C., secretary of the society, commented in a sympathetic, albeit slightly condescending, manner and perhaps with an unwitting nod to the nascent New Woman, 'I am […] glad to find that the lady students have been most vigorous, I had almost ventured to say, manfully insisted on women's rights, in carrying away a large number of prizes.'[19] The *Daily Express* in 1884 commended Purser's portraits as 'utterly free from the cut and dry effect of a conventional portrait'.[20] Writing in the *Irish Monthly* in 1889, the novelist Rosa Mulholland regretted what she saw as a dearth of impressive art in Ireland but praised Sarah Purser as a portrait painter who had 'done excellent work, and from whom much may be expected'.[21] The *Irish Times* in February 1914 wrote admiringly of Purser:

> Miss Purser is a member of a family which has been closely identified with art and literature in Ireland […] As a portrait painter Miss Purser has attained a considerable reputation. She has painted many leading families in Ireland and England, as well as a number of celebrated people […] her portraits may be seen in the Royal Irish Academy and in Trinity College. She is an honorary member of the Royal Hibernian Academy.[22]

Estella Solomons's work was also praised in various press reviews. For example, the *Irish Times* in April 1906 commented on Solomons's *Portrait* exhibited at the RHA that year as catalogue no. 222 and not for sale.[23] The reviewer wished to draw attention to it as it may have been passed over by visitors, and it was

> both interesting and clever […] There is no ambitious display of technical skill for its own sake, and all aggressiveness of colour has been studiously avoided […] the artist's effort has been not so much to paint a striking picture as to produce a study in personality […] [f]or all its quietness and unpretentiousness of style, there is a strength of characterisation in the work lifting it above the ordinary level.[24]

In February 1914, the *Irish Times* reviewer drew attention to a forthcoming exhibition of paintings, etchings and sculpture at Mills's Hall, 8 Merrion Row by Estella Solomons, Mary Duncan and Albert Power, to be opened on 7 February by the president of the RHA. Solomons sent 68 paintings to this exhibition, which the *Irish Times* promised 'should prove to be one of the most interesting of the season'.[25] The reviewer noted that 'Miss Estella Solomons, whose portrait work is already known to patrons of the Academy and other art exhibitions, contributes some studies of contemporary Irish writers and others'.[26] Her exhibited paintings also included *Parknasilla* (oil on board, 1911) depicting a female figure reading on a beach and on sale for five guineas.[27] The exhibition opening drew 'a large attendance, which included Mr George Russell, Captain White, and Miss Maud Gonne, and was representative of the artistic circles of Dublin'.[28]

In a later piece on Solomons in the magazine *Irish Life*, John Crampton Walker both praises Solomons as an artist and comments on a contemporary tendency to associate progressive art only with men:

> Amongst Irish women artists Miss Stella F. Solomons deserves to take a foremost place, representing, as she does, the progressive and advanced movement in art which is usually associated with men only; indeed, she is far more modern than many of the most prominent of our academicians.[29]

Crampton Walker comments favourably on Estella Solomons's reputation and skill as a portraitist, and he also draws attention to Solomons's important role in recording and commemorating literary figures of the time:

> At the present day she is chiefly known as a portrait painter, and has painted nearly all the young Irish poets and men of letters […] she is best in oils, and manages with singular felicity to catch the salient features that give the mental character as well as the physical expression of her subject […] a great asset to the portrait-painter in that it is the one great element which distinguishes the artist from the camera.[30]

Although Crampton Walker's review is sympathetic, he notably only draws attention to her portraits of male figures, yet some of her best portraits of readers depict women, who were celebrated as poets and novelists.

Reviewing a show by Estella Solomons, again with Mary Duncan, Thomas Bodkin writing in *The Irish Statesman* damns her with faint praise.[31] Bodkin notes that he found their art poor after visiting the National Gallery first but then returned and found himself 'charmed with many pieces […] This 'two-women' show is better far than the majority of the one-man shows to which we are accustomed in Dublin.' Bodkin praises Solomons's works as 'sincere' but goes on to comment that 'They all show evidence of plenty of feeling, and an almost complete absence of thought. They are, in short, studies […] in no proper sense of the word are they "pictures".'[32] The review displays ignorance of the modernity of Solomons's work, which eschews academic precision for tactile brushwork. The language also falls neatly into the cliché of women's emotionality and irrationality.

Solomons's portraits therefore were sometimes criticised for their tendency towards impressionistic brushwork, perceived as lacking finish and deficient in thought. Such commentary invoked stereotypes of women's emotionality, compared to men's rationalism. It displayed ignorance of the modernist painting techniques common in Paris and other European cities, or perhaps as Crampton Walker suggested, a reluctance to perceive women as progressive artists. Overall, however, the work of Purser and Solomons was given considerable publicity and mostly well-received in contemporary press reviews.

Sarah Purser: A studio of her own

Sarah Purser was born in 1848 in Kingstown, now Dun Laoghaire, into a middle-class non-conformist family.[33] Typical of professional and well-to-do Anglo-Irish families, the Pursers cultivated close connections with Europe. Between 1861 and 1863, aged 13–15, Purser attended the *Institution Evangélique de Montmirail* in Switzerland, learning French, Italian and German and was able to 'read widely in current European literature'.[34] Purser may have spent a period at the Royal Dublin Society School of Art in Kildare Street, Dublin, in the 1870s, the only art school in Ireland that accepted women students.[35] When her father fell bankrupt, she spent six months studying at the *Académie Julian* in Paris which offered women studio space, models and informal teaching. Unlike other Anglo-Irish travellers, she was not then well-off, having a total of £30.[36]

Purser obtained a fortuitous commission to paint members of the Gore-Booth family at Lissadell House, Co. Sligo and, following their recommendations, acquired further commissions from English aristocrats. Her work was hung in the Royal Academy and 'from that, I never looked back – I went through the British aristocracy like the measles'.[37] Purser showed on average eight paintings a year at the RHA exhibitions, more than most of her male colleagues, including William Orpen.[38] She became 'one of Ireland's leading portrait painters in the eighties and nineties', and much later, the first woman to be elected to membership of the RHA.[39]

Purser was able to earn a good living as a professional artist focusing on portraits, which were the best financial option.[40] Shearer West observes in her book *Portraiture* that women artists who gained a living from painting before the twentieth century were often portraitists. She believes this was partly not only because portraiture could be practised in an appropriate domestic setting but also because 'portraits were [...] considered a low and mechanical genre of art [...] and women were traditionally viewed as creatively limited and best at arts that required imitation'.[41] However, if portraiture had not generally enjoyed a high artistic status, this was not the case in Ireland in this period, when portraiture was an important means of representing individuals valued for their cultural and political contributions to a country consciously developing an independent identity. Furthermore, portraiture was a significant medium through which women artists in particular represented and affirmed other creative women and such portrayals in turn contributed to the formation of the idea of the New Woman.

Woolf pointed out the important connection between a woman's independence and her financial situation.[42] Purser managed to make herself quite wealthy. She profited both from her work and by clever financial management: 'Sarah Purser was an astute business operator. She made a lot of money from her paintings and shrewd investment in Guinness and on the Stock Exchange made her quite wealthy.'[43] Purser had a studio in Leinster Street, then from 1886 in Harcourt Terrace, separately from where she lived with her mother in a large house in Wellington Road.[44] In 1909, she and her brother leased Mespil House, a Georgian residence in Dublin south of the canal.[45] Mespil House had 'incredibly beautiful ceilings; the finest in Dublin that of her diningroom [*sic*], displaying the seasons and the elements in rich rococo exuberance', and the rooms contained 'an abundance of flowers – and pictures, Hone, Yeats and Osborn [*sic*] among the Irish, more modern ones […] Beside the immense, pillared drawingroom [*sic*] […] was her own study.'[46]

Although nominally Protestant, Purser was known for her rationalism.[47] The *Spectator* commented later on Sarah Purser that as well as her art: '[Purser] had every other conceivable interest in life: it spanned in date and interests from Edward Martyn [a Catholic playwright and nationalist] to Professor Tierney, ranged from philosophy to industry.'[48] Purser held a regular salon, presiding over mixed gatherings for artists and literati, where tea (but never alcohol) was served.[49] Brian Inglis, a relation, observed that the monthly meetings at Sarah Purser's home provided 'a bridge between unionists and nationalists, men and women who might wish to assassinate each other'.[50] The various visitors to her studio in Harcourt Terrace included AE, critic, writer, artist and nationalist, the sculptor John Hughes and writers and nationalist activists including Katharine Tynan, Jane Barlow, W. B. Yeats, Susan Mitchell, Douglas Hyde, Michael Davitt, John O'Leary and Maud Gonne.[51] Sarah Purser was a rare friend of Maud Gonne's in 1890s Dublin.[52] Many of these friends and acquaintances became the subjects of her portraits.

Brian Fallon noted that 'early in the century, literary and artistic Dublin was a little in awe of Sarah Purser', and that AE was 'scared' of her.[53] Purser may have been quite a forbidding character when she chose. According to Sarah Purser's nephew, Michael Purser, when Mabel O'Brien, aged 29, was engaged to Michael Purser's grandfather, Frank Purser, and she was introduced to Sarah Purser, O'Brien nervously provided 'a stream of social inanities' whereupon Sarah Purser responded shortly, 'Miss O'Brien. When you are married into this family you will realise that we Pursers only speak when we have something to say.'[54]

Sarah Purser was active in various literary/theatrical and artistic initiatives in Dublin, as well as participating in the contemporary political debates. Michael Purser believed that his aunt may have been 'apolitical' and the Pursers did not go in for politics.[55] He regarded his Aunt Sarah as 'too cosmopolitan to succumb to romantic nationalist enticements [...]. Politically Sarah was fairly neutral, perhaps inclining towards Home Rule rather than Unionism, but really more interested in the world of the intellect than that of politics.'[56] Sarah Purser was certainly passionate about the 'world of the intellect', but she was not apolitical. Her interests in Ireland are suggested by her financial support for the Land League.[57] She was in touch with Arthur Griffith who sent her his nationalist paper the *United Irishman*. The *Irish Press* in an obituary notice concluded that Sarah Purser was 'a Parnellite [an advocate of Irish Home Rule], closely associated with the literary revival and with the Gaelic League in its early days'.[58] Purser also had a 'lifelong interest in the Co-operative Movement' that began when she met the Gore-Booths.[59]

Sarah Purser was a guarantor of the Irish Literary Theatre, a basis for the Abbey Theatre established in 1904, where she habitually attended first nights.[60] She helped to found the Dublin Art Club in 1886 for exhibiting work by professional artists.[61] With her friend Sir Hugh Lane, Purser was ambitious to bring modern art to Ireland, and she organised an exhibition of impressionist paintings in Dublin in 1899 with AE.[62] In 1901, Purser helped to arrange an exhibition of the work of John B. Yeats and Nathaniel Hone, remarking, 'If we are ever to have a distinctively Irish School, it may perhaps finds its source in these large-hearted works.'[63] Hugh Lane, like Purser, had in mind the consolidation of an Irish school of modern art believing that 'critical judgement will recognise in the works shown a distinctive temperament which gives promise of the successful establishment of a recognised Irish school of painting'.[64] Lane organised a display of 64 Irish paintings for the Irish Village at the Franco-British exhibition of 1908 in London. Among 'distinguished artists' included, the *Irish Times* mentions Sarah Purser, John Lavery, William Orpen, Walter Osborne and J. B. Yeats.[65] Alongside Cecilia Harrison and others, Sarah Purser encouraged the establishment of the Municipal Gallery of Modern Art, based on Hugh Lane's personal collection. This constituted 'the first real attempt at a representative collection of Modern Art to be found in the British Isles'.[66]

Reflecting on Sarah Purser as an artist, the Irish author and poet Stephen Gwynn stated, 'Hers was a purely intellectual talent, and went with one of the keenest minds [...] of all Ireland.'[67] It is perhaps not surprising that the theme of a woman reader recurs in a number of Purser's sketches and paintings. Her sketches include a profile view of c. 1881 of her mother bent over a large book and a profile view of a young woman reading of c. 1887–1892. One of her sketches, of around 1891 or 1892, depicts a frontal view of an older woman dressed fashionably in a tilted hat and a coat with puffed shoulders reading at a table by lamplight. Wearing a pince-nez, she looks down to concentrate. Purser's biographer, John O' Grady, suggests that this was probably done in a library as the woman is in outdoor dress.[68]

Purser's oil paintings of women readers include *Young Lady in an Interior Reading a Book Wearing a Velvet Ermine Cloak and Silk Dress* (oil on panel, 1885–1886, Private Collection), *Miss Jane Barlow, D.Litt* (oil on canvas, 1894, Figure 29), *Young Woman Reading* (oil on canvas, c. 1895, Private Collection) and *The Afternoon Read* (c. 1915, Figure 15) discussed in Chapter 4.[69] *Young Lady in an Interior Reading a Book*, a slightly obscure portrait, depicts a woman standing with one hand on a chair, the other turning the page of a large illustrated book on a table covered untidily in a dark green velvet-fringed cloth. The woman looks quietly contented and seems to be in her own space. The curiously detailed sartorial title which directs the viewer's gaze to her garb is not typical of Purser's work and may have been given by an auctioneer when the painting was last sold privately in June 2016. However, the picture emphasises the figure's focus on the book, both through her gaze and the action of turning a page.

Sarah Purser was clearly a formidable and talented character, an intellectual and an activist who contributed much to Dublin's cultural life and art production. The next section examines one of her paintings of a woman reader, *Miss Jane Barlow, D.Litt.*, in detail.

A portrait of Jane Barlow

Miss Jane Barlow, D.Litt (Figure 29) is one of Purser's most intriguing portraits. Barlow and Purser developed a close relationship marked on Barlow's side by an extraordinary proliferation of correspondence. For example, in one month, January 1897, Jane Barlow wrote at least five letters to Sarah Purser on 4th, 12th, 14th, 18th and 22nd.[70] Barlow herself was a prominent figure in the intellectual life of contemporary Dublin as a successful author. She published novels, short stories, plays and poetry.[71] Barlow was elected vice president of the National Literary Society in 1897 and awarded an honorary degree of D.Litt. by Trinity College Dublin when it opened its doors to women in 1904. Born in 1856, Jane Barlow lived most of her life in Raheny, then a village north of Dublin, in 'The Cottage' which had a thatched roof, mud walls and climbing roses.[72] She later moved to Howth. Her mother, Mary Barlow, was also a writer.[73] Jane Barlow was educated by a governess and by her father, Rev. James William Barlow, who was vice-provost of Trinity College Dublin from 1899 until 1908. As well as an author, Barlow was a pianist and a linguist proficient in French and German. She travelled to the west of Ireland and in her twenties visited France, Greece and Turkey.[74] Barlow rejected religious institutions.[75] She belonged to the Society of Psychical Research, which aimed to investigate rather than confirm such phenomena, and she assured Purser that 'You need not fear that I am going to become spook-ridden. I am prosecuting my researches in a thoroughly sceptical and scientific spirit.'[76] As Purser's portrayal suggests, Barlow was a reader and she 'read copiously in her father's library [...] Across her path, once in a while, went the baying hounds and the galloping horses of the lighter moments of Somerville and Ross.'[77]

O'Grady believes that Barlow was 'almost a recluse'.[78] Certainly she had aspirations for a quiet life, but she attended social and public events. For example, Barlow was one of a small party of men and women to accompany the Countess of Aberdeen on a tour of Irish industries in the north and northwest of Ireland in June 1894.[79] Barlow never lived alone but with her family and several live-in servants. Her mother died on 20 December 1894 not long after Barlow's portrait was finished. At the time of the 1901 census, Barlow resided in Howth with her father, her sister and four brothers, and three resident servants, when the family's religion is given as Church of Ireland and that of the servants Roman Catholic.[80] The servants were evidently important to the Barlows' daily life. When her parlourmaid was ill and a nurse had been fetched, Barlow wrote to Purser that this 'is all an additional worry'.[81] In November 1897, Barlow explained that she was 'at present cookless', following quickly with another letter:

> My dear Sarah, A great many thanks for your offer of sandwiches, but as a cook arrives this evening, they would come too late for the relief of our present necessity [...] Maurice [Barlow's brother] is overwhelmed at your having brought him out tea, and is [...] talking gluttonously about the delicious flavour of your biscuits.[82]

This correspondence indicates both Sarah Purser's friendship and support, and the essential role that residential servants played in an Anglo-Irish Protestant household, enabling Jane Barlow to pursue her writing, although requiring her to take responsibility for their welfare.

Barlow supported moves to expand educational opportunities for women. Writing to Sarah Purser in 1895, she noted that Trinity College Dublin was about to increase access to examinations for women, which she approved and with gentle irony queried the outcome: 'The Board, I hear, has finally resolved to admit women experimentally to Honour and Moderatorship examinations in Michaelmas '96. I wonder whether they will be satisfied with this, or think it too thin an end of the wedge.'[83]

Barlow's political sympathies, like Purser's, were towards Irish nationalism, despite a cryptic comment to Purser in 1895 that she agreed with 'Miss Stephen' that 'the Union has been the strength and wealth of what she supposes to be Ireland'.[84] In January 1897, Barlow confided to Purser, 'My dear Sarah […] The other day I wrote a Fenian letter to Mr. O'Leary.'[85] The same year, Barlow told Purser that she had lately risen to be a vice president of the National Literary Society and that she had been invited to have her name on the Burke Commemoration Committee, but 'I wonder whether the Edmund Burke Centenary Commemoration Committee is a proper thing for a nationalist to be connected with'.[86] In a letter the following year, perhaps with reference to the imminent Boer War, Barlow comments, 'Are they going to war I wonder. I would <u>love</u> a good disgraceful British defeat.'[87] From these various remarks, it appears that Barlow, while recognising the power and productiveness of the Union, identified herself as an Irish nationalist with little sympathy for Britain. In December 1905, Barlow again contributed to the nationalist magazine the *Irish Homestead*, along with Alice Milligan and Jack B. Yeats.[88]

Irish Idylls

Consistent with her nationalist inclinations, Jane Barlow's writing looked to the west of Ireland for her themes. Her first book, *Irish Idylls*, was a collection of short stories about Irish peasant life. It was published in 1892, originally with photographic illustrations of cottages and everyday activities. *Irish Idylls* ran into nine editions and was read in France, Germany, Britain and America.[89] Barlow also wrote for Irish journals and magazines, including the *Alexandra College Magazine*, *The Nation*, *Hibernia* and AE's nationalist publication *The Irish Homestead*.[90] Her story 'A Celtic Christmas' for *The Irish Homestead* in 1902 was illustrated by Purser.[91] Barlow was also invited to contribute to various American and British publications including a Bostonian paper called *The Youth's Companion* which offered 'princely terms', and *The Lady's Realm*.[92] *The Lady's Realm* was an illustrated monthly magazine launched in 1896 and published in London which was aimed at the New Woman.

Barlow's fiction was not always understood to represent Irish life. In December 1897, she wrote wryly to Sarah Purser, who was then visiting London, that Mr Thomas Arnold had told a lady that 'the author of "Irish Idylls" had never set foot in Ireland in her life. So perhaps you may chance to fall in with her in London.'[93] Wilson Foster observed of *Irish Idylls* that 'the Connemara peasant is portrayed respectfully and fairly knowledgeably (the speech-patterns and idioms are there, even if rather unlocalized), though the note of condescension is impossible to miss'.[94] However, it may be contended that such condescension is in fact missing. Barlow knew the west coast of Ireland well, where she took walking holidays and where she studied the spoken English of the peasants.[95] The stories in *Irish Idylls* carefully describe the Connemara landscape with the stony ground difficult to till, and the peasants' relationships with one another in the face of extreme poverty. In 'Lisconnel', the first story in *Irish Idylls*, Barlow vividly evokes a landscape of vast brown bogland near the village, 'as if the weather-beaten fell of some huge primæval beast were stretched smoothly over the flat plain'.[96] She depicts strong women who mind the land after their husband's death, for example, in 'A Windfall'. 'Herself' is a moving story of a woman broken by the loss of her family to emigration and death and finally eviction from her cottage by red-coated dragoons, 'plumed and burnished'. The early inclusion of photographs must have added an air of verisimilitude to her stories, but Barlow's precise and evocative language itself presents a realistic and affecting picture of people subsisting in conditions of extreme hardship.

Strangers at Lisconnel: A Second Series of Irish Idylls was published in 1895. The London paper *The Morning Leader* drew attention to 'a new and fascinating group of peasant characters [...] Mrs [*sic*] Barlow has drawn some of the quaintest, and most humorous characters that ever delighted the reader of English fiction'.[97] Barlow's book was sympathetically and less condescendingly reviewed later by Benedict Kiely in the *Irish Times*: 'Lisconnel [...] was not a world that, in her opinion, should survive, because she saw its evils and had sound ideas about reform. But it was the world to which her heart belonged and it offered to her the material that she was really capable of using.'[98]

Despite her success as a writer and her contribution to the contemporary Irish Literary Renaissance, Jane Barlow was omitted from anthologies by editors such as W. B. Yeats, who observed disparagingly that Barlow wrote only of 'old women and hens'.[99] However, when Katharine Tynan Hinkson edited a revised and enlarged version of *The Cabinet of Irish Literature* (c. 1903) she included Barlow, whom she described as a 'new force in Irish literature'.[100] A review in *Irish Monthly* noted approvingly that for Barlow's entry, 'a fine full-page portrait [...] is followed by a short sketch of her uneventful life and a long list of her eventful works, from which are given forty-eight columns of delightful extracts'.[101]

Hinkson, a poet and prolific novelist, was a supporter and friend of both Barlow and Purser. Such mutually supportive networks were undoubtedly important in encouraging and enabling the work of creative women in Ireland at this time. Occasions such as the efforts to establish a gallery of modern art in Dublin again brought such women together, for example, in public appeals for funds. A funding appeal published in the *Irish Times* in January 1905 included artists and writers such as Cecilia Harrison, Edith Somerville and Jane Barlow.[102]

Jane Barlow's letters and her portrait

Barlow's letters demonstrate the close and mutually supportive relationship between herself and Sarah Purser. Barlow wrote frequently to Purser in the 1890s from her home at The Cottage, Raheny, Co. Dublin, her letters addressed to Miss Purser, 11 Harcourt Terrace, Dublin. All of these letters, written in an even, undemonstrative script, and later ones were retained by Purser and her family and now form a formidable pile at the National Library of Ireland. Barlow's correspondence with Purser is fluent and confidential in tone as if writing a diary, and her style is playful and ironic but sometimes a bit unhappy. She comments on the weather, her work, individuals, her health, the health of Sarah Purser and 'Mrs Purser', and on Sarah Purser's portraits, which she praises, encouraging her and warning her against working too hard, again evidence of women's mutual support for each other's creative work.

Barlow's letters throw light on the genesis of her portrait, and the extent to which Purser negotiated its character with her sitter.[103] The portrait may have been Sarah Purser's idea, as Barlow gently mocks Purser for choosing to portray her. Arranging a sitting, Barlow remarked with characteristic self-deprecation: 'This is, of course, assuming that you really do wish to waste your time on me.'[104] Sarah Purser was working on her portrait of Jane Barlow in 1893, when Barlow wrote to Purser, addressing her formally as 'Dear Miss Purser', to arrange a time: 'Would you rather have me in the morning than the afternoon? I could come just as well at 10 or 11, if that would be more convenient to you,' and she added, 'Of course I will wear the grey jacket, the sight of which you must, I should think, by this time hate.'[105] In an undated letter, possibly from an envelope postmarked 8 September 1894, and once more beginning 'Dear Miss Purser', Barlow asks, 'Would Thursday or Friday afternoon suit you for a sitting? I could come to you either at 3 or 4 o'clock on either of those days. If neither is convenient, I could come any afternoon next week.'[106] These comments imply that over 1893–1894, a number of sittings took place, partly organised by Barlow, and Barlow's reference to the 'grey jacket' suggests either that the artist had stipulated that the sitter's dress remained constant or that Barlow habitually wore her 'grey jacket'.

Barlow's letters suggest that Purser discussed the form of the portrait with her sitter. They indicate too Purser's apparent difficulty in undertaking life-sized portraits. For example, in an undated letter, Barlow writes,

> Since you are horrid enough to talk of my <u>orders</u>, they are: that you be
> entirely guided by your own judgement about the dimensions of your
> canvas. It is impossible but that you have some preference about the
> scale on which you paint it, and to me the size seems quite immaterial, it
> is sure to be lovely. [...] So just consider nothing except your own inclin-
> ation. I quite agree with you that it would not do at all to cut off any of
> the figure.[107]

Barlow adds in a postscript, 'I seem to remember your saying one time that
you found it tiring to paint life-sized pictures, and if so, I strongly recommend
the smaller dimensions.'[108] In an undated letter, Barlow now addressing Purser
as 'My dear Sarah', tells her that 'I shall be very glad to have my lovely picture,
but as you know, you are not to hurry or worry over it in the least.'[109]

Barlow's agreement about not cutting off the figure indicates that Purser
had asked her advice or preference about this. It also suggests that there was
an existing sketch or photograph being used as a basis for the painting. In a
letter with an envelope postmarked 30 January 1895, that is, after the completion of her portrait, Barlow asks Purser

> whether it would be a bother to you if some time [...] I got your photog-
> rapher to photograph your portrait. It is ridiculously too nice for me, but
> for that reason I should like to send it to some old people in England who
> are always lamenting over the badness of my photographs.[110]

Barlow's request to use Purser's photographer suggests that Purser had a
skilled photographer to hand, whose pictures she may have used for her portrait work.

Barlow's comments on payment for the portraits that Purser did of her
family suggest that Purser was not expecting payment as from a less intimate
client. For instance, Barlow wrote in February 1898,

> It will be a real pleasure to have these pictures. And, my dear, you must
> not be horrid, and you must let me send you a cheque for them just in
> the ordinary way of business, though I very well know that you have had
> a great deal more than ordinary trouble with them.[111]

Miss Jane Barlow, D.Litt

Sarah Purser's finished oil portrait, *Miss Jane Barlow, D.Litt.* (Figure 29), is
now in the Hugh Lane City Gallery, Dublin. As Logan Sisley, Acting Head
of Collections at the gallery, pointed out, it has a square format unusual for a

portrait.[112] This could be the result of some 'cutting' of the figure. The frame is simple but decorative in an Arts and Crafts mode, with an English motif of three oak leaves at each corner. The portrait, which has been cleaned, seems a little less bright, with a slightly faded air compared to its reproductions, but the figure of Jane Barlow is vibrant, bearing out Gwynn's compliment that '[Walter Osborne] could render the quality of draperies and the flush of colour on a face; but [Sarah Purser], at her best, set the living person on canvas'.[113]

In the portrait, focus is thrown onto the foreground figure of Jane Barlow with an indistinct patterned wallpaper or curtain in the background. The figure is close to the front of the canvas, resting her left elbow on a table and supporting her head in an attitude of thoughtfulness. Many of Purser's female models are serious or pensive, but the figure of Barlow turns to smile, as her blue eyes hold the viewer's with a steady gaze. Her red hair is drawn back, workmanlike, from her face. Barlow is carefully garbed in an elaborate high-necked dress, greenish in colour, with shoulder puffs and decorative front and cuffs of brown and beige with a touch of blue. The paint is applied in strokes of bottle and lighter green and dark tan, which together merge into a greenish-brown colour. This dress does not conform to the grey jacket mentioned in her letter to Purser, suggesting that the sitter's garb was changed, or that Sarah Purser modified it when finishing the portrait, or, less likely, that this is a different portrait. Kimberly Griffith has drawn attention to contemporary fashions similar to Barlow's garb.[114] An illustration by the writer and cartoonist George du Maurier titled *Fin de Siècle* shows two fashionable women, one in a long-sleeved jacket with slight puffs at the shoulder and turned-back cuffs not unlike Barlow's.[115] Barlow then seems to have been fashionably dressed according to contemporary Victorian styles.

The table is covered by a cloth in a similar colour mixture to the main part of Barlow's dress, with a light tan background and triangles of sienna and blues. On it are an open illustrated book and a vase of white, pink and blue flowers, perhaps chrysanthemums and love-in-the-mist. Jane Barlow's book is another splash of mixed bright colours – red, orange, blue, drawing attention to it and its possible identity as an art book, although what is illustrated is unclear. Another thicker book sits closed on the table. With the fingertips of her right hand, the figure steadies the open book. Her attitude indicates that she is an interrupted reader, and implies a return to this activity following the artist's/viewer's intervention.

Barlow herself, and viewers of her portrait, evidently admired it. Barlow's comment that her portrait was 'ridiculously too nice' shows that she was pleased with it and considered it somewhat flattering. In a letter dated 13 July without the year, Barlow, addressing 'My dear Miss Purser', remarks that Lady

Ferguson had visited and approved greatly of the (family) portraits by Sarah Purser 'especially mine', and 'Miss Newcombe seems to admire the painting of it very much'.[116] The portrait offered a positive image of a successful and independent woman author as reader. Barlow later donated her portrait to the Hugh Lane collection of Dublin municipality and when the Municipal Gallery of Modern Art opened in its new premises at Charlemont House on 19 June 1933, this portrait was on display.[117]

Estella Solomons: Reader, artist, activist

Estella Solomons, an artist and active Irish nationalist, was born in Dublin in 1882 into a well-established Jewish family. Her mother came from Yorkshire and her father's family had earlier moved from England. In June 1897, aged 15, Solomons was studying in Hanover. Her exercise books, inscribed Estella F. Solomons, show that she was following a fairly intensive introduction to English Literature, with individual pieces written, or dictated, on the works of a range of over 20 novelists and poets, as well as on literary figures of the eighteenth century, and 'The Rise of the Novel'.[118] All of these authors were men, with the one exception of the poet Elizabeth Barrett Browning. Visiting Amsterdam, Solomons particularly admired Rembrandt's art, and followed his example when she adopted etching.[119] She attended Alexandra College and Dublin Metropolitan School of Art where she was tutored by William Orpen. Solomons also attended the RHA schools under Walter Osborne and Chelsea Art School tutored by Orpen and by Augustus John whom she greatly admired.[120]

Beatrice Elvery, a fellow student at Dublin Metropolitan School of Art, noted that Orpen imported models for the life class from London to make up for a deficit in Dublin, and he allowed his students to smoke, one of the racy habits associated with the New Woman.[121] According to Elvery, there was an Irish nationalist tendency at the School of Art where 'it was difficult not to be swept away in a flood of patriotism'.[122] Solomons's formal art training, then, was received from a mix of continental, Anglo-Irish and Welsh tutors, and the informal curriculum was generally one of unconventionality, independence and support for Irish nationalism.

Like Sarah Purser, Solomons inhabited different, often opposing societies: 'She moved among Jewish and non-Jewish, English and Irish, Southern and Northern, literary, business and professional circles.'[123] Unlike Purser, Solomons did not depend on her art for a living and so she was able to paint portraits when and of whom she chose, or in Fallon's opinion, 'when she liked someone sufficiently to paint their portrait'.[124] She exhibited her work regularly, showing it at the Five Provinces Branch of the Gaelic League's shows held at 7 St Stephen's Green and designed to promote art in Dublin, and at the Annual Members' Exhibition of the RHA.[125]

Solomons's images of readers

Estella Solomons portrayed readers many times. Her sketchbooks frequently depict herself or family members reading, or occasionally writing.[126] Solomons was unsystematic about keeping her sketchbooks, so that many of her drawings are 'upside-down', but some individual sketches are carefully executed.[127] In one of her undated early sketchbooks, she has a finished pencil drawing of a seated woman with a serious expression, pen and papers in hand. This is likely to be a self-portrait, especially as the figure wears a long dark dress with a high neckline decorated with the same distinctive, long-scalloped, possibly net, collar, as that in her etching *Self-Portrait in a Window* (Figure 28).[128] In a sketchbook inscribed with Estella Solomons's name, her Dublin address, 26 Waterloo Road, and the date June 1906, there is a detailed head and bust in soft pencil of a bespectacled woman, likely to be of her mother Rosa reading a book.[129] In the same sketchpad is a half-length drawing of a bearded and moustached man in a waistcoat and jacket holding an open book, half-smiling and looking off to the side, perhaps her father Maurice.[130]

Further examples in subsequent sketchbooks include a pencil sketch of a woman reading; a seated woman looking up from her book, wearing the distinctive lace-collared dress and again most likely a self-portrait; a drawing of a woman in an armchair holding a book and turning around towards the viewer; a half-figure pencil sketch of an unidentified woman with a book; and a rough sketch of a possibly older slightly buxom woman seated perhaps on a cushion with a book open on her knee.[131] A loose page inserted in one sketchpad has three rough drawings of women reading, and another loose sheet depicts an unidentified woman sitting on a stool reading a book or magazine.[132] Various sketches of her partner Seumas O'Sullivan include a detailed drawing of him ensconced in a deckchair with his book.[133] Solomons again portrayed herself as a reader in her etching *Self-Portrait in a Window* (Figure 28). Her oil paintings of readers include *Seumas Reading by the Coast* (Figure 9); *A Woman Reading at a Desk by a Window* (Figure 17); *Portrait of a Woman* (Figure 19); and *Portrait of Alice Milligan* (Figure 30).

Reading, then, was an occupation that Solomons chose to represent repeatedly and which was clearly integral to her life and that of her family, including her partner Seumas O'Sullivan. As an independent artist, Solomons was in the mould of the New Woman, while her images of women readers contributed to the visual language that helped to constitute the New Woman in Ireland as an intellectual.

Solomons and political activism

Another aspect of the New Woman was political activism, whether in the cause of women's suffrage, improved educational provision or support for nationalism, and Solomons was a New Woman in this sense too. She was a committed Irish nationalist and she joined *Cumann na mBan* in Rathmines in 1915, the women's branch of the Irish National Volunteers, a militia established to combat the Ulster Volunteer Force. Although this was a radical act for a woman, membership of *Cumann na mBan* was not universally approved by feminists as it was regarded as colluding with male rule.[134] Solomons learned from a Sinn Féin agent called 'The Butterman' how to handle a revolver, and used her studio in Great Brunswick Street, now Pearse Street, to hide arms and ammunition.[135] She first met Kathleen Goodfellow, a poet and subject of her portraits, the following year while sheltering from bullets on Mount Street during the Easter Rising. Goodfellow also joined *Cumann na mBan*. Solomons's studio became a hideout for men on the run.[136]

In May 1916 following the Rising, an Irish National Aid Association was formed, and in August, John Lavery responded to Solomons's letter requesting 'a picture on [*sic*] blank canvas to be sold by public auction in Dublin for the benefit of the Irish National Aid Association [...] it would give me much pleasure to contribute a blank framed canvas if the proceeds of its sale were directed eventually to the alleviation of the distress in Dublin'.[137] Staying with her sister Sophie at the Grand Central Hotel in London in August 1916, Solomons wrote to O'Sullivan: 'What a world! Noise & hurry & dust & blood dripping from everyone's hands.'[138] The artist Jack Morrow, whose studio was a venue for plotting the Irish Rising, wrote warmly to Solomons when he was awaiting sentence at DMP Barracks, Great Brunswick Street, reassuring her, 'My good Stella, Don't worry I feel splendid & hopeful. I know that I have good friends' and sending his love to her and O'Sullivan.[139] Solomons looked after Jack Morrow's daughter Moppy while he was a political prisoner.[140]

Following the establishment of the Irish Free State, Solomons and O'Sullivan held Sunday afternoon gatherings for friends and colleagues who were artists and writers. Describing those held later at Morehampton Road from the late 1930s, A. J. Leventhal noted that many were Trinity graduates but some came from the National University, so that 'a cultural ecumenism was already sprouting in the Starkey drawing-room'.[141] Leventhal said, 'There was talk. About the arts. All of them', and he observed that

One was usually invited. It was not open house […] Seumas as host was as charming as his wife and as easily conventional. He smoked his pipe after tea. No one sat on the floor […] The cake was ceremoniously passed round. There was almost an air of ritual. One came and left at the right hour.

This careful adherence to society etiquette was a large contrast to their previous tendency to unconventionality and political activism.

A Portrait of Alice Milligan

Solomons's *Portrait of Alice Milligan* (oil on canvas, 1918, Figure 30) is one of her most moving and best-known portrayals. The subject, Alice Milligan, was an author, editor, designer and feminist. Like Solomons, Milligan was a fervent Irish nationalist and like her an exemplar of the New Woman. Milligan was born near Omagh in 1866 to Methodist parents who worked in the Irish linen trade. She attended Methodist College, Belfast and studied English history and literature for a year at King's College London before training as a teacher.[142] Milligan and her father, Seaton, a self-taught antiquarian and naturalist, co-wrote *Glimpses of Erin* (1888), a history and tourist guide with reflections on Irish/English relations.[143] Her father's politics were unionist and 'the "Erin" of the title constituted the north-east corners of Ulster'.[144] However, in Dublin in 1891 Milligan underwent a 'political epiphany' while travelling in a tram up O'Connell Street.[145] She became an important figure in the Irish cultural revival as a novelist, poet, editor and journalist, as well as a dramatist and designer of theatre costumes. Milligan learnt Irish, studied Irish folklore and offered lecture tours to the Gaelic League, covering 'every conceivable sort of lecture, History, Scenery, Antiquities & Irish Industry & Country Life'.[146] Milligan's activism included supporting Irish political prisoners and she explored in her art 'what it was to be "othered" and to have empathy with "the other"'.[147] Milligan edited *The Northern Patriot*, and with her friend Anna Johnston [Ethna Carbery] in 1896 she founded and co-edited a nationalist monthly journal, the *Shan Van Vocht*, 'the poor old woman', an early name for Ireland, with the by-lines,

Yes, Ireland shall be free

From the centre to the sea,

And hurrah for liberty

Says the Shan Van Vocht.[148]

Milligan believed that 'The worth and glory of a nation may well be measured and adjudged by the typical character of its womanhood.'[149] In 1897 she formed the Irish Women's Centenary Union to campaign for women to have a voice in marking the 1898 centenary.[150] Milligan created silent *tableaux vivants*, representing figures from Irish folklore, such as the warrior queen, Maeve, that were intended to reach across linguistic and religious barriers.[151] Their performance also enabled political expression by women friends who, Milligan lamented, 'were not called upon to have a opinion whatsoever'.[152] Milligan found her creative work undermined by financial difficulties and by other duties laid upon her. For some years before the Easter Rising, she cared for her parents and her brother, and had to refuse offers to lecture and to write for publication, explaining that 'I have only written one poem in a period of eighteen months & as at present I am residing in lodgings with my mother & an invalid brother. I have not an hour's seclusion.'[153]

Solomons's *Portrait of Alice Milligan* (Figure 30), like Purser's portrait of Jane Barlow, depicts an 'interrupted reader', but it represents a very different engagement with the fictive viewer. At this time, Milligan had suffered many deaths among family and friends. In 1902 her sister drowned and her close friend Anna Johnston died; her parents died early in 1916.[154] She had witnessed the defeat of the 1916 Rising and the cruel execution of her friend Roger Casement by the British.

In Solomons's portrait, Milligan is carefully dressed in dark-toned clothes, a bottle-green dress and hat with a matching veil thrown back. Solomons emulates Rembrandt's use in portraiture of a simple dark background of grey-green. The chair is upholstered in bottle-green with a tan back that picks up the red colour of Milligan's hair. There is no window, and aside from the chair, no furnishing or ornament of any kind. The bleak surround perhaps fits the theme of Milligan's losses. Milligan leans anxiously forward from her chair, with a look both sad and plaintive, one hand grasping the chair-arm. Her other hand points to a small book perhaps of poetry open on her lap. Light from an unidentified source falls on her face and hands, and onto her book. The book stands out against the dark green fabric of her dress, and its edges are also green, so that it seems to be both a salient object and an organic part of the figure.

Solomons exhibited her portrait of Alice Milligan in March 1919 at the Annual Exhibition of the RHA.[155] Solomons's work was criticised by the reviewer for *The Freeman's Journal* in terms again suggesting ignorance of the modernity of Solomons's work:

It is clear that as an artist she is primarily interested in character [...] From a technical point of view Miss Solomons, having got her impression, is inclined to leave other things hanging in the air rather than run the risk of disturbing it. This explains, though it cannot be held to justify, the summary treatment of the hands which mars so penetrating a study as the portrait of Miss Alice Milligan.[156]

The requirement for technical finish suggests that for this reviewer, a criterion of academic competency applicable to academicians, by definition mostly male, is being applied to a painting by Solomons that is a little more modernist in style. However, the *Irish Times* reviewer for the exhibition commented favourably that 'Miss Estella Solomons contributes some excellent work, mostly portraits of prominent figures in Irish life. The best of her subjects is Miss Alice Milligan, a picture boldly treated without over-zealous regard for accuracy of detail.'[157]

Conclusion

While women remained legally and politically marginalised in Irish society, Sarah Purser and Estella Solomons gained considerable professional standing as artists, as well as contributing to the artistic, cultural and political life of Dublin at this time. Both did achieve a 'room of their own'. Sarah Purser was a prominent and much-lauded artist and an important cultural leader in contemporary Dublin. She helped to establish key Irish art institutions such as the Dublin Art Club and the Municipal Gallery of Modern Art and personally hosted regular gatherings, bringing together artists, intellectuals and politicians from different religious and political persuasions. In 1914, Sarah Purser was appointed by the Lord Lieutenant a governor and guardian of the National Gallery of Ireland,[158] an appointment renewed by the Lords Justices in 1919 for another five-year term.[159] With Sir John Purser Griffith, Sarah Purser founded the Purser-Griffith scholarship in the history of modern art, awarded in turn by Trinity College Dublin and University College Dublin.[160] Estella Solomons was a courageous political activist committed to Irish independence. As an artist, she represented prominent literary and political figures and, importantly, evocative pictures of readers, especially women.

Despite their social standing, Purser and Solomons were not fully acknowledged in the public sphere in Ireland. For example, women were not admitted to full membership of the Royal Hibernian Academy until the 1920s. Purser was made an Honorary Royal Hibernian Academician in 1890, the best that could be offered to a woman artist, and a member in 1924. Solomons was elected an associate member of the RHA in 1925.

The four women, Purser, Barlow, Solomons and Milligan, contributed to a flourishing of creative and political activity among women in Dublin at this time. This was nurtured by supportive networks of friendship and, in the case of Barlow and Purser, also copious correspondence. Ideas of the New Woman and demands for female suffrage were being exchanged among artists and activists in Ireland, Britain and the European continent. In Ireland, such ideas were germinated in a context of social and political ferment, and hope among many for a new independent, fair and equal polity. Books were integral to the development of the New Woman in Ireland and elsewhere, as the foundation for her independence, self-education, creativity and political activism. It is not surprising then that Purser and Solomons should paint Barlow and Milligan as readers. Yet, as argued in this volume, such portraits remained a peculiarly Irish and even Anglo-Irish phenomenon.

Portraits of women readers were often bought privately and might then disappear from public view. They were finally for domestic rather than public display, and they did not usually become part of public portraiture which remained a predominantly masculine sphere.[161] Nonetheless, they had been exhibited and publicly reviewed. They were also available to be purchased by and circulated among the professional middle classes, adding to a collective imagery of women as serious readers. Some of them, including Purser's and Solomons's marvellous portraits of Jane Barlow and Alice Milligan, have fortunately been lodged in public galleries in Ireland.[162]

CONCLUSION

In summary, this volume has examined an intriguing and distinctive group of Irish portraits of reading figures from the long nineteenth century, mostly depicting female figures and mainly by women artists. The many images of women readers found in European art at this time, generally by male artists, emphasise women's bodily appearance for an admiring viewer, rather than the act of reading. The Irish portraits, by contrast, present a woman engaged in independent solitary reading, while the fictive viewer is excluded, although drawn in, or briefly interrupts her occupation.

Women were legally and politically marginalised in Ireland's patriarchal political and social system, and they were undermined by widespread ideological constructions of them as weak, irrational and dependent. The Catholic Church in particular at this time promoted an exclusively maternal vision of women's lives. However, some women and men in Ireland participated in transnational movements demanding women's suffrage and access to higher education. Early campaigners for women's rights recognised the necessary link between women's social and political advancement and reading. Campaigning and reading both became features of the nascent New Woman in Ireland, alongside a burgeoning of art and literature. Stories and novels included New Women as protagonists, while portrayals of independent women readers created an original visual imagery for the New Woman in Ireland.

Contemporary Irish portraits of men rarely show them reading. The patriarchal society prevalent in Europe, but with its peculiar formations in Ireland, promoted ideals of manliness that discouraged reading for pleasure. In Ireland the landowning Anglo-Irish patriarchy held a British imperial ideal of manliness that postulated an aggressive and naturally hegemonic masculine nature. Their culture, fostered by public school team games and burnished with ancient epics, revolved around sport, politics and the military. Such manliness was based on decisive action, with little value placed on reflective activities such as reading, especially fiction. When a male figure is portrayed with a book, such as a Bible, this commonly signifies a professional status or a figure of authority, thus reinforcing men's ownership of political and social power.

Although the Anglo-Irish overall constituted a privileged class, they were not a homogeneous social group and not all endorsed the dominant values of the Ascendancy. Some men indulged in the unmanly pursuit of reading fiction, and they tend to be depicted in attitudes that suggested an absence of authoritativeness.

Patriarchal ideology was not confined to the Anglo-Irish, whose dominance was opposed by a growing body of Irish nationalists who wished to restore the Irish language and rejected English and Anglo-Irish Protestant culture. Irish-Irelanders took Catholicism as Ireland's religion, and focused on the west of Ireland as an originary locus of pure Irishness. Reading was valued insofar as it celebrated such a conception of Irishness and in place of Homeric myths, ancient Gaelic tales provided models for men's valour.

The portraits of reading figures examined in this volume were generally by women from the affluent Anglo-Irish professional classes. Despite impediments, women artists and writers in Dublin in this period won a considerable degree of cultural and social power, encouraging one another through informal and international networks of friendship and activism. Some supported Irish nationalist goals including Home Rule for Ireland, and their social circles included Catholics and other non-Anglicans as well as religious sceptics. Nationalist women authors such as Jane Barlow took the rural west as their subject matter, or like Alice Milligan studied and reworked Irish folk tales. However, they also tried to give a strong voice to women, while Barlow, far from reifying the West, showed its poverty. While such women did not necessarily share the dominant Ascendancy culture, they were advantaged nevertheless by their situation among the privileged and well-connected echelons and institutions of Irish society. Through travel and training abroad, they could become familiar with European languages and writing, and many shared in the growing transnational campaigns for the advancement of women's rights.

As we have seen, the idea of the New Woman emerged in Ireland from a confluence of factors, and predominantly among the Anglo-Irish. The nationalist Ladies' Land League, led by Anna Parnell from a prominent Anglo-Irish family, publicly demonstrated women's ability to organise and work for reform across the country, and Parnell herself was the model for a fictional New Woman. Unlike the Irish-Irelanders, who focused exclusively on Ireland, the Anglo-Irish nurtured close historical and cultural ties with Britain, as well as with the European continent. Campaigns for women's suffrage and for access to higher education took place in Dublin and London with exchanges of speakers, and men as well as women took part. The idea of the New Woman partly grew out of such campaigns and it was a transnational concept constituted across various cities including Dublin, London and Paris.

The New Woman became a protagonist in both literature and visual art. The English magazine *Punch* published numerous caricatures of the New Woman which often presented her as a bicyclist in an exaggerated version of rational dress, sometimes with an athletic build but always as a joke. Bicycling became something of a linchpin for the definition of the New Woman, as well as a trope for cartoonists. Despite the mockery of *Punch*, such images vividly publicised the notion of a woman willing to contravene social conventions and embodied the nascent New Woman. There was an early welcome in Dublin for women cyclists in rational dress.

The New Woman had many other significant interests, however, including a concern for women's civil rights and a commitment to educative and imaginative reading, as well as to her own work, whether writing in a range of genres or creating visual art of her own. Reading offered not only greater general knowledge but also the opportunity to enter the fictional lives of independent characters. Contemporary fiction from various countries including Ireland represented female protagonists who challenged social conventions and questioned the patriarchy. As we have seen, the new habit of silent reading, together with the genesis and spread of the novel, offered women fresh intellectual and imaginative possibilities, as well as freedom from masculine oversight.

This volume has argued that in Ireland these new and independent reading habits were given visual form. The Irish portraits depicted absorbed, contemplative readers in their own space, oblivious to being viewed as a spectacle, and subtly evoking women's developing sense of autonomy. The fictive viewer might not even have an imaginary place in this private scene, although the reader's absorption in a text would draw them in. Portrayals of an interrupted reader, their attention momentarily distracted but with a finger at the page, only served to emphasise the urgency of their reading. These portraits provided a countervailing visual imagery of the New Woman to that of cartoonists, as well as to that of the woman reader depicted merely as an alluring sight.

Although Anglo-Irish women artists tended to train in Paris and other European cities and were therefore well-acquainted with modernist art, the Irish portraits, with some exceptions, are often muted in colour and fairly traditional in style. This treatment was one way of conveying a quiet or studious setting which would not startle the viewer. The serious female reader was expressive of education and independence, and an important visual embodiment of the New Woman as an engaged and thinking individual. In this way, Irish portraits of women readers drew on and helped to reframe ideas about women, their intellectual capacities, and their social and domestic role.

As noted in the introduction to this volume, scholarly studies of reading and readers in this period speak of history and literature, but visual art tends to be neglected, and where visual art is a focus, Irish examples are rare. This study therefore adds an important dimension to such work. Although commonly regarded as ideologically innocent, art like literature embodies and conveys ideologies. Portraits of male figures, accompanied by status markers like scrolls or Bibles, collectively reinforce the idea of patriarchal power. However, the female portraits discussed in this volume also carry a message, of women's resistance to their common classification as objects for masculine viewing, and of women as independent and intellectual, that is, a type of the New Woman.

Throughout this study, a cross-disciplinary approach has proved fruitful, for example, in exploring the interconnections between literary and visual representations of the New Woman. An examination of the contemporary concept and practice of silent reading helped to elucidate the focused occupation of the depicted readers. The art historical practice of considering the role and placement of a fictive viewer and the critical notion of 'absorption', applied to reading, assists in explaining how these images of absorbed, solitary women might engage the viewer. The contextualisation of the Irish portraits with reference to the transnational campaigns for women's civil rights has also proved useful. Indeed, this explorative study spawned an unexpectedly complex array of issues. The Irish portraits have been subjected to perhaps an unusually complicated but productive reading which has provided a fresh approach to the history and visualisation of the New Woman.

This study highlighted both the dominance and the diversity of Anglo-Irish culture in this period. It probed the masculine ethos of the Ascendancy with its surprisingly clear rejection of the reading of fiction as a worthwhile activity, and it showed how, by contrast, many Anglo-Irish women valued reading, especially as educational opportunities were denied them. The considerable productivity and cultural contributions of Anglo-Irish women at this time became clear, including their efforts to help create public institutions such as the Municipal Gallery of Modern Art, Dublin, which continues to flourish. The work of some of these women, such as Cecilia Harrison and Estella Solomons, deserves to be better known.

Some recognition of women's autonomy, with pledges of universal suffrage as well as religious and civil liberty, was to be briefly embodied in the Proclamation that accompanied the Irish Rising of 1916, but the promise of women's equality was subsequently eroded in the dominant Catholic and masculine ethos of the Irish Free State and later Republic. However, the idea of the New Woman had been widely sown in Ireland and elsewhere. It has a quiet but persistent life in these portraits of the New Woman as thinker and intellectual, and those images remain captivating and relevant in Ireland today.

NOTES

Introduction

1   For instance, the work of the poet W. B. Yeats was well known, but that of his brother, the painter Jack B. Yeats, was scarcely recognised outside Ireland.

2   D. S. McColl quoted in Hugh P. Lane, 'Prefatory Notes'.

3   Flint, *The Woman Reader*, 4.

4   Docherty, 'Women as Readers: Visual Interpretations', 339.

5   O'Toole, *The Irish New Woman*.

6   Barr, Buckley and O'Cinneide, *Literacy, Language and Reading*.

7   Luddy, *Women in Ireland: A Documentary History*.

8   Brown, *Women Readers in French Painting*, 12.

9   Cullen, *The Irish Face*, 12.

10   See Cullen, *The Irish Face*, 11–12.

11   Cullen, *The Irish Face*, 11–12.

12   See Kenny, 'Ireland and the British Empire', 1–25.

13   Leerssen, 'Lebowski's Rug and the Book', 335.

14   Hall, 'Cultural Identity', 68.

15   Ferris, *The Romantic National Tale*, 14; previously, terms like 'English-Irish', 'Anglo-Hibernian' or just 'Irish' were used: Ferris, *The Romantic National Tale*, 14.

16   McNally, 'Protestant Perspectives', 80.

17   F. E., letter to Marx, 23 May 1856, 83, 85.

18   Dooley, *Decline of the Big House*, 10–12, 289–91: Appendix II.

19   Vaughan, *Landlords and Tenants in Ireland*, 5.

20   McConville, *Ascendancy to Oblivion*, 243.

21   Fitzpatrick, 'Ireland and the Empire', 503. Irish history was excised from primary school books: Murphy, *Ireland, Reading and Cultural Nationalism*, 7, 10, 66.

22   See https://www.irishtimes.com/about-us/the-irish-times-trust. Accessed 7 January 2020.

23   Morris, 'Irish Methodism and the Religious Press', 66–67. The *Irish Christian Advocate*, another Irish Methodist title was established in 1883: Morris, 'Irish Modernism and the Religious Press', 66–67.

24   Morgan, *National Identities and Travel*, 93. On anti-Catholic prejudice, see Duffy, 'Colonial Spaces and Sites of Resistance', 23.

25   Somerville and Ross, *The Real Charlotte*, 87, 268. Julie Anne Stevens has drawn attention to the anti-Catholic tendencies of Ascendancy Protestantism and to the social class aspect of Mullen's snobbish hostility to Catholics: email communication to author, 19 February 2021; Stevens, *The Irish Scene*, 61.

26   A Lady, 'Talk of Town', *Irish Times*, 2 February 1895, 5.

27 Fletcher, 'A Young Nationalist', unpaginated.
28 William Orpen (1878–1931) was born in Co. Dublin, trained at Dublin Metropolitan School of Art and the Slade School of Fine Art, London. He worked in London and Dublin and in 1901 married Grace Knewstub, the subject of his painting illustrated as Figure 13. For further details, see Upstone, *William Orpen.*
29 David Hicks, 'Behind the Faces on the Canvas: Irish Country Houses – Portraits & Painters', *Irish Times*, 2 December 2014, accessed 7 January 2020, https://www.iri shtimes.com/culture/books/behind-the-faces-on-the-canvas-irish-country-houses-portraits-painters-1.2022762.
30 Sir Vere Foster quoted in Coalter, 'Reviews: Museum Eye', unpaginated.
31 Cooke, 'Dublin Mechanics' Institute', 19.
32 Wilson, 'Constructions of Irishness', 110.
33 Smyth, *The Novel and the Nation*, 15.
34 *Drawn to the Page.*
35 *The Irish People* 1, no. 1, 28 November 1863, 5.
36 Murphy, *Ireland, Reading and Cultural Nationalism*, 135.
37 Sullivan and Sullivan, *Irish Readings*, 3–4.
38 See Cusack, *Riverscapes and National Identities*, 167–73.
39 Tilley, '*Dublin Penny Journal*', 88–89.
40 *The Irish People* 1, no. 1, 28 November 1863.
41 'Anna Maria Hall', *Drawn to the Page.*
42 An Irish Protestant, 'A Young Protestant Party', 3.
43 Brown, 'The Question of Irish Nationality', 635, 641.
44 Walker, 'Portrait of the Artist', 106.
45 Purser, *Jellett, O'Brien, Purser and Stokes*, 116.
46 Biletz, 'Women and Irish-Ireland', 59.
47 Hardwick, *The Yeats Sisters*, 177; Lewis, *The Yeats Sisters*, 3.
48 Devereaux, 'Finding Cottie', 121–23.
49 Pyle, *Cesca's Diary*, 7; Fletcher, 'A Young Nationalist', unpaginated.
50 Pyle, *Cesca's Diary*, xix.
51 De Markievicz, Lecture to Students' National Literary Society, Dublin, unpaginated.
52 Breen, 'The Making and Unmaking of an Irish Woman of Letters', Abstract.
53 Murphy, *Ireland, Reading and Cultural Nationalism*, 74.
54 For instance, Daniel Maclise illustrated some of Charles Dickens's Christmas books: *Drawn to the Page.* Harry Clarke illustrated Hans Christian Andersen's fairy tales, published in London.
55 Fitzpatrick, 'Ireland and the Empire', 503. Irish history was excised from primary schoolbooks: Murphy, *Ireland, Reading and Cultural Nationalism*, 7, 10, 66.
56 Breen, 'The Making and Unmaking of an Irish Woman of Letters', 3.
57 Ó Ciosáin, 'Varieties of Literacy', 18, 20.
58 Ó Ciosáin, 'Varieties of Literacy', 22.
59 Kaestle, 'History of Literacy', 22.
60 See Carleton, *Father Butler*, 126–27.
61 Marsh's Library Catalogue, accessed 7 January 2020, https://www.marshlibrary.ie/ catalogue/.
62 Marsh's Library, ML.1., Visitor Book 1826–83.
63 Amy Boylan, assistant librarian, Marsh's Library, St Patrick's Close, Dublin: email communication to author, 7 October 2020.

64 Marsh's Library, ML.2. Visitor Book 1863–64.

65 Marsh's Library, ML.2. Visitor Book 1863–64.

66 These may have been prestige items brought out for visitors: Amy Boylan, assistant librarian, Marsh's Library, St Patrick's Close, Dublin: email communication to author, 7 October 2020.

67 Diary of Robert Travers, assistant librarian, Marsh's Library, ML.4, Visitor Book 1871–86.

68 Diary of Robert Travers, assistant librarian, Marsh's Library, ML.4, Visitor Book 1871–86.

69 Potter, 'Limerick City Municipal Library', 102. Later, the Scottish-American philanthropist, Andrew Carnegie, donated generous funds allowing many new libraries to be built in Ireland.

70 Frances Clarke, duty librarian, National Library of Ireland, email communication to author, 10 November 2020.

71 No record of Purser visiting Marsh's then, for example, was found: Amy Boylan, assistant librarian, Marsh's Library, St Patrick's Close, Dublin: email communication to author, 7 October 2020. Sarah Purser is discussed in some detail in Chapter 5.

72 Carton, 'Novels and Novel Readers', 239. *Irish Monthly* was a literary journal founded in 1873 by Fr. Matthew Russell, S.J., who edited it until his death in 1912. He encouraged women writers and contributors with a range of backgrounds and beliefs.

73 Somerville and Ross *The Real Charlotte*, 258.

74 Murphy, *Ireland, Reading and Cultural Nationalism*, 6–7, 60.

75 Barr, Buckley and O'Cinneide, *Literacy, Language and Reading*, 11.

76 For example, see O'Toole, *The Irish New Woman*, 110–13; Kelso, 'The Body as Interface'.

1. Imperial Man, Manly Nationalism and the Unmanly Reader

1 Brookes, *Manliness and Culture*, 29–30 (emphasis in the original).

2 Brookes, *Manliness and Culture*, 31, 33.

3 Beynon, *Masculinities and Culture*, 28.

4 Springhall, 'Baden-Powell and the Scout Movement', 935.

5 Beynon, *Masculinities and Culture*, 26.

6 Beynon, *Masculinities and Culture*, 27, 35.

7 Beynon, *Masculinities and Culture*, 27, 35.

8 Jackson, *Unmasking Masculinity*, 234.

9 Valente, *The Myth of Manliness*, 2.

10 Valente, *The Myth of Manliness*, 2–4.

11 Valente, *The Myth of Manliness*, 7.

12 Valente, *The Myth of Manliness*, 8–10.

13 Morgan, *National Identities and Travel*, 91, 93.

14 See Curtis, *Apes and Angels*.

15 Foster, *Paddy and Mr Punch*, 192–93.

16 Renan, 'La Poésie des races celtiques', 478.

17 Arnold, *Study of Celtic Literature*.

18 Valente, *The Myth of Manliness*, 10–11.

19 Meath, *Memories*, 337; Meath, *Brabazon Potpourri*, 93–103.

20   Butler, 'Irishwomen and the Home Language', 5; Valente, *The Myth of Manliness*, 19.

21   Hagerman, *Britain's Imperial Muse*, 101.

22   Beynon, *Masculinities and Culture*, 41; Watson, Weir and Friend, 'Development of Muscular Christianity', 1.

23   Charles Kingsley quoted in Watson, Weir and Friend, 'Development of Muscular Christianity', 1–2.

24   Beynon, *Masculinities and Culture*, 42; Watson, Weir and Friend, 'Development of Muscular Christianity', 2.

25   Drücker, 'Hunting and Shooting', 125–26.

26   Stevens, *Two Irish Girls in Bohemia*, 16–17.

27   Somerville-Large, *The Irish Country House*, 298–300.

28   Fitzpatrick, 'Ireland and the Empire', 511.

29   See: *Kilrush Herald*, 5 June 1879; *Kilrush Herald and Kilkee Gazette*, 10 July 1879; 'The Zulu War', *Kilrush Herald and Kilkee Gazette*, 3 and 17 July 1879.

30   *Irish Times*, 23 May 1877, 4.

31   'The Zulu War', *Irish Times*, 11 February 1879, 5.

32   *Kilrush Herald*, 5 June 1879; *Kilrush Herald and Kilkee Gazette*, 10 July 1879; 'The Zulu War', *Kilrush Herald and Kilkee Gazette*, 3 and 17 July 1879.

33   Somerville-Large, *The Irish Country House*, 298.

34   Arthur, *Advice to Young Men*, 62.

35   Arthur, *Advice to Young Men*, 46.

36   Arthur, *Advice to Young Men*, 60–61.

37   Arthur, *Advice to Young Men*, 61.

38   Arthur, *Advice to Young Men*, 70.

39   Greg, 'False Morality of Lady Novelists', 83–84.

40   Brookes, *Manliness and Culture*, 66, 90 [emphasis in original].

41   Brookes, *Manliness and Culture*, 93 [emphasis in original].

42   Carton, 'Novels and Novel Readers', 237; 'Novels and Novel Readers – II', 309.

43   Carton, 'Novels and Novel Readers', 239, 247–48.

44   Carton, 'Novels and Novel Readers – II', 309–18, 310; M. R., 'Judge Carton. In Memoriam', 419.

45   Gerardine Meaney (1991) quoted in O'Toole, *The Irish New Woman*, 9. See also Cusack, 'Introduction: Art, Nation and Gender', 1–11.

46   Quinn, 'The *Nation*', 53–54.

47   Murphy, *Ireland, Reading and Cultural Nationalism*, 36.

48   Tomas Davis quoted in Murphy, *Ireland, Reading and Cultural Nationalism*, 37.

49   Cairns and Richards, *Writing Ireland*, 36–37.

50   Murphy, *Ireland, Reading and Cultural Nationalism*, 44.

51   Henry McManus's biography is a bit uncertain. He was born c. 1810 in Monaghan or Dublin, becoming an artist, art teacher and head of the Dublin Society School in 1849, where he introduced classes for women (Chapter 3).

52   Quinn, 'The *Nation*', 62.

53   Quinn, 'The *Nation*', 57.

54   Smyth, *The Novel and the Nation*, 15–16.

55   Thomas D'Arcy McGee (1847) quoted in Quinn, 'The *Nation*', 60.

56   *The Irish People* 1, no. 1, 28 November 1863, 9. Downloaded courtesy of Digital Library, Villanova University.

57   Joyce, 'Ireland's Trained and Marshalled Manhood', 76–77.

58   Valente, *The Myth of Manliness*, 19, 21–25.
59   Joyce, 'Ireland's Trained and Marshalled Manhood', 71–72.
60   Joyce, 'Ireland's Trained and Marshalled Manhood', 70, 75.
61   McDevitt, 'Muscular Catholicism', 277, 280, n. 9.
62   Brady, 'Home and Away', 28.
63   However, Catholic clergy disapproved of the IRB, with its strong interest in the organisation: McDevitt, 'Muscular Catholicism', 281, n. 14.
64   McDevitt, 'Muscular Catholicism', 264.
65   McDevitt, 'Muscular Catholicism', 264–65.
66   See McDevitt, 'Muscular Catholicism', 262, 268.
67   Brady, 'Home and Away', 28.
68   McDevitt, 'Muscular Catholicism', 275.
69   John Sheehan (1902), quoted in O'Connor, *The Irish Dancing*, 29.
70   Ward, *Unmanageable Revolutionaries*, 50–51.
71   Ward, *Unmanageable Revolutionaries*, 67–68.
72   Margaret Ward observed in 2003 that '[t]he role of women in revolutionary Irish nationalist movements is still under-researched and underestimated', Introduction to McCoole, *No Ordinary Women*, 11.
73   McCoole, *No Ordinary Women*, 26.
74   'Old Fogey', 'National Economics'.
75   Yeats, *Fairy and Folk Tales*, 5.
76   MacManus [pseud. Ethna Carbery], *In the Celtic Past*. Her father, Robert Johnston, was an executive member of the IRB.
77   Wilson Foster, *Irish Novels*, 10, 12–13, 15.
78   Sullivan and Sullivan, *Irish Readings*, I: 4–5.
79   O'Donnell, 'On the Rampart', 190–92.
80   Sullivan and Sullivan, *Irish Readings*, II: 73.
81   For a discussion of the historical role of men and the allegorical use of women in art, see Cusack, *Art, Nation and Gender*, 1–11.
82   Sisley, 'Portraits of National Interest', 37.
83   Sisley, 'Portraits of National Interest', 63.
84   Yeldham, *Maria Spilsbury*, 21–22.
85   Gwynn, 'Henry Grattan', 579.
86   Lord Brougham, quoted in 'British Parliamentary Orators', 206; see also 'Henry Grattan', 215.
87   Yeldham, *Maria Spilsbury*, 123.
88   Yeldham, *Maria Spilsbury*, 20–21. Moravian evangelism influenced Evangelicalism, a Protestant movement that took root in London and in the Anglican Church of Ireland. Evangelicalism promoted an individual's personal relation to the Bible, instead of formal mediation by an ecclesiastical hierarchy. It is possible that Maria Spilsbury herself was no longer a member of the Moravian Church when she moved to Ireland: see ibid., 20.
89   Hamilton, 'History of the Moravian Church', 161.
90   Yeldham, *Maria Spilsbury*, 18.
91   See Yeldham, *Maria Spilsbury*.
92   *Bible Reading*, which is alternatively titled *Family Group before a Thatched Cottage*, is illustrated in Yeldham, *Maria Spilsbury*, 70, and in Page and Smith, *Women, Literature, and the Domesticated Landscape*, 100, with a colour detail on the cover.

93   The first portrait of Kelly (c. 1815) is illustrated in Yeldham, *Maria Spilsbury*, 126. The second can be viewed at: https://www.adams.ie/86977/MARIA-SPILSB URY-TAYLOR-1776-1820-Portrait-of-the-Rev-Thomas-Kelly-of-Kellyville-Athy-seated-in-his-study.

94   *Brief Memorials of the Rev. B.W. Mathias*, 7–8.

95   Donald M. Lewis, quoted in Yeldham, *Maria Spilsbury*, 127.

96   J.H.S. 'Preface', *Brief Memorials of the Rev. B.W. Mathias*, xx–xxi. Mathias's dissenting beliefs led to his exclusion from preaching in the Established Church though this was later revoked: J.H.S. 'Preface', *Brief Memorials of the Rev. B.W. Mathias*, xviii.

97   Yeldham, *Maria Spilsbury*, 16.

98   Yeldham, *Maria Spilsbury*, 17, 20.

99   Murphy, *Patrick Tuohy*, 161.

100 Purser's friend and admirer, the author Jane Barlow, wrote to tell her, 'I think your Dr Ingram is quite splendid. A great portrait of a great man': Letters Jane Barlow to Sarah Purser 1897 [Barlow's emphasis], NLI MSS 8186 (7).

101 Barrett, 'John Kells Ingram', 6–7.

102 Ingram, *The Memory of the Dead*, 1843, fourth stanza, lines 5–8.

103 Barrett, 'John Kells Ingram', 10.

104 Barrett, 'John Kells Ingram', 15.

105 Jack B. Yeats, an Anglo-Irish nationalist, has become known as Ireland's national painter. He was born in London and spent his childhood between London and Sligo in the west of Ireland. Yeats trained at South Kensington and Chiswick Schools of Art and initially worked as an illustrator. He lived in England, later returning to Ireland, first to Greystones, Co. Wicklow then to Dublin. For further details, see Cusack, ''Tis the Wild Things' and 'Migrant Travellers'; Arnold, *Jack Yeats*.

106 See: Cusack, 'Migrant Travellers', 201. *The Man from Aranmore* is discussed in Cusack, ''Tis the Wild Things', 84.

107 Arnold, *Jack Yeats*, 179.

108 Birmingham, *Irishmen All*, 158.

109 Birmingham, *Irishmen All*, 158, 162–68.

110 Pyle, *Jack B. Yeats: Catalogue Raisonné*, 1: 62.

111 Pierre Macherey observed that the meaning of a statement might be found in its absences, as well as what was present: 'Silences shape all speech […] Can we make this silence speak? What is the unspoken saying?' Macherey, *Theory of Literary Production*, 96.

112 Carleton, *Father Butler*, 4.

113 Carleton, *Father Butler*, 7. The Roman Breviary is a liturgical book of the Roman Catholic Church containing prayers, hymns, psalms and lessons.

114 Carleton, *Father Butler*, 56.

115 Carleton, *Father Butler*, 141.

116 Somerville and Ross, *The Real Charlotte*, 68, 120, 122–23.

117 Somerville and Ross, *The Real Charlotte*, 277.

118 Somerville and Ross, *The Real Charlotte*, 122–23.

119 Photography early aspired to the status of art and the 1871 census classed professional photographers in the Dublin area with artists, engravers and sculptors.

120 Julie Anne Stevens, email correspondence with author, 31 May 2020. The *Skibbereen Eagle* was founded in 1857 as a monthly then weekly paper.

121 Julie Anne Stevens, email correspondence with author, 31 May 2020.

122 A *canapé à confidante* is a sofa with a triangular seat each end.

123   In Düsseldorf and in Paris, Somerville said she learnt to work rapidly in art following her first impression: Stevens, *Two Irish Girls in Bohemia*, 23.

124   This picture had the name Roderic O'Conor verso and was held at auction by Biddle & Webb in Birmingham UK on 13 September 2013 (present location unknown). O' Conor was born in Co. Roscommon in 1860. He trained at the Metropolitan School of Art, Dublin and the Académie Royale des Beaux-Arts, Antwerp before moving to Paris. For further details, see Benington, *Roderic O' Conor*.

125   Walter Osborne (1859–1903) was born in Dublin into a well-off Protestant family. He was educated at the Royal Hibernian Academy Schools, Dublin, the Metropolitan School of Art and the Académie Royale des Beaux Arts, Antwerp and worked in England and France as well as Ireland. He was a founding member of Dublin Art Club: Sheehy, *Walter Osborne*, 8.

126   Leventhal, 'Seumas O' Sullivan', 10.

127   Estella Solomons is discussed in some detail in Chapter 5.

128   Kennedy, 'Estella Solomons', 13.

129   'P.E.N. Tribute to Dr Starkey', n.t., n.d. TCD MSS Press Cuttings, Box 4652e(1). PEN is an acronym for 'Poets, Essayists, Novelists' an international organisation founded in 1921 to protect literary freedoms.

130   Sketches by Estella Solomons of Seumas O'Sullivan reading include, for instance, one in head and shoulders reading a book: Sketchbooks of Estella Solomons (1905–1953), TCD, MSS 4522, loose sheet at folio 35 recto. Another pencil sketch of O'Sullivan depicts his head and shoulders and introduces his hand supporting a book: Sketchbooks of Estella Solomons (1905–1953), TCD, MS 4511, p. 24. A pencil sketch in profile/back view shows O'Sullivan bent over a table writing or reading, his pipe lying on the table and his feet ensconced in sandals: Sketchbooks of Estella Solomons (1905–1953), TCD, MS 4522, p. 12. In another sketch of O'Sullivan, he is shown with his pipe reading a book by a window offering a country view of a barn, stone wall and low hill: Sketchbooks of Estella Solomons (1905–1953), TCD, MS 4517, p. 55 verso.

131   Sketchbooks of Estella Solomons (1905–1953), TCD, MS 4517; inserted near the related sketch, p. 34.

132   O'Sullivan, 'Prelude to an Autobiography', 26.

133   Arthur Griffith, 17 Fownes Street, Dublin, printed sheet dated 28 July 1903, Press Cuttings, TCD, MSS 4652a–f.

134   O'Sullivan, 'Prelude to an Autobiography', 22.

135   Sketchbooks of Estella Solomons (1905–1953), TCD, MS 4522, p. 19.

136   Sketchbooks of Estella Solomons (1905–1953), TCD, MS 4522, p. 19.

137   Leventhal, 'Seumas O'Sullivan', 16.

138   Somerville and Ross, *The Real Charlotte*, 123.

139   Conlon, 'Men Reading Women Reading', 43.

140   Leventhal, 'Seumas O'Sullivan', 18–19.

2. 'Creatures of a Different Breed': Women Readers and Patriarchal Discourse

1   John Lavery, born in Belfast, was baptised a Roman Catholic. He trained and worked in Glasgow and Paris and had a successful career in London. Lavery remained

attached to Ireland and Irish independence. For more details see McConkey, *Sir John Lavery*; Shaw-Sparrow, *John Lavery*.

2   Foucault, *History of Sexuality*, 18, 33, 53.

3   Foucault, *History of Sexuality*, 24.

4   Digby, 'Women's Biological Straitjacket', 193, 208.

5   Foucault, *History of Sexuality*, 104.

6   Connell, *Masculinities*, 164.

7   Cobbe, 'Address to Women Concerning the Suffrage', 3.

8   Greg, 'False Morality of Lady Novelists', 83–84.

9   Greg, 'False Morality of Lady Novelists', 84.

10 Carton, 'Novels and Novel Readers', 239. Greene's bookshop was opened in Clare Street Dublin in 1843. Charles Eason and son acquired their Dublin bookshop in 1886.

11 Greg, 'False Morality of Lady Novelists', 87.

12 Greg, 'Why Are Women Redundant?', 281.

13 Greg, 'Why Are Women Redundant?', 282.

14 Ellis, *The Daughters of England*, author's preface.

15 Ellis, *The Daughters of England*, 8.

16 Ellis, *The Daughters of England*, 11.

17 Carton, 'Novels and Novel Readers', 240.

18 Johann Adam Bergk (1799) quoted in Bollmann, *Reading Women*, 25.

19 Jack, *The Woman Reader*, 2.

20 Dr John Harvey Kellog (1882) quoted in Golden, *Images of the Woman Reader*, 37.

21 Cusack, 'This Pernicious Tea Drinking Habit', 178–209. However, in the case of tea consumption, criticism was confined to women of low status, ibid.

22 Madden, 'On Insanity', 68.

23 Present Writer, The, 'Harmless Novels', 206.

24 Eccles, 'A Plea for the Modern Woman – II', 326.

25 Eccles, 'A Plea for the Modern Woman – II', 323, 329.

26 Eccles, 'A Plea for the Modern Woman – II', 324.

27 Eccles, 'A Plea for the Modern Woman – II', 319.

28 Eccles, 'A Plea for the Modern Woman – II', 324–25.

29 Eccles, 'A Plea for the Modern Woman – II', 328.

30 Woolf, *A Room of One's Own*, 33.

31 Stevens, *Two Irish Girls in Bohemia*, 15.

32 Camplin and Ranauro, *Books Do Furnish a Painting*, 173.

33 Information about this painting seems to be scant. It is in the public domain but only at very low resolution. It can be viewed at: https://commons.wikimedia.org/wiki/File:Avy,_Reading.jpg.

34 *Femme lisant* can be viewed at: https://www.christies.com/en/lot/lot-6073951.

35 *Young Girl Reading* can be viewed at: https://commons.wikimedia.org/wiki/File:Renoir_-_young-girl-reading-1895.jpg!PinterestLarge.jpg.

36 Docherty, 'Women as Readers', 335–88.

37 *Girl Reading* can be viewed at: https://www.pinterest.nz/pin/520517669429878052/.

38 *The Afternoon Rest* can be viewed at: https://books0977.tumblr.com/post/146324068027/the-afternoon-rest-john-morgan-british.

39 *Sweet Solitude* can be viewed at: https://commons.wikimedia.org/wiki/File:Edmund_Blair_Leighton_-_Sweet_solitude.jpg.

40 *Reading in a Sailing Boat* can be viewed at: https://thelongvictorian.com/2016/04/15/painting-a-girl-reading-in-a-sailing-boat/.

41 Manet apparently contributed to finishing the figure of the mother.

42 Brown, *Women Readers in French Painting*, 25.

43 Camplin and Ranauro, *Books Do Furnish a Painting*, 177.

44 Camplin and Ranauro, *Books Do Furnish a Painting*, 176.

45 *Girl in a Red Dress* can be viewed at: https://gallerix.org/storeroom/142764965/N/241/.

46 *Mary Auras* can be viewed at: https://www.sothebys.com/en/auctions/ecatalogue/2008/the-irish-sale-l08120/lot.148.html.

47 *Mary Black-Hawkins* can be viewed at: https://www.christies.com/en/lot/lot-6062462.

48 The picture is also titled *Girl in Hammock* according to a note verso of the painting.

49 Ortner, 'Is Female to Male as Nature is to Culture?', 12.

50 For a note on Walter Osborne, see Chapter 1.

51 It is notable that even the artist and active revolutionary, Countess Constance Markievicz, is portrayed by Casimir Dunin Markievicz as a society lady lounging in a long white dress in *The Artist's Wife* (oil on canvas, 1899).

52 *On the Cliff* can be viewed at: https://www.sothebys.com/en/auctions/ecatalogue/2009/the-irish-sale-l09680/lot.14.html.

53 O'Grady, *Life and Work of Sarah Purser*, 112.

3. The Shaping of the New Woman in Ireland

1 Quinlan, 'Onward Hand in Hand', 21–23.

2 Quinlan, 'Onward Hand in Hand', 23.

3 Cappock, 'Sarah Cecilia Harrison', 78; Lane, 'The International Story of the Women's Suffrage Movement'.

4 Lane, 'The International Story of the Women's Suffrage Movement'.

5 Haslam, *The Women's Advocate*, 270–71.

6 Quinlan, ''Onward Hand in Hand', 25.

7 A Lady, 'Talk of Town', *Irish Times*, 2 February 1895, 5.

8 A Lady, 'Talk of Town', *Irish Times*, 2 February 1895, 5.

9 'Minute Book of the Dublin Women's Suffrage Association/Irish Women's Suffrage and Local Government Association (1876–1913)', National Archives, accessed 4 January 2021, https://www.nationalarchives.ie/article/minute-book-dublin-womens-suffrage-association-irish-womens-suffrage-local-government-association-1876-1913. An Irish Poor Law Act in 1838 divided the country into 130 poor law unions, each managed by a board of poor law guardians: 'Guide to the Archives of the Poor Law': https://www.nationalarchives.ie/article/guide-archives-poor-law/.

10 'Women's Suffrage and Poor Law Guardians Association', *Irish Times*, 8 July 1898, 2.

11 'Irish Women's Suffrage Association', *Irish Times*, 1 February 1904, 7.

12 'Dublin Municipal Elections. Some Surprises. League Candidates Defeated. First Lady Councillor Returned', *Irish Times*, 16 January 1912, 8.

13 O'Neill, 'Sarah Cecilia Harrison', 66–67, 69.

14 Harrison's closeness to Lane is indicated by the fact that she was one of a few named beneficiaries of his will apart from family members, when Lane left her ¤100, 'Sir Hugh Lane's Will. Large Bequests to Dublin. The Modern Art Gallery and a Codicil', *Irish Times*, 4 October 1915, 4.

15 Thomas Bodkin (1910) quoted in O' Neill, 'Sarah Cecilia Harrison', 68.

16 Barry, 'Female Suffrage from a Catholic Standpoint', 282.

17 Ward, *Unmanageable Revolutionaries*, 70.

18 Ryan, 'The "Irish Citizen"', 105.

19 Ryan, 'The "Irish Citizen", 109.

20 Grand, 'The New Aspect of the Woman Question', 272.

21 See Cusack, 'This Pernicious Tea Drinking Habit', 184.

22 Sutherland, *In Search of the New Woman*, 14.

23 Beeton, *Etiquette for Ladies*, 36.

24 W. B. Yeats quoted in Lewis, *The Yeats Sisters*, 86; Hardwick, *The Yeats Sisters*, 70.

25 Lewis, *The Yeats Sisters*, 85. Alexandra College offered girls further education.

26 Lewis, *The Yeats Sisters*, 85.

27 O'Riordan, 'Leisure with a Purpose', 211.

28 Susan L. Mitchell (1903), quoted in MacPherson, 'The Myriad-Minded Woman', 18. *The Irish Homestead* was founded by The Irish Agriculture Organization Society in 1895, a 'weekly newspaper for farmyard, field and fireside': Devereux, 'Cultural Virtues', 568.

29 Houston, *The Emancipation of Women*, 35.

30 *Dublin Review* 52, no. 103, 38–39.

31 Ferguson, 'Alexandra College, Dublin', 129; 'Alexandra College Dublin: Mission, Ethos, Values and Philosophy': https://www.alexandracollege.eu/Mission-Ethos-and-Philosophy/. Its values still include empowering girls and women and independent thinking, and it still needs a certain level of affluence to attend.

32 In 1909 it was replaced by the National University of Ireland.

33 'Minute Book of the Ladies' Institute', 141.

34 Provost & President, George Salmon 1888–1904 (c. 1819–1904), accessed 5 March 2020, https://www.tcd.ie/provost/history/former-provosts/g_salmon.php.

35 Parkes, ed., *A Danger to the Men?* 24. Thanks to Ellen O'Flaherty, Assistant Librarian (College Archives), Manuscripts & Archives Research Library, Trinity College Dublin, for this reference.

36 'Final Report of the Commissioners', 144.

37 'Honorary Degrees for Women', *Irish Times*, 9 July 1904, 18.

38 Women had been admitted to the University of London since 1868, but were only eligible to receive a Certificate of Proficiency.

39 'Honorary Degrees for Women', *Irish Times*, 9 July 1904, 18.

40 McManus reported in Turpin, 'The Royal Dublin Society', 6.

41 Turpin, 'The Royal Dublin Society', 7.

42 Fallon, 'Estella Solomons, Painter', 32.

43 'Irish Women Artists', 7. Walker's claim that 'It is an honourable fact that there has been no discrimination against women as artists, either professionally or politically, in Ireland' is somewhat overstated: Walker, 'Portrait of the Artist', 106.

44 'Irish Women Artists', 2.

45 O'Toole, *The Irish New Woman*, 2.

46 Ernest Renan argued in a paper delivered at the Sorbonne in 1882 that forgetting inconvenient history was a key factor in the formation of a nation: Renan, *Qu'est-ce Qu'une Nation?* (What Is a Nation?), 25.

47 Meaney, O'Dowd and Whelan, *Reading the Irish Woman*, 13, 14.

48 Dobbs, 'The Blue-Stockings', 81.

49 O' Toole, *The Irish New Woman*, 69.

50 McCabe, *Freeman's Journal*, 262–63. Archbishop McCabe was also quoted in 'Belfast News-Letter', 14 March 1881: see Ward, *Unmanageable Revolutionaries*, 23.

51 *Times*, October 1881, quoted in Ward, *Unmanageable Revolutionaries*, 22.

52 Valente, *The Myth of Manliness*, 47, 50.

53 Some of Lolly Yeats's own artwork survives, although little is in public collections, or reproduced.

54 Hardwick, *The Yeats Sisters*, viii, 65.

55 Hardwick, *The Yeats Sisters*, 63.

56 Hardwick, *The Yeats Sisters*, 65.

57 Hardwick, *The Yeats Sisters*, 61; Walker, 'Portrait of the Artist', 106; Lane, *Origins of Modern Irish Socialism*, 112–13: members of the Contemporary Club included Douglas Hyde, John B. Yeats and W. B. Yeats.

58 Lewis, *The Yeats Sisters*, 4.

59 Stevens, *Two Irish Girls in Bohemia*, 53.

60 Tusan, 'Inventing the New Woman', 169, 170.

61 Tusan, 'Inventing the New Woman', 170.

62 *Shafts* 1 (1892), quoted in Flint, *The Woman Reader*, 153.

63 Tusan, 'Inventing the New Woman', 170.

64 Tusan, 'Inventing the New Woman', 174.

65 Nelson, *A New Woman Reader*, ix; O'Toole, *The Irish New Woman*, 3.

66 Heilmann, *New Woman Strategies*, 4.

67 Heilmann, *New Woman Strategies*, 239n.17.

68 Grand, 'The New Aspect of the Woman Question', 271.

69 Ouida, 'The New Woman', 610–19.

70 Grand, 'The New Aspect of the Woman Question', 270–71.

71 Mitchell, 'The "New Woman" as Prometheus', 4.

72 Ouida, 'The New Woman', 613.

73 Ouida, 'The New Woman', 614.

74 Tusan, 'Inventing the New Woman', 175.

75 Sutherland, *In Search of the New Woman*, 5.

76 'New Light on the "New Woman"', 548.

77 Nelson, *A New Woman Reader*, ix.

78 Butler, 'Irishwomen and the Home Language', 6.

79 Butler, 'Irishwomen and the Home Language', 4.

80 Austen, *Pride and Prejudice*, 39.

81 Austen, *Mansfield Park*, 15.

82 Eliot, *Adam Bede*, 148.

83 Cruse, *The Victorians and Their Reading*, 349.

84 Cobbe, 'Our Policy: An Address to Women Concerning the Suffrage', 3-8; Cobbe, 'Why Women Desire the Franchise', 1–4; Cruse, *The Victorians and Their Reading*, 344–45; Cruse, *The Victorians and Their Reading*, 350.

85 'Lily Yeats Books', *Anne Yeats gift (1996)*, National Gallery of Ireland: Yeats Archive, 346–47.

86 Stevens, *Two Irish Girls in Bohemia*, 32.

87 Humphry, *A Word to Women*, 61–62.

88 Humphry, *A Word to Women*, 13.

89 Murdoch, *Daily Life of Victorian Women*, 158.

90 Humphry, *A Word to Women*, 73.

91 Humphry, *A Word to Women*, 79.

92 See Flaubert, *Madame Bovary*, 47; Tolstoy, *Anna Karenina*, 98.

93 James, *Portrait of a Lady*, v–xviii.

94 O' Toole, *The Irish New Woman*, 70–71; Gifra-Adroher and Hurtley, *Hannah Lynch and Spain*, 41n.40.

95 Gifra-Adroher and Hurtley, *Hannah Lynch and Spain*, 15; O'Toole, *The Irish New Woman*, 71.

96 Gifra-Adroher and Hurtley, *Hannah Lynch and Spain*, 17.

97 Lynch, *The Prince of the Glades – II*, 12–13.

98 Grand, 'The Undefinable', 37.

99 Grand, 'The Undefinable', 38.

100 Grand, 'The Undefinable', 49.

101 Grand, 'The Undefinable', 50.

102 Stevens, *Two Irish Girls in Bohemia*, 65.

103 Somerville and Ross, *The Real Charlotte*, 88.

104 Somerville and Ross, *The Real Charlotte*, 301, 353.

105 Somerville and Ross, *The Real Charlotte*, 15.

106 Somerville and Ross, *The Real Charlotte*, 32.

107 Rains, 'Irish Media History'.

108 Rains, 'Irish Media History'.

109 Pollock, *Mary Cassatt*, 144.

110 *La fille de Montmartre* can be viewed at: https://www.pinterest.co.uk/pin/4035648 16594576681/.

111 Mitchell, 'The "New Woman" as Prometheus', 8.

112 Examples cited by Brown of women readers depicted in Parisian cafes are all by male artists: see Brown, *Women Readers in French Painting*, 30–39, figures 1.6–1.10. The association of the New Woman with public café life was much less common in Dublin at this time than in Paris. Eighteenth-century Dublin had a lively café culture with a male clientele, but by the early nineteenth century they were replaced by taverns, hotels and restaurants: Kennedy, 'Dublin's Coffee Houses', 37. Ernest Bewley's first Oriental Cafes, patronised by the Protestant elite, opened in the 1890s.

113 Brown, *Women Readers in French Painting*, 206.

114 Collins, 'Athletic Fashion', 315, 321, 326.

115 Stevens, *The Irish Scene*, 75.

116 Collins, 'Athletic Fashion, 311.

117 The Latin phrase *nosce te ipsum* means 'know yourself'.

118 Collins, 'Athletic Fashion, 331–32.

119 Scully, 'A Comic Empire', 8; Introduction to this volume.

120 A Lady, 'Talk of Town', *Irish Times*, 2 February 1895, 5.

4. The Silent Reader and the Fictive Viewer

1   Bollmann, *Reading Women*, 26–27.
2   Potter, 'Limerick City Municipal Library', 100; Ó Ciosáin, 'Varieties of Literacy', 15.
3   Jajdelska, *Silent Reading*, 3.
4   Jajdelska, *Silent Reading*, 3.
5   See Jajdelska, *Silent Reading*, 4.
6   James, *Portrait of a Lady*, Preface, xiii.
7   Henry James quoted in Vanderlaan, 'The Painter Henry James Might Have Been', 3.
8   Vanderlaan, 'The Painter Henry James Might Have Been', 3.
9   James, *Portrait of a Lady*, Preface, xvii.
10   Greg, 'False Morality of Lady Novelists', 83–84.
11   Tucker, 'The "Invisible Movement That Reading Is" ', 309.
12   Tucker, citing Johann Adam Bergk, 'The "Invisible Movement That Reading Is" ', 315.
13   Bollmann, *Reading Women*, 23.
14   Leerssen, 'Lebowski's Rug and the Book', 334.
15   Lynch, *Loving Literature*, 4.
16   Rothman, 'The History of "Loving" to Read'.
17   Lynch, *Loving Literature*, 9–10.
18   Murphy, 'Lady Charlotte Stopford', 239.
19   Murphy, 'Lady Charlotte Stopford', 243.
20   Benedict Anderson argued that people's collective sense of reading the same newspapers contributed to the formation of national identities: Anderson, *Imagined Communities*, 34–36.
21   Fried, *Absorption and Theatricality*, 50.
22   Abbé Marc-Antoine Laugier (1753) quoted in Fried, *Absorption and Theatricality*, 11.
23   Crary, *Techniques of the Observer*, 5–6, 15.
24   See Foucault, *History of Sexuality*.
25   Contemporary press reports of women's exhibited work provide examples (see Chapter 5).
26   Fried, *Absorption and Theatricality*, 103. In his preface to the Penguin edition of *Portrait of a Lady*, Henry James similarly refers to casting 'a spell' on the attention of the audience: James, *Portrait of a Lady*, Preface, xv.
27   Scott, 'Victorian Yellowbacks', 266–67. Sensation novels were a Victorian literary genre of the 1860s–1880s that depended on dramatic and shocking plots.
28   John Butler Yeats was born in Co. Down in 1839. He was educated at Trinity College and the King's Inns, Dublin, becoming a barrister, before switching to art and attending Heatherley's Academy, the Slade School of Fine Art and the Royal Academy Schools in London. He moved to Howth, Co. Dublin, then Dublin and later to the United States. For further details, see: Murphy, *Prodigal Father*.
29   Docherty, 'Women as Readers', 340.
30   Docherty, 'Women as Readers', 363.
31   Docherty, 'Women as Readers', 370.
32   Golden, *Images of the Woman Reader*, 141.
33   Golden, *Images of the Woman Reader*, 150–55.
34   *The Writer* can be viewed at: https://www.adams.ie/68321/Estella-Frances-Solomons-HRHA-1882-1968-The-Writer.

35   The National Portrait Gallery, London has 13 photographic portraits of Georgina Hariot. This one can be seen at: https://www.npg.org.uk/collections/search/portr ait/mw184987/Hariot-Georgina-ne-Rowan-Hamilton-Marchioness-of-Dufferin-and-Ava?LinkID=mp52511&role=sit&rNo=5.

36   John B. Yeats himself was a reader, his library including books on art, mathematics and travel writing: 'John Butler Yeats Library', *National Gallery of Ireland, Anne Yeats gift (1996), National Gallery of Ireland: Yeats Archive*, IE/NGI/Y1, 24.3, 343–45.

37   Yeats, *Essays Irish and American*, 5, 7.

38   The black mantilla can also indicate widowed status, but the artist, Maria Spilsbury, pre-deceased Henrietta's husband Henry by a few days in June 1820.

39   She wears a black dress and red-edged cap with a red shawl: colours in the portrait are referenced in O'Grady, *Life and Work of Sarah Purser*, 195.

40   Purser, *Jellett, O'Brien, Purser and Stokes*, caption to Plate 3. Michael Purser recalled that Sarah Purser and her mother were 'not on good terms' according to his aunt, Dr Honor Purser, Sarah Purser's doctor: postcard to author, n.d.

41   O'Connor, *The Irish Dancing*, 8.

42   Schapiro, *Words and Pictures*, 38–39.

43   Schapiro, *Words and Pictures*, 45. The context in which each is used is important and there will be an interplay between context and features that typically characterise the form: Schapiro, *Words and Pictures*, 45.

44   Schapiro, *Words and Pictures*, 39.

45   Sketchbook C, 1881, Gorry Collection Dublin: details and illustration in: O'Grady, *Sarah Purser*, 176–77.

46   *Study of a Young French Woman* can be viewed at: https://www.adams.ie/Sarah-Cecilia-Harrison-1863-1941-Study-of-a-young-French-woman.

47   Whytes, 'Portrait of a Young Lady Reading', accessed 12 November 2020, https://www.whytes.ie/art/portrait-of-a-young-lady-reading/146418/?SearchString=&LotNumSearch=&GuidePrice=&OrderBy=HL&ArtistID=&ArrangeBy=list&NumPerPage=1000&offset=23.

48   Sonstroem, 'Teeth in Victorian Art', 363, 365.

49   Lipstick was commercially manufactured in Paris by the late nineteenth century.

50   Mulholland, 'Irish Painters', 484.

51   O'Conor was introduced in Chapter 1 and Solomons is discussed in some detail in Chapter 5. Little is known about Katherine McCausland and writing about her seems scant. She was born in Dublin in 1859 into a professional legal family. She studied at the Académie Julian, Paris and moved to France, although she retained connections with Ireland. For further details, see Campbell, 'Compagnons de Voyage'.

52   *Girl Reading* can be viewed at: https://www.sothebys.com/en/auctions/ecatalogue/2018/irish-art-l18134/lot.16.html.

53   O'Conor was educated at a Catholic boys' boarding school in York. As heir to an estate of 1,800 acres and recipient of a family allowance, O'Conor did not have to earn a living from his art: Benington, *Roderic O'Conor*, 19–21, 23.

54   See Crary, *Techniques of the Observer*, 92.

55   Solomons also painted her younger brother Bethel sitting in his coat with a fur collar.

56   Gorry Gallery Exhibition Catalogue, 38.

57   Campbell, 'Compagnons de Voyage', 100, 102.

58   Campbell, 'Compagnons de Voyage', 100, 103. She lent a painting of Breton women to Hugh Lane for his 'Exhibition of Irish Art' in London in 1904: ibid., 103.

59   *Paul César Helleu.* Drypoint involved drawing or incising a design on a copper plate.
60   Paul Cesar Helleu also depicted his wife in emphatic hats, for instance, *Madame Helleu au chapeau bleu* (Madame Helleu in a blue hat).
61   *Ellen à la lecture* (c. 1902–3) would also form a nice contrast, but was not available to reproduce.
62   This is the case in certain European images of women readers, as observed in Chapter 2.
63   Eitner, citing A. W. Schlegel, 'The Open Window', 286.
64   Estella Solomons and her work are considered in some detail in Chapter 5.
65   Barnaby, 'Dresses and Drapery', 99.
66   For instance, in the work of the German artists, Georg Friedrich Kersting and Franz Ludwig Catel. A swag was a decorative curtain draped in a curve between two points.
67   See Cieraad, 'Dutch Windows', 47.
68   Kathleen Goodfellow sometimes took a male pseudonym, Michael Scot.

5. A Room of Her Own: Four New Women in Dublin

1   Woolf, *A Room of One's Own*, 2.
2   Woolf, *A Room of One's Own*, 34–35, 105–6.
3   Woolf, *A Room of One's Own*, 5–6.
4   Hardwick, *The Yeats Sisters*, 70.
5   Lewis, *The Yeats Sisters*, 2.
6   John B. Yeats, quoted in Lewis, *The Yeats Sisters*, 41.
7   *Irish Women's Writing Network.*
8   Stevens, *Two Irish Girls in Bohemia*, 26.
9   Colman, 'Far from Silent', 203–4. The *Irish Monthly* encouraged women's writing: ibid., 204.
10   Colman, 'Far from Silent', 206.
11   Morris, *Alice Milligan*, 18–19.
12   Ward, *Maud Gonne*, 67.
13   Marsh's Library Catalogue, accessed 7 January 2020, http://marshlibrary.ie/catalo gue/Search/Results?lookfor=Poisoners+and+propagandists and http://marshlibr ary.ie/catalogue/Search/Results?lookfor=+Angelica+Kauffmann It is probable that works produced in the late nineteenth century would have been bought for the library soon after publication: Amy Boylan, Assistant Librarian, Marsh's Library, St Patrick's Close, Dublin: email communication to author, 7 October 2020.
14   Fallon, 'Estella Solomons, Painter', 38.
15   Sisley, 'Portraits of National Interest', 37.
16   'Social Notes' quoted in Cappock, 'Sarah Cecilia Harrison', 78.
17   'Royal Hibernian Academy: Opening of Exhibition', *Irish Times*, 5 March 1912, 6.
18   'Royal Dublin Society School of Art: Distribution of Prizes', *Irish Times*, 29 February 1876, 6.
19   'Royal Dublin Society School of Art: Distribution of Prizes', *Irish Times*, 29 February 1876, 6.
20   *Daily Express* (1884) quoted in O'Grady, *Life and Work of Sarah Purser*, 60.
21   Mulholland, 'Irish Painters', 481, 483.
22   'National Gallery of Ireland: A Lady Governor', *Irish Times*, 3 February 1914, 4.
23   Royal Hibernian Academy Exhibition catalogue, 77th Annual Exhibition, 1906. *Royal Hibernian Academy of Arts: Index of Exhibitors 1826-1979, III.*

24 'An Irish Lady Portraitist', *Irish Times*, 20 April 1906, 7. It has not been possible to identify this portrait.

25 Exhibition catalogue listing paintings and etchings by Estella Solomons and works by Mary Duncan and Albert Power, TCD MSS 4649a/4567; 'Exhibition of Paintings, Etchings, and Sculpture', *Irish Times*, 4 February 1914, 9.

26 'Exhibition of Paintings, Etchings, and Sculpture', *Irish Times*, 4 February 1914, 9.

27 Exhibition catalogue listing paintings and etchings by Estella Solomons and works by Mary Duncan and Albert Power, TCD MSS 4649a/4567. *Parknasilla* can be viewed at: http://adams.auctioneersvault.com/catalogues/70714/files/assets/common/downloads/page0059.pdf.

28 'News of the Week: Dublin', *Irish Times*, 14 February 1914, 2.

29 Crampton Walker, 'Our Picture Gallery', 353.

30 Crampton Walker, 'Our Picture Gallery', 354.

31 Solomons later painted Bodkin's portrait, now in The Model gallery, Sligo, Ireland.

32 'The Art of Estella Solomons and Mary Duncan' by Thomas Bodkin, *The Irish Statesman*, 1 November 1919, 464, in Seumas O' Sullivan and Estella Solomons, Press Cuttings, TCD MSS 4652b.

33 O' Grady, *Life and Work of Sarah Purser*, 15.

34 O' Grady, *Life and Work of Sarah Purser*, 21–22.

35 O' Grady, *Life and Work of Sarah Purser*, 23.

36 Kimberly Griffith, 'Miss Jane Barlow D.Litt.', Online Coffee Conversation, Hugh Lane Gallery, 17 June 2020.

37 Sarah Purser quoted in Lindie Naughton, 'I Went Through British Aristocracy Like Measles Claimed Irish Artist Sarah Purser', *The Herald*, 8 March 1917, 6.

38 Kimberly Griffith, 'Miss Jane Barlow D.Litt.', Online Coffee Conversation, Hugh Lane Gallery, 17 June 2020.

39 'Famous Irish Woman Artist Dead', *Sunday Independent*, 8 August 1943.

40 Walker, 'Portrait of the Artist', 106.

41 West, *Portraiture*, 145.

42 Woolf, *A Room of One's Own*, 105–6.

43 *Co-op Ireland*, 9.

44 Purser, *Jellett, O' Brien, Purser and Stokes*, 117.

45 O' Grady, *Life and Work of Sarah Purser*, 106.

46 'Leader Page Parade', *Spectator*, n.d., c. 1943 [extract in Hugh Lane Gallery archives]. Mespil House was later demolished and some of its grand ceilings reused for the State Apartments of Dublin Castle: 'Taoiseach unveils plaque', *Irish Times*, 21 July 1976, 11.

47 Brian Fallon, 'A Painter and a Fighter', *Irish Times*, 17 December 1996.

48 'Leader Page Parade', *Spectator*, n.d., c. 1943 [extract in archives of Hugh Lane Gallery].

49 Michael Purser, Sarah Purser's nephew, personal conversation, 22 October 2019.

50 Brian Inglis (1962) quoted in 'Taoiseach unveils plaque', *Irish Times*, 21 July 1976, 11.

51 Brian Fallon, 'A painter and a fighter', *Irish Times*, 17 December 1996.

52 Ward, *Maud Gonne*, 52.

53 Brian Fallon, 'The Female Vision', *Irish Times*, 1 May 1990, 9.

54 Purser, *Jellett, O'Brien, Purser and Stokes*, 115.

55 Michael Purser, Sarah Purser's nephew, conversation with author, 22 October 2019.

56 Purser, *Jellett, O'Brien, Purser and Stokes*, 116, 120.

57 O'Grady, *Life and Work of Sarah Purser*, 66.

58   'Death of Miss Sarah Purser', *Irish Press*, 9 August 1943.

59   *Co-op Ireland*, 9.

60   'Death of Miss Sarah Purser', *Irish Press*, 9 August 1943.

61   O'Grady, *Life and Work of Sarah Purser*, 55.

62   Purser, *Jellett, O'Brien, Purser and Stokes*, 117.

63   Sarah Purser quoted in O'Grady, *Life and Work of Sarah Purser*, 97–98.

64   'Irish Art Gallery at Franco British Exhibition', *Irish Times*, 1 July 1908, 7.

65   'Irish Art Gallery at Franco British Exhibition', *Irish Times*, 1 July 1908, 7.

66   D.S. McColl quoted in Hugh P. Lane, 'Prefatory Notes'. Lane was subsequently angered by the failure of Dublin Corporation to provide a permanent building and bequeathed works to the London National Gallery and other property to the National Gallery of Ireland instead of the Dublin Modern Art Gallery, 'Sir Hugh Lane's Will. Large Bequests to Dublin. The Modern Art Gallery and a Codicil', *Irish Times*, 4 October 1915, 4–5. Lane's will and codicil were disputed. Later, Purser's suggestion that Charlemont House, recently occupied by a government department, should house the Municipal Gallery of Modern Art was taken up by William Cosgrave and others who donated the building to Dublin Corporation for an art gallery: O'Grady, *Life and Work of Sarah Purser*, 136.

67   Stephen Gwynn (London 1926), quoted in O'Grady, *Life and Work of Sarah Purser*, 78.

68   O'Grady, *Life and Work of Sarah Purser*, 211. Women readers frequented Marsh's Library Dublin, but a search in the Visitors' Books for 1891–1892 found Sarah Purser had not visited: Amy Boylan, Assistant Librarian, Marsh's Library, email correspondence with author, 7 October 2020.

69   *Young Lady in an Interior* can be viewed at: http://www.artnet.com/artists/sarah-henrietta-purser/young-lady-in-an-interior-reading-a-book; *Young Woman Reading* is catalogued in O' Grady, *Life and Work of Sarah Purser*, 233, cat. n. 318, but no image is available.

70   Letters Jane Barlow to Sarah Purser 1897, NLI MSS 8186 (7).

71   Barlow's play 'A Bunch of Lavender' was performed in Dublin in December 1911, 'Theatre of Ireland. Production of Two Plays', *Irish Times*, 19 December 1911, 8.

72   Griffith, "Miss Jane Barlow D.Litt.'.

73   Griffith, "Miss Jane Barlow D.Litt.'.

74   Griffith, "Miss Jane Barlow D.Litt.'.

75   Clarke, 'Jane Barlow'.

76   Letters Jane Barlow to Sarah Purser 1895, NLI MSS 8186 (4).

77   Benedict Kiely, 'Lisconnell on the Bog: Ninety Years Ago', *Irish Times*, 20 April 1984, 12.

78   O'Grady, *Life and Work of Sarah Purser*, 73. See also: Tynan, *Memories*, 291.

79   'Lady Aberdeen in the North. Visit to Inniskeen', *Irish Times*, 12 June 1894, 5; 'Lady Aberdeen's Tour. Visit to Glencolumbkille', *Irish Times*, 15 June 1894, 5.

80   Residents of a house 2 in Ballyhoey [sic] (Howth, Dublin), http://www.census.nationalarchives.ie/ (accessed 15 November 2019). At the time of the 1911 census, Jane Barlow lived with her father, her sister, two brothers and five resident servants: Residents of a house 1 in Ballyhoy (Howth, Dublin), http://www.census.nationalarchives.ie/ (accessed 15 November 2019).

81   Letters Jane Barlow to Sarah Purser 1895, NLI MSS 8186 (4).

82   Letters Jane Barlow to Sarah Purser 1897, NLI MSS 8186 (9). Purser's friendship with Barlow lasted until Barlow's death in 1917: Letters to Sarah Purser from Katherine Barlow: Sarah Purser Papers, 1848–1943, NLI MSS 10,201 (2).

83 Letters Jane Barlow to Sarah Purser 1895, NLI MSS 8186 (4).

84 Letters Jane Barlow to Sarah Purser 1895, NLI MSS 8186 (3).

85 Letters Jane Barlow to Sarah Purser 1897, NLI MSS 8186 (7).

86 Letters Jane Barlow to Sarah Purser 1897, NLI MSS 8186 (7).

87 Letters Jane Barlow to Sarah Purser 1898, NLI MSS 8186 (10).

88 'A Celtic Christmas', *Irish Times*, 6 December 1905.

89 Clarke, 'Jane Barlow'. The idea and title for *Irish Idylls* were suggested to her by Sir William Robertson Nicoll, a Scottish Free Church minister and literary editor, who sent her a copy of J. M. Barrie's book, *Auld Licht Idylls*: 'Obituary' [Miss Jane Barlow], *The Irish Book Lover* 8, nos. 11–12 (June–July 1917): 141–42.

90 The fourth number of the *Alexandra College Magazine*, with one of the main items a story by Barlow, was warmly anticipated, *Irish Times*, 2 June 1894, 5.

91 O'Grady, *Life and Work of Sarah Purser*, 99, 243.

92 Letters Jane Barlow to Sarah Purser 1897, NLI MSS 8186 (9).

93 Letters Jane Barlow to Sarah Purser 1897, NLI MSS 8186 (9).

94 Wilson Foster, *Irish Novels*, 3.

95 Clarke, 'Jane Barlow'.

96 Barlow, *Irish Idylls*, 1–2.

97 'Jane Barlow's Irish Idylls', *The Morning Leader*, 27 January 1896, Press cutting for Miss J. Barlow, Durant's Press Cuttings, NLI MSS 8186 (3).

98 Benedict Kiely, 'Lisconnell on the Bog: Ninety Years Ago', *Irish Times*, 20 April 1984, 12.

99 W .B. Yeats quoted in Clarke, 'Jane Barlow'.

100 Griffith, "Miss Jane Barlow D.Litt.'.

101 M. R., 'Cabinet of Irish Literature', 339. The date usually cited for the revised edition is 1905. However, this review was published in 1903.

102 Cappock, 'Sarah Cecilia Harrison', 73.

103 Letters Jane Barlow to Sarah Purser 1894, NLI MSS 8186 (2); 1888-1893, NLI MSS 8186 (1).

104 Letters Jane Barlow to Sarah Purser 1894, NLI MSS 8186 (2).

105 Letters Jane Barlow to Sarah Purser 1888–1893, NLI MSS 8186 (1).

106 Letters Jane Barlow to Sarah Purser 1894, NLI MSS 8186 (2).

107 Letters Jane Barlow to Sarah Purser 1888–1893, NLI MSS 8186 (1).

108 Letters Jane Barlow to Sarah Purser 1888–1893, NLI MSS 8186 (1).

109 Letters Jane Barlow to Sarah Purser 1888-1893, NLI MSS 8186 (1). The content of this letter suggests it might have been written in 1894, despite its filing as before 1893.

110 Letters Jane Barlow to Sarah Purser 1895, NLI MSS 8186 (3).

111 Letters Jane Barlow to Sarah Purser 1898, NLI MSS 8186 (10).

112 Logan Sisley, conversation with author at the Hugh Lane Gallery, 29 January 2020.

113 Stephen Gwynn (London 1926), quoted in O'Grady, *Life and Work of Sarah Purser*, 78.

114 Griffith, "Miss Jane Barlow D.Litt.'.

115 George du Maurier, *Fin de Siècle*, scanned by George P. Landow for *Victorian Web*: www.victorianweb.org/art/illustration/dumaurier/47.html.

116 Letters Jane Barlow to Sarah Purser 1894, NLI MSS 8186 (2). This was written in 1894 according to the library file, so either the oil portrait of Jane Barlow had been completed by July or more than one portrait of her had been executed. It is more likely the year was 1895 as in a black-bordered letter of 9 December 1894 Jane

Barlow thanks Sarah Purser for pictures received safely of her mother (painted posthumously) and her father.

117 O'Grady, *Life and Work of Sarah Purser*, 82, 136.

118 Commonplace Books, TCD, MSS (4499–4508), 4500, 4501.

119 John Crampton Walker, 'Our Picture Gallery', *Irish Life*, 1917, 354.

120 The *Cork Examiner* interviewing Estella Solomons later in her life reported that she 'expressed admiration for [Augustus] John as a great artist and as a teacher who inspired his pupils': 'Art of Estella Solomons', *Cork Examiner*, 27 February 1935.

121 Beatrice Elvery, quoted in Dalton, *Irish Women Artists*, 56.

122 Róisín Kennedy, 'Estella Solomons: A portrait of the artist as a Republican', *Irish Independent*, 21 January 2016, 13.

123 Pyle, *Portraits of Patriots*, 6.

124 Fallon, 'Estella Solomons, Painter', 34.

125 'Gaelic League Art Exhibition', *Irish Times*, 23 October 1911, 10; Pyle, *Estella Solomons*, 10.

126 Sketchbooks of Estella Solomons (1905–1953), TCD, (MSS 4509-31), MS 4509, 6 verso. In the same sketchbook, there is a woman standing with a book in her hands, roughly executed in soft purple pencil: Sketchbooks of Estella Solomons (1905-1953), TCD, MS 4509, 21 verso.

127 Sketchbooks of Estella Solomons (1905–1953), TCD, MSS 4509-31. Her handwriting similarly seems impulsive and forceful, straying from the margins: see for example: Handwritten letter from Gr. Central Hotel, London, to James Starkey, 80 Rathmines Road, Dublin, postmarked 21 August 1916, TCD MSS 4630-4649, 4631/375.

128 Sketchbooks of Estella Solomons (1905–1953), TCD, MSS 4509-31, MS 4509, 6 verso.

129 Sketchbooks of Estella Solomons (1905–1953), TCD, MSS 4526, 19 verso.

130 Sketchbooks of Estella Solomons (1905–1953), TCD, MSS 4526, 20 verso.

131 Sketchbooks of Estella Solomons (1905-1953), TCD, MSS 4515, 7 recto; 4519, 5 recto; 4522, 46 verso; 54 recto; 58 verso.

132 Sketchbooks of Estella Solomons (1905–1953), TCD, MSS 4521, loose sheets, n.p.

133 Sketchbooks of Estella Solomons (1905-1953), TCD, MS 4522, 19 recto.

134 Ryan, 'The "Irish Citizen"', 107.

135 Kennedy, 'Estella Solomons', 13.

136 Pyle, *Portraits of Patriots*, 22.

137 Handwritten letter from John Lavery, 5 Cromwell Place, London S.W., to Miss Estella F. Solomons, Irish National Aid Association, 10 Exchequer Street, Dublin, 21 August 1916, TCD MSS 4630-4649, 4631/374.

138 Handwritten letter from Gr. Central Hotel, London, to James Starkey, 80 Rathmines Road, Dublin, postmarked 21 August 1916, TCD MSS 4630-4649, 4631/375.

139 Handwritten note in pencil addressed on one side to 'Miss Solomons' and signed 'Jack', n.d., TCD MSS 4630-4649, 3863.

140 Solomons did many sketches and an oil portrait of Moppy; one of her sketches shows Moppy in a deckchair: Sketchbooks of Estella Solomons (1905-1953), TCD, MSS 4521, loose sheet, n.p.

141 Leventhal, 'Seumas O' Sullivan', 12.

142 Morris, *Alice Milligan*, 24–25.

143 Milligan and Milligan, *Glimpses of Erin*.

144   Morris, *Alice Milligan*, 26.

145   Morris, *Alice Milligan*, 29.

146   Alice Milligan quoted in Pyle, 'Alice Milligan', 92.

147   Morris, *Alice Milligan*, 15.

148   Morris, *Alice Milligan*, 35, Johnston, *Alice*, 70–71.

149   Quoted in Morris, *Alice Milligan*, 47.

150   Morris, *Alice Milligan*, 206.

151   Pyle, 'Alice Milligan', 93.

152   Alice Milligan quoted in Pyle, 'Alice Milligan', 93.

153   Alice Milligan quoted in Morris, *Alice Milligan*, 48.

154   Morris, *Alice Milligan*, 48.

155   'Estella Frances Solomons ARHA', catalogue no. 217, *Royal Hibernian Academy of Arts: Index of Exhibitors 1826–1979, III*.

156   'Art in Dublin. Exhibition by Miss E. Solomons and Miss M. Duncan', *Freeman's Journal*, 27 October 1919, 4.

157   'The Royal Hibernian Academy. Annual Exhibition.', *Irish Times*, 31 March 1919, 4.

158   'National Gallery of Ireland: A Lady Governor', *Irish Times*, 3 February 1914, 4.

159   'National Gallery of Ireland', *Irish Times*, 15 February 1919, 2.

160   'Death of Miss Sarah Purser', *Irish Press*, 9 August 1943.

161   See Cullen, *The Irish Face*, 2004.

162   Barlow's portrait is in the Hugh Lane Gallery Dublin and Milligan's is at the Ulster Museum, Belfast.

WORKS REFERENCED

Archival Sources

Hugh Lane City Gallery, Dublin: Archives library
    Miscellaneous files relating to Sarah Purser
Marsh's Library, Dublin
    Visitor Books, 1860s–1890s
National Archives
    Minute Book of the Dublin Women's Suffrage Association / Irish Women's Suffrage
        and Local Government Association (1876–1913).
National Gallery of Ireland, Dublin
    Yeats Archive, IE/NGI/Y1
National Library of Ireland, Dublin: Manuscripts library
    Letters: Jane Barlow to Sarah Purser, 1893–1916, – NLI MSS 8186–8188
    Sarah Purser Papers, 1848–1943, NLI MSS 10,201 (2)
Trinity College, Dublin: Manuscripts and Archives library
    Commonplace Books – Estella Solomons, TCD MSS 4499–4508.
    Press Cuttings Seumas O'Sullivan and Estella Solomons, TCD MSS 4652a–f.
    Sketchbooks of Estella Solomons, TCD MSS 4509–4531.
    Solomons papers TCD MSS 4630–4649b

Printed Sources

Anderson, Benedict. *Imagined Communities: Reflections on the Origin and Spread of Nationalism*, London: Verso, rev. edn, 1991.
'Anna Maria Hall author of "Lights and Shadows of Irish Life"', *Drawn to the Page: Irish Artists and Illustration 1830–1930*. Accessed 30 July 2019. https://dttp.tcd.ie/catalog/illustration%20114.
Arnold, Bruce. *Jack Yeats*, New Haven, CT: Yale University Press, 1998.
Arnold, Matthew. *The Study of Celtic Literature*, popular edn, London: Smith, Elder & Co., [1867] 1891. Accessed 10 October 2020. http://www.gutenberg.org/files/5159/5159-h/5159-h.htm.
'Art of Estella Solomons', *Cork Examiner*, 27 February 1935.
Arthur, Timothy Shay. *Advice to Young Men on Their Duties and Conduct in Life*, Boston, MA: N.C. Barton, 1848.
Austen, Jane. *Pride and Prejudice*, London: Penguin Classics, [1813] 2003.

————. *Mansfield Park*, Ware, Hertfordshire: Wordsworth Editions, [1814] 1992.

Barlow, Jane. *Irish Idylls*, New York: Dodd, Mead & Co. Leopold Classic Library [1894, facsimile].

Barnaby, Alice. 'Dresses and Drapery: Female Self-Fashioning in Muslin, 1800–1850'. In *Crafting the Woman Professional in the Long Nineteenth Century: Artistry and Industry in Britain*, edited by Kyriaki Hadjiafxendi and Patricia Zakreski, 89–106. London: Routledge, [2013] 2016.

Barr, Rebecca Anne, Sarah-Anne Buckley and Muireann O'Cinneide, eds, *Literacy, Language and Reading in Nineteenth-Century Ireland*, Liverpool: Liverpool University Press, 2019.

Barrett, Sean D. 'John Kells Ingram (1823–1907)', *Hermathena*, no. 164 (Summer 1998): 5–30.

Barrie, J. M. *Auld Licht Idylls*, [1888], London: Hodder and Stoughton, 1929.

Barry, David. 'Female Suffrage from a Catholic Standpoint', *Irish Ecclesiastical Record* 27, September 1909. In *Women in Ireland, 1800–1918: A Documentary History*, edited by Maria Luddy, 280–83. Cork: Cork University Press, 1995.

Beeton, Samuel Orchart. *Etiquette for Ladies: A Complete Guide to Visiting, Entertaining, and Travelling, with Hints on Courtship, Marriage, and Dress*, Oxford: Old House, [1876] 2011.

Benington, Jonathan. *Roderic O'Conor: A Biography, with a Catalogue of His Work*, Dublin: Irish Academic Press, 1992.

Beynon, John. *Masculinities and Culture*, Buckingham: Open University Press, 2002.

Biletz, Frank A. 'Women and Irish-Ireland: The Domestic Nationalism of Mary Butler', *New Hibernia Review* 6, no. 1 (Spring 2002): 59–72.

Birmingham, George A. *Irishmen All*, London: T. N. Foulis, 1913.

Bollmann, Stefan. *Reading Women*, London: Merrell, 2006 [first published in Munich, 2005 as *Frauen, die lessen, sind gefährlich: Women Who Read Are Dangerous*].

Brabazon, Reginald, 12th Earl of Meath. *Memories of the Nineteenth Century*, London: John Murray, 1923.

————. *Brabazon Potpourri*, London: Hutchinson, [1902] 1928.

Brady, Sara. 'Home and Away: The Gaelic Games, Gender, and Migration', *New Hibernia Review* 11, no. 3 (Autumn 2007): 28–43.

Breen, Mary Catherine. 'The Making and Unmaking of an Irish Woman of Letters', PhD thesis, Linacre College Oxford, 2012.

Brief Memorials of the Rev. B.W. Mathias, Late Chaplain, Bethesda Chapel, Dublin: William Curry, 1842.

'British Parliamentary Orators: Sir Robert Peel, Daniel O'Connell, Henry Grattan', *Illustrated Magazine of Art* 4, no. 22 (1854): 205–6.

Brookes, John. *Manliness and Culture*, 3rd edn, London: James Blackwood, 1877.

Brown, Kathryn. *Women Readers in French Painting 1870–1890: A Space for the Imagination*, London: Routledge, [2012] 2016.

Brown, Stephen J. 'The Question of Irish Nationality', *Studies: An Irish Quarterly Review* 1, no. 4 (December 1912): 634–54.

Butler, Mary E. L. 'Irishwomen and the Home Language', *All Ireland Review* 1, no. 50 (15 December 1900): 6; no. 52 (29 December 1900): 4–5.

Cairns, David, and Shaun Richards. *Writing Ireland: Colonialism, Nationalism and Culture*, Manchester: Manchester University Press, 1988.

Campbell, Julian. 'Compagnons de Voyage'. *Irish Arts Review* 25, no. 4 (Winter 2008): 100–103.

Camplin, Jamie, and Maria Ranauro. *Books Do Furnish a Painting*, London: Thames and Hudson, 2018.

Cappock, Margarita. 'Sarah Cecilia Harrison: Artist, Social Campaigner and City Councillor'. In *Revolutionary States: Home Rule and Modern Ireland*, edited by Logan Sisley, 71–89. Dublin: Hugh Lane Dublin City Gallery, 2012.

Carleton, William. *Father Butler: The Lough Dearg Pilgrim. Being Sketches of Irish Manners*, Dublin: William Curry Jun, 1829.

Carton, Richard Paul, K. C., Judge, the Late. 'Novels and Novel Readers', *Irish Monthly* 35, no. 407 (May 1907): 237–49.

———. 'Novels and Novel Readers Part II', *Irish Monthly* 35, no. 408 (June 1907): 309–18.

Cieraad, Irene. 'Dutch Windows: Female Virtue and Female Vice'. In *At Home: An Anthropology of Domestic Space*, edited by Irene Cieraad, 31–52. Syracuse New York: Syracuse University Press, [1999] 2006.

Clarke, Frances. 'Jane Barlow', *The Dictionary of Irish Biography*. Accessed 1 December 2021. https://dib.cambridge.org/viewReadPage.do?articleId=a0374&searchClicked=clicked&quickadvsearch=yes.

Coalter, Mark. 'Reviews: Museum Eye', *History Ireland* 13, no. 4 (2005). Accessed 1 December 2021. https://www.historyireland.com/volume-13/museum-eye-4/.

Cobbe, Frances Power. 'Our Policy: An Address to Women Concerning the Suffrage', *LSE Selected Pamphlets* (1870).

———. 'Why Women Desire the Franchise', *LSE Selected Pamphlets* (1877).

Collins, Tracy J.R. 'Athletic Fashion, "Punch" and the Creation of the New Woman', *Victorian Periodicals Review* 43, no. 3 (Autumn 2010): 309–35.

Colman, Anne. 'Far from Silent: Nineteenth-Century Irish Women Writers'. In *Gender Perspectives in Nineteenth-Century Ireland: Public and private spheres*, edited by Margaret Kelleher and James H. Murphy, 203–11. Dublin: Irish Academic Press, 1997.

Conlon, James. 'Men Reading Women Reading: Interpreting Images of Women Readers', *Frontiers: A Journal of Women Studies* 26, no. 2 (2005): 37–58.

Connell, R. W. *Masculinities*, Cambridge: Polity Press, 1995.

Cook, Faith. 'Thomas Kelly', *Evangelical Times*, May 2005. Accessed 1 December 2021. https://www.evangelical-times.org/26579/thomas-kelly/2005.

Cooke, Jim. 'The Dublin Mechanics' Institute, 1824–1919', *Dublin Historical Record* 52, no. 1 (Spring 1999): 15–31.

Co-op Ireland: The Irish Co-operative Journal, August 1980.

Crampton Walker, John. 'Our Picture Gallery', *Irish Life* (1917): 353–54.

Crary, Jonathan. *Techniques of the Observer: On Vision and Modernity in the Nineteenth Century*, Cambridge, MA: MIT Press, [1990] 1992.

Cruse, Amy. *The Victorians and Their Reading*, Cambridge: Riverside Press, 1935.

Cullen, Fintan. *The Irish Face: Redefining the Irish Portrait*, London: National Portrait Gallery, 2004.

Curtis, L. Perry, Jr. *Apes and Angels: The Irishman in Victorian Caricature*, Washington, DC: Smithsonian Institution Press, [1971] 1997.

Cusack, Tricia. ' "Tis the Wild Things That Have the Real Beauty": Jack B. Yeats, Modernity and Other Worlds', *Irish Review: Film and the Visual Arts in Ireland* 21 (1997): 75–91.

———. 'Migrant Travellers and Touristic Idylls: The Paintings of Jack B. Yeats and Post-Colonial Identities', *Art History* 21, no. 2 (June 1998): 201–18.

———. 'Introduction: Art, Nation and Gender'. In *Art, Nation and Gender: Ethnic Landscapes, Myths and Mother-Figures*, edited by Tricia Cusack and Síghle Bhreathnach-Lynch, 1–11. London: Routledge, [2003] 2018.

———. ' "This Pernicious Tea Drinking Habit": Women, Tea, and Respectability in Nineteenth-Century Ireland', *Canadian Journal of Irish Studies* 41 (2018): 178–209.

————. *Riverscapes and National Identities*, Syracuse: Syracuse University Press, [2010] 2019.

Dalton, Claire. *Irish Women Artists 1870–1970*, Dublin: Adams, 2014.

Devereux, Rosemary. 'Cultural Virtues', *Irish Arts Review* 33, no. 4 (Winter 2016): 568–71.

————. 'Finding Cottie', *Irish Arts Review* 36, no. 1 (Spring 2019): 120–23.

Digby, Anne. 'Women's Biological Straitjacket'. In *Sexuality and Subordination: Interdisciplinary Studies of Gender in the Nineteenth Century*, edited by Susan Mendus and Jane Rendall, 192–220. London: Routledge, 1989.

Dobbs, Jeannine. 'The Blue-Stockings: Getting It Together', *Frontiers: A Journal of Women's Studies* 1, no. 3 (Winter 1976): 81–93.

Docherty, Linda J. 'Women as Readers: Visual Interpretations', *Proceedings of the American Antiquarian Society* (1998): 335–88.

Dooley, Terence. *The Decline of the Big House in Ireland*, Dublin: Wolfhound Press, 2001.

Drawn to the Page: Irish Artists and Illustration 1830–1930. Accessed 30 July 2019. https://dttp.tcd.ie.

Drücker, Nicola. 'Hunting and Shooting: Leisure, Social Networking and Social Complications: Microhistorical Perspectives on Colonial Structures and Individual Practices: The Grehan Family, Clonmeen House, Ireland, late Nineteenth and Early Twentieth Century'. In *Was Ireland a Colony? Economics, Politics and Culture in Nineteenth-Century Ireland*, edited by Terrence McDonough, 117–44. Dublin: Irish Academic Press, 2005.

Dublin Review 52, no. 103 (1863).

Duffy, Paddy. 'Colonial Spaces and Sites of Resistance: Landed Estates in Nineteenth-Century Ireland'. In *(Dis)Placing Empire: Renegotiating British Colonial Geographies*, edited by Lindsay J. Proudfoot and Michael M. Roche, 15–40. Aldershot, UK: Ashgate, 2005.

Eccles, Charlotte O'Conor. 'A Plea for the Modern Woman – II', *Irish Monthly* 32, no. 372 (June 1904): 319–32.

Eitner, Lorenz. 'The Open Window and the Storm-Tossed Boat: An Essay in the Iconography of Romanticism', *Art Bulletin* 37, no. 4 (December 1955): 281–90.

Ellis, Mrs [Sarah Stickney]. *The Daughters of England: Their Position in Society, Character and Responsibilities*, New York: D. Appleton, 1842.

Eliot, George. *Adam Bede*, London: Penguin, [1859] 2008.

Estella Solomons: Portraits of Patriots with a Biographical Sketch of the Artist by Hilary Pyle, Dublin: Allen Figgis, 1966.

Fallon, Brian. 'Estella Solomons, Painter'. In *Retrospect: The Work of Seumas O'Sullivan 1879–1958 and Estella F. Solomons 1882–1968*, edited by Liam Miller, 32–48. Dublin: Dolmen Press, 1973.

F. E. [Frederick Engels]. Letter to Marx, 23 May 1856. Translated from German. In *Karl Marx and Frederick Engels: Ireland and the Irish Question*, 83–85. Moscow: Progress, 1971.

Ferguson, M. C. 'Alexandra College, Dublin'. In *The Woman's World*, edited by Oscar Wilde, 129. London: Cassell, 1888.

Ferris, Ina. *The Romantic National Tale and the Question of Ireland*, Cambridge: Cambridge University Press, 2002.

'Final Report of the Commissioners of the Royal Commission on Trinity College, Dublin, and the University of Dublin HC 1907 xli'. In *Women in Ireland, 1800–1918: A Documentary History*, edited by Maria Luddy, 144–45. Cork: Cork University Press, 1995.

Fitzpatrick, David. 'Ireland and the Empire'. In *The Oxford History of the British Empire – III: The Nineteenth Century*, edited by Andrew Porter, 494–521. Oxford: Oxford University Press, 1999.

Flaubert, Gustave. *Madame Bovary*, independently published, [1857] 2015.

Fletcher, Anthony. 'A Young Nationalist in the Easter Rising', *History Today* 56, no. 4, April 2006, unpaginated. Accessed 1 December 2021. https://www.historytoday.com/archive/young-nationalist-easter-rising.

Flint, Kate. *The Woman Reader 1837–1914*, Oxford: Clarendon Press, 1995.

Foster, R. F. *Paddy and Mr Punch: Connections in Irish and English History*, London: Allen Lane, 1993.

Foucault, Michel. *The History of Sexuality: An Introduction*, translated by Robert Hurley. London: Penguin, [1976] 1990.

Fried, Michael. *Absorption and Theatricality: Painting and Beholder in the Age of Diderot*, Chicago: University of Chicago Press, [1980] 1988.

Gifra-Adroher, Pere, and Jacqueline Hurtley, eds. *Hannah Lynch and Spain: Collected Journalism of an Irish New Woman, 1892–1903*, Venice: Edizioni Ca'Foscari, 2018.

Golden, Catherine J. *Images of the Woman Reader in Victorian British and American Fiction*, Gainesville: University Press of Florida, 2003.

Gorry Gallery. Exhibition catalogue, '18th–21st Century Irish Paintings', 5–19 February 2003.

Grand, Sarah. 'The New Aspect of the Woman Question', *North American Review* 158, no. 448 (March 1894): 270–76.

———. 'The Undefinable', October 1894. In *A New Woman Reader: Fiction, Articles, and Drama of the 1890s*, edited by Carolyn Christensen Nelson, 35–51. Peterborough ON: Broadview Press, 2001.

Greg, William Rathbone. 'False Morality of Lady Novelists'. In *Literary and Social Judgments*, by W. R. Greg, 82–112. London: Trübner, 2nd edn, 1869.

———. 'Why Are Women Redundant?' In *Literary and Social Judgments*, by W. R. Greg, 280–316. London: Trübner, 2nd edn, 1869.

Griffith, Kimberly. 'Miss Jane Barlow D.Litt.'. Online Coffee Conversation, Hugh Lane Gallery, 17 June 2020.

Gwynn, Denis. 'Henry Grattan and Catholic Emancipation', *An Irish Quarterly Review* 18, no. 72 (December 1929): 576–92.

Hagerman, C. A. *Britain's Imperial Muse: The Classics, Imperialism, and the Indian Empire, 1784–1914*, Houndmills: Palgrave Macmillan, 2013.

Hall, Stuart, 'Cultural Identity and Cinematic Representation', *Framework: The Journal of Cinema and Media*, no. 36 (1989): 68–81.

Hamilton, J. Taylor. 'A History of the Church Known as the Moravian Church, or The Unitas Fratrum, or The Unity of the Brethren, during the Eighteenth and Nineteenth centuries', *Transactions of the Moravian Historical Society* 6 (1900): i–xii, 1–632.

Hardwick, Joan. *The Yeats Sisters: A Biography of Susan and Elizabeth Yeats*, London: HarperCollins, 1996.

Haslam, Thomas. '*The Women's Advocate*, 1 April 1874'. In *Women in Ireland, 1800–1918: A Documentary History*, edited by Maria Luddy, 269–71. Cork: Cork University Press, 1995.

Heilmann, Ann. *New Woman Strategies: Sarah Grand, Olive Schreiner, Mona Caird*, Manchester: Manchester University Press, 2004.

'Henry Grattan', *All Ireland Review* 2, no. 28 (31 August 1901): 215.

Houston, Arthur. *The Emancipation of Women from Existing Industrial Disabilities: Considered in Its Economic Aspect*, London: Longman, Green, Longman, and Roberts; Dublin: McGlashan & Gill, 1862.

Humphry, Mrs C. E. *A Word to Women*, London: James Bowden, 1898.

Ingram, John Kells. *The Memory of the Dead*, 1843.

Irish People, The, 1, no. 1, 28 November 1863. Downloaded courtesy of Digital Library, Villanova University.

Irish Protestant, An, 'A Young Protestant Party', *The United Irishman: A National Weekly Review*, 7 February 1903, 3.

Irish Times, The, 29 February 1876–2 December 2014.

'Irish Women Artists from the Archives'. National Gallery of Art Dublin, 2020.

Irish Women's Writing (1880–1920) Network. 'Research Pioneers 1: John Wilson Foster: Research Pioneers in Irish Women's Writing: An Interview Series'. Accessed 1 December 2021. https://irishwomenswritingnetwork.com/2019/10/07/research-pioneers-1-john-wilson-foster/.

Jack, Belinda. *The Woman Reader*, New Haven, CT: Yale University Press, 2013.

Jackson, David. *Unmasking Masculinity: A Critical Autobiography*, Abingdon: Routledge, [1990] 2015.

Jajdelska, Elspeth. *Silent Reading and the Birth of the Narrator*, Toronto: University of Toronto Press, 2007.

J.H.S. 'Preface', *Brief Memorials of the Rev. B.W. Mathias*, 1842 (i–xxiii).

James, Henry. *The Portrait of a Lady*, Harmondsworth: Penguin, [1881] 1971.

Johnston, Sheila Turner. *Alice: A Life of Alice Milligan*, Newtownards: Colourpoint, [1994] 2009.

Joyce, Toby. '"Ireland's Trained and Marshalled Manhood": The Fenians in the Mid-1860s'. In *Gender Perspectives in Nineteenth-Century Ireland: Public and Private Spheres*, edited by Margaret Kelleher and James H. Murphy, 70–80. Dublin: Irish Academic Press, 1997.

Kaestle, Carl F. 'The History of Literacy and the History of Readers', *Review of Research in Education* 12 (1985): 11–53.

Kelso, Charlotte. 'The Body as Interface: New Woman Identity in George Egerton's "The Regeneration of Two"', *Australasian Journal of Victorian Studies* 23, no. 1 (2019): 80–93.

Kennedy, Máire. 'Dublin's Coffee Houses of the Eighteenth Century', *Dublin Historical Record* 63, no. 1 (Spring 2010): 29–38.

Kennedy, Róisín. 'Estella Solomons: A Portrait of the Artist as a Republican', *Irish Independent*, 21 January 2016, 13.

Kenny, Kevin. 'Ireland and the British Empire: An Introduction'. In *Ireland and the British Empire*, edited by Kevin Kenny, 1–25. Oxford: Oxford University Press, 2004,

Kilrush Herald; *Kilrush Herald and Kilkee Gazette*, 5 June–17 July 1879.

Lane, Fintan. *The Origins of Modern Irish Socialism 1881–1896*, Cork: Cork University Press, 1997.

Lane, Hugh P. 'Prefatory Notes, Dublin, December 1907', *Illustrated Catalogue with Biographical and Critical Notes By S.C.H.*, Municipal Gallery of Modern Art, 17 Harcourt Street, Dublin, 1908.

Lane, Leeann. 'The International Story of the Women's Suffrage Movement'. Accessed 27 March 2020. https://www.rte.ie/centuryireland/index.php/articles/female-activists-the-international-story-of-the-womens-suffrage-movement?imz_s=7kkj9eas1bukum7fu13c97acf4.

Leerssen, Joep. 'Review Article: Lebowski's Rug and the Book in Nineteenth Century Ireland', reviewing James H. Murphy, *The Oxford History of the Irish Book, Volume IV. The Irish Book in English, 1800–1891*, *Irish Historical Studies* 38, no. 150 (November 2012): 332–36.

Leventhal, A. J. 'Seumas O'Sullivan'. In *Retrospect: The Work of Seumas O'Sullivan 1879–1958 and Estella F. Solomons 1882–1968*, edited by Liam Miller, 7–20. Dublin: Dolmen Press, 1973.

Lewis, Gifford. *The Yeats Sisters and the Cuala*, Dublin: Irish Academic Press, 1994.

Lodge, John. *The Peerage of Ireland: Or a Genealogical History of the Present Nobility of That Kingdom with Engravings of Their Paternal Coats of Arms*, updated in 1789, Dublin: James Moore.

Luddy, Maria. *Women in Ireland, 1800–1918: A Documentary History*, Cork: Cork University Press, 1995.

Lynch, Deirdre Shauna. *Loving Literature: A Cultural History*, Chicago: University of Chicago Press, [2015] 2018.

Lynch, Hannah. *The Prince of the Glades*, II, London: Methuen, 1891.

Macherey, Pierre. *A Theory of Literary Production*, translated by Geoffrey Wall. Abingdon: Routledge, [1966] 2006.

MacManus, Anna [Ethna Carbery]. *In the Celtic Past*, Dublin, 1904, republished by Dodo Press, Gloucester, 2008.

MacPherson, D. A. J. 'The Myriad-Minded Woman: Public and Private Worlds in the Journalism of Susan L. Mitchell', *Irish Review* 42 (2010): 18.

Madden, Thomas More. 'On Insanity, and the Criminal Responsibility of the Insane'. Paper read before the Medical Society of the College of Physicians in Ireland. Dublin: John Falconer, 1866.

Markievicz, Constance de. Lecture to Students' National Literary Society, Dublin, *Women, Ideals and The Nation*, pamphlet, Dublin 1909.

McCabe, Archbishop, *Freeman's Journal*, 12 March 1881. In *Women in Ireland, 1800–1918: A Documentary History*, edited by Maria Luddy, 262–63. Cork: Cork University Press, 1995.

McConkey, Kenneth. *Sir John Lavery*, Edinburgh: Canongate, 1993.

McConville, Michael. *Ascendancy to Oblivion: The Story of the Anglo–Irish*. London: Phoenix, 2001.

McCoole, Sinéad. *No Ordinary Women: Irish Female Activists in the Revolutionary Years 1900-1923*, Dublin: O'Brien Press, [2003] 2015.

McDevitt, Patrick F. 'Muscular Catholicism: Nationalism, Masculinity and Gaelic Team Sports, 1884–1916', *Gender & History* 9, no. 2 (August 1997): 262–84.

McNally, P. 'Protestant Perspectives: Presbyterians, Patriots and Unionists', *Irish Studies Review* 7, no. 1 (1999): 79–82.

Meaney, Gerardine, Mary O'Dowd and Bernadette Whelan. *Reading the Irish Woman: Studies in Cultural Encounter and Exchange, 1714–1960*, Liverpool: Liverpool University Press, 2013.

Miller, Liam, ed. *Retrospect: The Work of Seumas O'Sullivan 1879–1958 and Estella F. Solomons 1882–1968*, Dublin: Dolmen Press, 1973.

Milligan, Seaton F., MRIA and Alice L. Milligan. *Glimpses of Erin*, London: Marcus Ward, n.d.

'Minute Book of the Ladies' Institute, Belfast, Victoria College, Belfast'. In *Women in Ireland, 1800–1918: A Documentary History*, edited by Maria Luddy, 141–42. Cork: Cork University Press, 1995.

Mitchell, Dolores. 'The "New Woman" as Prometheus: Women Artists Depict Women Smoking', *Woman's Art Journal* 12, no. 1 (Spring–Summer 1991): 3–9.

Morgan, Marjorie. *National Identities and Travel in Victorian Britain*, Basingstoke, UK: Palgrave Macmillan, 2001.

Morris, Catherine. *Alice Milligan and the Irish Cultural Revival*, Dublin: Four Courts Press, 2013

Morris, Nicola. 'Watchmen to the House of Israel? Irish Methodism and the Religious Press'. In *Literacy, Language and Reading in Nineteenth-Century Ireland*, edited by Rebecca Anne

Barr, Sarah-Anne Buckley and Muireann O'Cinneide, 66–86. Liverpool: Liverpool University Press, 2019.

Mulholland, Rosa. 'Irish Painters in This Present Year', *Irish Monthly* 17, no. 195 (September 1889): 481–86.

Murdoch, Lydia. *Daily Life of Victorian Women*, Santa Barbara, CA: Greenwood, 2014.

Murphy, Andrew. *Ireland, Reading and Cultural Nationalism 1790–1930: Bringing the Nation to Book*, Cambridge: Cambridge University Press, 2018.

Murphy, Patrick J. *Patrick Tuohy: From Conversations with His Friends*, Dublin: TownHouse, 2004.

Murphy, Rachel. 'Lady Charlotte Stopford: A Lady of Leisure?' In *Leisure and the Irish in the Nineteenth Century*, edited by Leeann Lane and William Murphy, 226–44. Liverpool: Liverpool University Press, 2016.

Murphy, William M. *Prodigal Father: The Life of John Butler Yeats, 1839–1922*, Syracuse, NY: Syracuse University Press, 2001.

M. R. 'The Cabinet of Irish Literature', *Irish Monthly* 31, no. 360 (June 1903): 335–40.

———. 'Judge Carton, K.C. In Memoriam', *Irish Monthly* 35, no. 410 (August 1907): 417–22.

Nelson, Carolyn Christensen, ed. *A New Woman Reader: Fiction, Articles, and Drama of the 1890s*, Peterborough, ON: Broadview Press, 2001.

'New Light on the "New Woman", A', *British Medical Journal* 2, no. 1758 (8 September 1894): 548.

'Obituary' [Miss Jane Barlow], *The Irish Book Lover* 8, nos. 11–12 (June–July 1917): 141–42.

Ó Ciosáin, Niall. 'Varieties of Literacy in Nineteenth-Century Ireland: Gender, Religion and Language'. In *Literacy, Language and Reading in Nineteenth-Century Ireland*, edited by Rebecca Anne Barr, Sarah-Anne Buckley and Muireann O'Cinneide, 15–27. Liverpool: Liverpool University Press, 2019.

O'Connor, Barbara. *The Irish Dancing: Cultural Politics and Identities 1900–2000*. Cork: Cork University Press, 2013.

O'Donnell, John. 'On the Rampart: Limerick'. In *Irish Readings*, edited by A. M. Sullivan, M. P. and T. D. Sullivan, M. P., 190–92. Dublin: M.H. Gill, 1913.

O'Grady, John. *The Life and Work of Sarah Purser*, Dublin: Four Courts Press, 1996.

'Old Fogey'. 'National Economics and the New Universities', *Sinn Féin*, 22 August 1908.

O'Neill, Marie. 'Sarah Cecilia Harrison: Artist and City Councillor', *Dublin Historical Record* 42, no. 2 (1989): 66–81.

O'Riordan, Maeve. 'Leisure with a Purpose: Women and the Entertaining Practices of the Irish Landed Elite, c. 1860–1914'. In *Leisure and the Irish in the Nineteenth Century*, edited by Leeann Lane and William Murphy, 209–25. Liverpool: Liverpool University Press, 2016.

Ortner, Sherry B. 'Is Female to Male as Nature is to Culture?' *Feminist Studies* 1, no. 2 (Autumn 1972): 5–31.

O'Sullivan, Seumas. 'Prelude to an Autobiography' [1944]. In *Retrospect: The Work of Seumas O'Sullivan 1879–1958 and Estella F. Solomons 1882–1968*, edited by Liam Miller, 21–31. Dublin: Dolmen Press, 1973.

O'Toole, Tina. *The Irish New Woman*, Houndmills: Palgrave Macmillan, 2013.

Ouida. 'The New Woman'. *North American Review* 158, no. 450 (May 1894): 610–19.

Page, Judith W., and Elise L. Smith. *Women, Literature, and the Domesticated Landscape: England's Disciples of Flora, 1780–1870*, Cambridge: Cambridge University Press, 2014.

Parkes, Susan M., ed. *A Danger to the Men?: A History of Women in Trinity College Dublin 1904–2004*, Dublin: Lilliput Press, 2008.

Paul César Helleu 1859–1927. London: Editions Graphiques Gallery, n.d.

Pollock, Griselda. *Mary Cassatt: Painter of Modern Women*, London: Thames and Hudson, 1998.

Potter, Matthew, 'The Establishment and Evolution of Limerick City Municipal Library, 1889-1938'. In *Leisure and the Irish in the Nineteenth Century*, edited by Leeann Lane and William Murphy, 99–116. Liverpool: Liverpool University Press, 2016.

Present Writer, The. 'Harmless Novels', *Irish Monthly* 14, no. 154 (April 1886): 206–14.

Provost & President: George Salmon, 1888–1904 (c.1819–1904). Accessed 1 December 2021. https://www.tcd.ie/provost/history/former-provosts/g_salmon.php.

Purser, Michael. *Jellett, O'Brien, Purser and Stokes: Seven Generations, Four Families*, Dublin: Prejmer Verlag, 2004.

Pyle, Hilary. *Estella Solomons: Portraits of Patriots, with a Biographical Sketch of the Artist*, Dublin: Allen Figgis, 1966.

———. *Jack B. Yeats: A Catalogue Raisonné of the Oil Paintings*, London: Andre Deutsch, 1992.

———. *Estella Solomons HRHA (1882–1968)*, Dublin: Frederick Gallery, 1999.

———. *Cesca's Diary 1913–1916: Where Art and Nationalism Meet*, Dublin: Woodfield Press, 2005.

———. 'Alice Milligan Centre Stage', *Irish Arts Review* 29, no. 2 (Summer, 2012): 90–93.

Quinlan, Carmel. ' "Onward Hand in Hand": The Nineteenth Century Irish Campaign for Votes for Women'. In *Irish Women and the Vote: Becoming Citizens*, edited by Louise Ryan and Margaret Ward, 21–44. Newbridge: Irish Academic Press, [2007] 2018.

Quinn, James. 'The *Nation*, History, and the Making of National Citizens'. In *Literacy, Language and Reading in Nineteenth-Century Ireland*, edited by Rebecca Anne Barr, Sarah-Anne Buckley and Muireann O'Cinneide, 53–65. Liverpool: Liverpool University Press, 2019.

Rains, Stephanie. 'Irish Media History: "Lady of the House", 1890-1923'. Accessed 1 May 2020. https://irishmediahistory.com/2015/09/29/lady-of-the-house-1890-1923/.

Renan, Ernest. 'La Poésie des races celtiques', *Revue des Deux-Mondes*, 1854, 478. Accessed 30 March 2020. https://fr.wikisource.org/wiki/La_Po%C3%A9sie_des_races_celtiques.

———. *Qu'est-ce Qu'une Nation?* Paris: R. Helleu, [1882] 1934.

Rewald, Sabine. *Rooms with a View: The Open Window in the 19th Century*, New York: Metropolitan Museum of Art, 2011.

Rothman, Joshua, 'The History of "Loving" to Read', *New Yorker*, 2 February 2015. Accessed 1 December 2021. https://www.newyorker.com/culture/cultural-comment/history-loving-read.

Royal Hibernian Academy. Catalogue. 77th Annual Exhibition, 1906. Dublin: Brown and Nolan.

Royal Hibernian Academy of Arts: Index of Exhibitors 1826–1979, III N-Z, compiled by Ann M. Stewart.

Ryan, Louise. 'The "Irish Citizen" ', 1912–1920', *Saothar* 17 (1992): 105–11.

Schapiro, Meyer. *Words and Pictures: On the Literal and the Symbolic in the Illustration of a Text*. The Hague: Mouton, 1973.

Scott, Patrick. 'Reviewed Work(s): Victorian Yellowbacks & Paperbacks, 1849–1905. Vol. 1: George Routledge by Chester W. Topp', *Papers of the Bibliographical Society of America* 87, no. 2 (1993): 266–68.

Scully, Richard. 'A Comic Empire: The Global Expansion of Punch as a Model Publication', *International Journal of Comic Art [IJOCA]* (Fall 2013): 6–35.

Shaw-Sparrow, Walter. *John Lavery and His Work*, Boston: Dana Estes, 1912: Facsimile: London: Forgotten Books, 2012.

Sheehy, Jeanne. *Walter Osborne*, Dublin: National Gallery of Ireland, 1983.

Sisley, Logan. 'Portraits of National Interest'. In *Revolutionary States: Home Rule and Modern Ireland*, edited by Logan Sisley, 37–63. Dublin: Hugh Lane Dublin City Gallery, 2012.

Smyth, Gerry. *The Novel and the Nation: Studies in the New Irish Fiction*, London: Pluto, 1997.

Somerville, E. Œ. and Martin Ross. *The Real Charlotte*, London: Oxford University Press, [1894] 1948.

Somerville-Large, Peter. *The Irish Country House: A Social History*, London: Sinclair-Stevenson, 1995.

Sonstroem, David. 'Teeth in Victorian Art', *Victorian Literature and Culture* 29, no. 2 (2001): 351–82.

Springhall, John. 'Baden-Powell and the Scout Movement before 1920: Citizen Training or Soldiers of the Future?' *English Historical Review* 102, no. 405 (October 1987): 934–42.

Stevens, Julie Anne. *The Irish Scene in Somerville and Ross*, Dublin: Irish Academic Press, 2007.

———. *Two Irish Girls in Bohemia: The Drawings and Writings of E. Œ. Somerville and Martin Ross*, Bantry: Somerville Press, 2017.

Sullivan, A. M., M. P., and Sullivan, T. D., M. P., eds. *Irish Readings*, Dublin: M. H. Gill, 1913.

Sutherland, Gillian. *In Search of the New Woman: Middle-Class Women and Work in Britain 1870-1914*, Cambridge: Cambridge University Press, [2015] 2018.

Tilley, Elizabeth. 'The *Dublin Penny Journal* and Alternative Histories'. In *Literacy, Language and Reading in Nineteenth-Century Ireland*, edited by Rebecca Anne Barr, Sarah-Anne Buckley and Muireann O'Cinneide, 87–103. Liverpool: Liverpool University Press, 2019.

Tolstoy, Leo. *Anna Karenina*, Wordsworth Editions, [1878] 1995.

Tucker, Brian. 'The "Invisible Movement That Reading Is": Metaphors of Motion in the Reading Debates around 1800'. *Colloquia Germanica* 47, no. 4 (2014): 309–28.

Turpin, John. 'The Royal Dublin Society and Its School of Art, 1849–1877'. *Dublin Historical Record* 36, no. 1 (1982): 2–20.

Tusan, Michelle Elizabeth. 'Inventing the New Woman: Print Culture and Identity Politics during the Fin-de-Siecle'. *Victorian Periodicals Review* 31, no. 2 (Summer 1998): 169–82.

Tynan, Katharine. *Memories*, London: Eveleigh, Nash & Grayson, 1924.

Upstone, Robert. *William Orpen: Politics Sex & Death*, London: Philip Wilson, 2005.

Valente, Joseph. *The Myth of Manliness in Irish National Culture, 1880–1922*. Urbana, Chicago: University of Illinois Press, 2011.

Vanderlaan, Kimberly. 'The Painter Henry James Might Have Been', *American Literary Realism* 41, no. 1 (2008): 1–13.

Vaughan, W. E. *Landlords and Tenants in Ireland, 1848–1904*, Dundalk: Economic and Social History Society of Ireland and Dundalgan Press, 1994.

Walker, Dorothy. 'Portrait of the Artist as a Young Woman', *Crane Bag* 4, no. 1 (1980): 106–11.

Ward, Margaret. *Maud Gonne: A Life*, London: Pandora, 1993.

———. *Unmanageable Revolutionaries: Women and Irish nationalism*, London: Pluto, [1989] 1995.

Watson, Nick J., Stuart Weir and Stephen Friend. 'The Development of Muscular Christianity in Victorian Britain and Beyond', *Journal of Religion & Society* 7 (2005): 1–21.

West, Shearer. *Portraiture*, Oxford: Oxford University Press, 2004.

Wilson, Ann. 'Constructions of Irishness in a Collection of Early Twentieth-Century Picture Postcards', *Canadian Journal of Irish Studies* 39, no. 1 (2015): 92–117.

Wilson Foster, John. *Irish Novels 1890-1940: New Bearings in Culture and Fiction*, Oxford: Oxford University Press, 2008.

Woolf, Virginia. *A Room of One's Own and Three Guineas*, London: William Collins, [1929] 2014.

Yeats, John Butler, R. H. A. *Essays Irish and American, with an Appreciation by AE*, Dublin: Talbot Press, 1918.

Yeats, W. B. *The Book of Fairy and Folk Tales of Ireland* [orig. 2 vols: 1888, 1892], London: Slaney Press, 1994.

Yeldham, Charlotte. *Maria Spilsbury (1776–1820): Artist and Evangelical*, Farnham: Ashgate, 2010.

www.ingramcontent.com/pod-product-compliance
Ingram Content Group UK Ltd.
Pitfield, Milton Keynes, MK11 3LW, UK
UKHW021816150726
7214IPUK00016B/152